Making the GRADE

Everything Your 3rd Grader Needs to Know

by
Micki Pflug

This Book Belongs To Zachary Meuse.

This book

"zachary Hi! Meuse

BARRON'S

About the Author

Micki Pflug has been active in the publishing arena for more than 10 years. She has created educational books and materials in reading, language arts, social studies, math, and science for learners of all ages. Micki holds a B.A. in journalism and a B.A. in anthropology from the University of Iowa.

All inquiries should be addressed to:
Barron's Educational Series, Inc.
250 Wireless Boulevard
Hauppauge, New York 11788
http://www.barronseduc.com

Library of Congress Catalog Card No. 2002043984

International Standard Book No. 0-7641-2478-1

Library of Congress Cataloging-in-Publication Data
Pflug, Micki.
    Making the grade everything your 3rd grader needs to know / Micki Pflug.
        p. cm.
    At head of title: Barron's.
    Includes bibliographical references and index.
    ISBN 0-7641-2478-1 (alk. paper)
    1. Third grade (Education)—Curricula—United States—Handbooks,
manuals, etc. 2. Home schooling—Curricula—United States—Handbooks,
manuals, etc. 3. Curriculum planning—United States—Handbooks, manuals,
etc. I. Title.

    LB15713rd .P45 2003
    372.19–dc13   2002043984

Printed in Hong Kong
9 8 7 6 5 4 3 2 1

Table of Contents

 **MATH**

How to Use This Book

Welcome to the *Making the Grade* series! These seven books offer tools and strategies for hands-on, active learning at the kindergarten through sixth-grade levels. Each book presents real-world, engaging learning experiences in the core areas of language arts, math, science, and social studies at age-appropriate levels.

Who should use this book?

Whether you're a stay-at-home or working parent with children in school, a homeschooler who's guiding your children's education, or a teacher who's looking for additional ideas to supplement classroom learning experiences, this book is for you.

- If you have children in school, *Making the Grade* can be used in conjunction with your child's curriculum because it offers real-world, hands-on activities that exercise the concepts and topics he or she is being taught in school.
- If you're a homeschooler who's guiding your children's education, this series presents you with easy-to-access, engaging ways to interact with your child.
- If you're a teacher, this book also can be a source for additional activities.

This book is your passport to a whole new world, one that gives you enough support to be a successful educator while encouraging independent learning with one child or shared learning among your children.

What is *Making the Grade*?

We're glad you asked! First, we'd like to tell you what it's not. It's not a textbook series. Rather, each book in the series delivers age-appropriate content in language arts, math, science, and social studies in an open-ended, flexible manner that incorporates the "real" world. You can use this book as a supplement to your core learning instruction or use it to get a jump start on the fundamentals.

Each subject section presents lessons comprised of both "teaching" pages and "student" pages. And each book in the *Making the Grade* series is perforated for flexible learning so that both you and your child can tear out the pages that you're working on and use one book together.

How do the lessons work?

The teaching and student pages work together. The lesson instruction and teaching ideas for each specific lesson appear first. Then activities that offer opportunities for your child to practice the specific skills and review the concepts being taught follow. Creativity and imagination abound! Throughout each lesson, hands-on activities are incorporated using concepts that are meaningful and relevant to kids' daily lives. The activities account for all kinds of learners—that is, visual, auditory, or kinesthetic learning. For more information on learning styles, see the Glossary on page 351.

Objective and Background

Each lesson opens with an objective that tells you exactly what the lesson is about. The background of the lesson follows, giving you the rationale behind the importance of the material being addressed. Each lesson is broken down for you so that you and your student can see how the skills and concepts taught are useful in everyday situations.

Materials and Vocabulary

Have you ever done a project and found out you're missing something when you get to the end? A list of materials is given up front so you'll know what you need before you begin. The lessons take into account that you have access to your local library, a computer and the Internet, writing instruments, a calculator, and a notebook and loose paper, so you won't find these listed. The materials are household items when possible so that even the most technical of science experiments can be done easily. The *Making the Grade* series paves the way for your learning experience whether you and your student are sitting side by side on the couch or in a classroom, at the library, or even on vacation!

Following the materials list, vocabulary words may be given offering clear, easy-to-understand definitions.

Let's Begin

Let's Begin is just that, "Let's Begin!" The instructional portion of the lesson opens with easy, user-friendly, numbered steps that guide you through the teaching of a particular lesson. Here you'll find opportunities to interact with your student and engage in discussions about what he or she is learning. There also are opportunities for your student to practice his or her critical-thinking skills to make the learning experience richer.

In the margins are interesting facts about what you're studying, time-savers, or helpful ideas.

Ways to Extend the Lesson

Every lesson concludes with ways to extend the lesson—teaching tips, such as hints, suggestions, or ideas, for you to use in teaching the lesson or a section of the lesson. Each lesson also ends with an opportunity for you to "check in" and assess how well your student has mastered the skill or grasped the concepts being taught in the lesson. The For Further Reading section lists books that you can use as additional references and support in teaching the lesson. It also offers your student more opportunities to practice a skill or a chance to look deeper into the content.

Student Learning Pages

Student Learning Pages immediately follow the teaching pages in each lesson. These pages offer fun opportunities to practice the skills and concepts being taught. And there are places where your student gets to choose what to do next and take ownership of his or her learning.

Visual Aids

Throughout the book you'll see references to the Venn Diagram, Comparison Chart, Web, Sequence Chain, and Writing Lines found in the back of the book. Many lessons incorporate these graphic organizers, or visual methods of organizing information, into the learning. If one is used in a lesson, it will be listed in the materials so that prior to the lesson you or your student can make a photocopy of it from the back of the book or you can have your student copy it into his or her notebook. See the Glossary for more information on graphic organizers.

What about field trips or learning outside the classroom?

One very unique feature of the *Making the Grade* series is the In Your Community activities at the end of each subject section. These activities describe ways to explore your community, taking advantage of your local or regional culture, industry, and environment while incorporating the skills learned in the lessons. For example, you can have your student help out at a farmer's market or with a local environmental group. These unique activities can supplement your ability to provide support for subjects. The activities give your student life experiences upon which he or she can build and expand the canvas upon which he or she learns.

These pages are identified in the Table of Contents so that you can read them first as a way to frame your student's learning.

How do I know if my student is learning the necessary skills?

Although each lesson offers an opportunity for on-the-spot assessment, a formalized assessment section is located in the back of this book. You'll find a combination of multiple-choice and open-ended questions testing your student on the skills, concepts, and topics covered.

Also, at the end of every subject section is a We Have Learned checklist. This checklist provides a way for you and your student to summarize what you've accomplished. It lists specific concepts, and there is additional space for you and your student to write in other topics you've covered.

Does this book come with answers?

Yes. Answers are provided in the back of the book for both the lessons and assessment.

What if this book uses a homeschooling or educational term I'm not familiar with?

In addition to the vocabulary words listed in the lessons, a two-page Glossary is provided in the back of the book. Occasionally terms will surface that may need further explanation in order for the learning experience to flourish. In the Glossary, you'll find terms explained simply to help you give your student a rewarding learning experience free from confusion.

Will this book help me find resources within the schools for homeschoolers?

In Communicating Between Home and School, there are suggestions for how to take advantage of the opportunities and resources offered by your local schools and how these benefits can enhance your homeschooling learning experiences.

I'm new to homeschooling. How can I find out about state regulations, curriculum, and other resources?

In For Homeschoolers on the following page, you'll find information about national and state legislation, resources for curriculum and materials, and other references. Also included is a comprehensive list of online resources for everything from homeschooling organizations to military homeschooling to homeschooling supplies.

How can I use this book if my student attends a public or private school?

Making the Grade fits into any child's educational experience—whether he or she is being taught at home or in a traditional school setting.

For Homeschoolers

Teaching children at home isn't a new phenomenon. But it's gaining in popularity as caregivers decide to take a more active role in the education of their children. More people are learning what homeschoolers have already known, that children who are homeschooled regularly succeed in college, the workplace, and society.

Whether you're new to homeschooling or have been educating your children at home for quite some time, you may have found the homeschooling path to have occasional detours. This book hopes to minimize those detours by offering information on state regulations, homeschooling approaches and curriculum, and other resources to keep you on the path toward a rewarding learning experience.

Regulations

There never has been a federal law prohibiting parents from homeschooling their children. A homeschooler isn't required to have a teaching degree, nor is he or she required to teach children in a specific location. Nonetheless, each state has its own set of regulations, educational requirements, and guidelines for those who homeschool.

Some states and areas of the United States have stricter regulations than others. Alabama; Alaska; Arizona; California; Delaware; Guam; Idaho; Illinois; Indiana; Kansas; Kentucky; Michigan; Mississippi; Missouri; Montana; Nebraska; New Jersey; New Mexico; Oklahoma; Puerto Rico; Texas; Virgin Islands; Washington, D.C.; Wisconsin; and Wyoming are considered to have a low level of regulation. Maine, Massachusetts, Minnesota, Nevada, New York, North Dakota, Pennsylvania, Rhode Island, Utah, Vermont, Washington, and West Virginia are considered to have a high level of regulation. The remaining states and areas not mentioned are considered to have a moderate level of homeschooling regulation.

But what do low, moderate, and high regulation mean? These classifications indicate the level of regulation that a particular state can enforce upon someone who has chosen to teach a child at home. Within each of these levels, there also are varying rules and laws.

These regulations begin with how to enter the world of homeschooling. Some states, such as New Jersey, don't require parents to notify the school of their intent to teach their children at home, yet a letter of intent often is submitted out of courtesy. New Jersey's regulations note that all children of compulsory school age must be in an instructional program equivalent to that provided in the public schools. Similarly, in Texas, another state that's considered to have a low level of regulation, parents don't have to notify anyone of their intent to homeschool their children. Texas homeschools are considered private schools and aren't subject to state regulation.

States with moderate levels of regulation often require that letters of intent to homeschool be submitted, as well as regular logs of instruction be kept, and other guidelines be followed. Florida, for example, requires that parents send a letter of intent to their local superintendent. Florida homeschoolers also have to log schoolwork and have the child annually evaluated using one of the methods of evaluation.

Other "moderate" states ask different requirements of their homeschoolers. In South Carolina, parents who are intending to homeschool their children must have either a high school diploma or have passed the GED (general educational development) test. Parents have three choices when it comes to homeschooling in this state: (1) they can maintain instruction under the supervision of their local school district, which would vary by district, (2) they can homeschool under the direction of the South Carolina Association of Independent Home Schools (SCAIHS), which would require them to pay annual dues, have their child tested annually, and have their curriculum reviewed, or (3) they must be accountable to one of the state homeschooling associations.

States that are considered to have a high level of homeschooling regulation often require parents who teach their children at home to follow guidelines throughout the school year. Pennsylvania has a strict policy for homeschoolers, and requires parents to submit a notarized affidavit of intent to homeschool, along with medical records and learning objectives for certain subjects. Note that the school only has the authority to say whether the required documentation was submitted, not determine whether the homeschooling plan of instruction is acceptable or unacceptable. The parents also must keep records of instruction and of attendance during the year. At the end of the school year, the child must be evaluated by either a certified teacher or a licensed psychologist, a portfolio of schoolwork needs to be submitted, and in certain grades the child must take a standardized test. Also, parents who plan to teach their children at home must have a high school education. Pennsylvania, however, does offer another homeschooling option. Parents can have children homeschooled by a tutor who is a certified teacher, in which case the parents only need to submit the tutor's credentials and criminal record.

Parents intending to homeschool their children in New York, another state considered to have a high level of regulation, must file a letter indicating their intentions and submit an IHIP (Individualized Home Instruction Plan). As in Pennsylvania, the school doesn't have the authority to determine the acceptability of the IHIP, only whether information was submitted as outlined by the state. The parents also must submit quarterly reports during the year and engage the child in at least 900 hours of instruction per year for grades K–6. At the end of each school year, the homeschooled child must be assessed, which can mean taking a standardized assessment test in some years and having the parents provide a narrative of assessment in others. In Minnesota, another state that has a high level of regulation, parents must submit the names and birth dates of the children they plan to homeschool annually. The parents also must have a bachelor's degree, or else they will have to submit quarterly report cards to the school. Parents also must provide supporting documentation about the subject matter that is being taught, although the information needed may vary from school district to school district. In addition, homeschooled children in this state must be tested annually, but the school doesn't need to see the test results.

No matter what level of regulation your state has, there are ways to operate your homeschool with success. Here are a few tips as you negotiate the homeschooling waters:

- Be aware of your district's and state's requirements.
- All of these laws, rules, and regulations may seem like more trouble than they're worth. The National Home Education Network (NHEN) may be able to help. Go to the association's Web site at *http://www.nhen.org*. For even more information on your state's laws and related references, see the Homeschooling Online Resources that follow. They can help you find information on your specific state and may be able to direct you to local homeschooling groups.
- Veteran homeschoolers in your area can be a fountain of practical knowledge about the laws. Consult a variety of homeschoolers for a clear perspective, as each family has an educational philosophy and approach that best suits it.

Homeschooling Military Families

Frequently moving from location to location can be exhausting for families with one or more parent in the military. If you have school-age children, it can be even more complicated. Schools across states and U.S. schools in other countries often don't follow the same curriculum, and states often can have varying curriculum requirements for each grade.

The Department of Defense Dependent Schools (DoDDS) is responsible for the military educational system. There are three options for military families in which they can educate their children:

1. attend school with other military children
2. if in a foreign country, attend the local school in which the native language is spoken, although this option may require approval
3. homeschool

Homeschooling can provide consistency for families that have to relocate often. The move itself, along with the new culture your family will be exposed to, is a learning experience that can be incorporated into the curriculum. Note that military families that homeschool must abide by the laws of the area in which they reside, which may be different from where they claim residency for tax purposes. If your relocation takes your family abroad, one downside is the lack of curriculum resources available on short notice. Nonetheless, military homeschoolers may be able to use resources offered at base schools.

Approaches and Curriculum

If you're reading this book, you've probably already heard of many different approaches and methods to homeschooling, which some homeschoolers sometimes refer to as *unschooling* (see the Glossary for more information). It's important that you choose one approach or method that works best for you—there's no right or wrong way to homeschool!

The curriculum and materials that are used vary from person to person, but there are organizations that offer books, support, and materials to homeschoolers. Many homeschoolers find that a combination of methods often works best. That's why *Making the Grade* was created!

Support Groups and Organizations

Homeschooling has become more popular, and the United States boasts a number of nationally recognized homeschooling organizations. Also, nearly every state has its own homeschooling organization to provide information on regulations in addition to other support. Many religious and ethnic affiliations also have their own homeschooling organizations too, in addition to counties and other groups.

Homeschooling Online Resources

These are some of the online resources available for homeschoolers. You also can check your phone book for local organizations and resources.

National Organizations

Alliance for Parental Involvement in Education
http://www.croton.com/allpie/

Alternative Education Resource Organization (AERO)
http://www.edrev.org/links.htm

American Homeschool Association (AHA)
http://www.americanhomeschoolassociation.org/

Home School Foundation
http://www.homeschoolfoundation.org

National Coalition of Alternative Community Schools
http://www.ncacs.org/

National Home Education Network (NHEN)
http://www.nhen.org/

National Home Education Research Institute (NHERI)
http://www.nheri.org

National Homeschooling Association (NHA)
http://www.n-h-a.org

Homeschooling and the Law

Advocates for the Rights of Homeschoolers (ARH)
http://www.geocities.com/arhfriends/

American Bar Association
http://www.abanet.org

Children with Special Needs

Children with Disabilities
http://www.childrenwithdisabilities.ncjrs.org/

Institutes for the Achievement of Human Potential (IAHP)
http://www.iahp.org/

National Challenged Homeschoolers Associated Network (NATHHAN)
http://www.nathhan.com/

Military Homeschooling

Department of Defense Dependent Schools/Education Activity (DoDDS)
http://www.odedodea.edu/

Books, Supplies, Curriculum

Federal Resources for Educational Excellence
http://www.ed.gov/free/

Home Schooling Homework
http://www.dailyhomework.org/

Home School Products
http://www.homeschooldiscount.com/

Homeschooler's Curriculum Swap
http://theswap.com/

HomeSchoolingSupply.com
http://www.homeschoolingsupply.com/

General Homeschooling Resources

A to Z Home's Cool
http://www.gomilpitas.com/

Family Unschoolers Network
http://www.unschooling.org

Home Education Magazine
http://www.home-ed-magazine.com/

Home School Legal Defense Association (HSLDA)
http://www.hslda.org

Homeschool Internet Yellow Pages
http://www.homeschoolyellowpages.com/

Homeschool Central
http://www.homeschoolcentral.com

Homeschool World
http://www.home-school.com/

Homeschool.com
http://www.homeschool.com/

HSAdvisor.com
http://www.hsadvisor.com/

Unschooling.com
http://www.unschooling.com/

Waldorf Without Walls
http://www.waldorfwithoutwalls.com/

Communicating Between Home and School

For homeschoolers, often there is limited contact with the schools beyond that which is required by the state. Yet a quick glance at your local schools will reveal opportunities, resources, and benefits that can offer you flexibility and that can supplement your child's total learning experience.

Special Needs

If you have a child with special needs, such as dyslexia or ADHD (attention deficit hyperactivity disorder), taking advantage of the programs and services your public school provides can expand your support system and give you some relief in working with your child. In many instances, the easy access and little or no cost of these services makes this a viable option for homeschoolers.

Depending on your child's diagnosed needs, some school districts may offer full services and programs, while some may only provide consultations. Some school districts' special education departments have established parent support networks that you may be able to participate in as a homeschooler. States and school districts vary in terms of what homeschoolers are allowed to participate in, so check with your local school administrator and then check with your state's regulations to verify your eligibility.

Two organizations, the Home School Legal Defense Association (HSLDA) and the National Challenged Homeschoolers Association Network (NATHHAN), offer a wide range of information and assistance on services and programs available for special needs children. Check them out on the Internet at *http://www.hslda.org* and *http://www.nathhan.com*. Your local homeschooling group—especially veteran homeschoolers—also will have practical information you can use.

Additionally, some homeschooling parents combine the resources of a school with those offered by a private organization to maximize support.

Gifted Children

If your child is considered gifted, your local public school may have programs available for students who require additional intellectual attention. Check with your local school administrator and your state's regulations first. In addition to providing information on special needs children, HSLDA and NATHHAN offer resources for parents of gifted children.

Don't be afraid to check out the colleges in your area, too. Many times colleges, especially community colleges, offer classes or one-time workshops that might be of interest to your child. Check with your local schools to see how you can take advantage of these opportunities.

Extracurricular Activities

Locations of other homeschooling families in the area, schedules, and different homeschooling approaches can make creating clubs specifically for homeschoolers challenging. Nonetheless, extracurricular activities at your local schools can give your child opportunities for peer interaction, and can help him or her develop new skills and interests that homeschooling situations can't always provide. For example, if your child has shown an interest in music and wants to play in a band, many communities don't have youth bands or orchestras (or if they do, the child must play at a certain level); in a school setting, your child might be able to play in the school band at his or her own level. Sometimes taking music lessons from a school's band leader is also an option.

Other extracurricular activities, such as Girl Scouts and Boy Scouts or 4-H (or if your child is older, a language club or an academic club, such as one for math, science, or debate), might offer additional opportunities for your homeschooler to interact with his or her peers and have a worthwhile learning experience at the same time. These types of groups often need parent volunteers as leaders, which can provide you with additional interaction with the school. If your homeschooled child is interested in extracurricular athletics, towns might not offer community-based athletics at a competitive level, so participating in school sports may be an option to consider, especially for your older child.

Your school also might have other resources that are suited to your needs. For example, the school library may be a better place than your community library to go to for the materials you need. Many schools also have certain times of the week or season when the gymnasium is open to the community for use. And some schools even host special seasonal activities for students during holiday breaks. Contact your local school district before participating.

Returning to School

If you plan on having your child return to school, taking advantage of the programs and opportunities offered can help ease the transition back into the classroom. Your child will already experience a sense of familiarity with his or her surroundings and peers, which can help smooth the transition to a different structure of learning.

Meet Your Third Grader

Third graders tend to be a lively bunch. Happier and more outgoing than he or she was in second grade, a third-grade child naturally plays and works hard. Of course, each child is unique and proceeds through the stages of growth at an individual pace—sometimes faster and sometimes slower. Your eight- to nine-and-a-half-year-old child may be accurately described here or may be working through a growth stage more commonly attributed to children one or two years younger or older. These variations between children are normal and expected. Whatever stage your child is in, recognizing the behavior patterns common to his or her age group can make your relationship healthier and more enjoyable.

Embrace Outgoing Nature

Some children at this age exchange their rather withdrawn second-grade demeanor for a new and very outgoing personality, ready to take on each new challenge (whatever that may be). Some third graders, in regard to play, experience this gusto for life combined with a bit of cockiness and an increased sense of physical ability. This can propel some children at this age to be fearless and play until exhausted. Active games and team sports are popular. Unfortunately, broken bones and accidents can often happen in this age group.

Your third-grade child has expanded his or her confidence and willingness to experience new things. This excitement propels everyday life into hyperdrive. Eating, talking, moving, playing—everything is done at increased speed. In his or her enthusiasm, a third grader may tend to do too much, become overstimulated, and appear flighty and unfocused. Understanding the high level of energy your child is experiencing and finding ways to help your third grader focus can subdue the craziness and ease overstimulation.

Your third grader may resist direct commands from adults, wanting to feel that he or she is making the decisions. However, third graders like to talk in code or secret languages. Developing an understood language of codes may improve his or her reception to guidance. One-word cues that you agree upon such as "breathe," or gestures such as folding your hands over your chest, can be used as a signal to gently help your third grader focus.

Guide Relationships

Your child is working on the emotional aspect of his or her relationships with others and may develop a small group of close friends or one best friend. Third graders are striving to develop interpersonal skills, which are as fundamental at this age as writing and math. Because of this, most third-grade children prefer working on projects in cooperative groups instead of working alone.

Third graders, however, are aware of differences and similarities. Naturally sensitive and intuitive, third-grade children are internally attuned to the idea of respect and are quick to respond positively to adult role modeling of tolerant behavior and compassion. This is a good age for parents and teachers to address the issue of multicultural relations and to encourage third-grade children to recognize the Untied States as a culturally diverse country with many different kinds of people.

A child at this age is reaching out to others. Very perceptive and visually astute, the third-grade child is able to assess verbal communication against emotional clues. If you're dishonest with a third grader, he or she will know it at some level, which can cause confusion. Honesty, authenticity, and self-awareness in parents and teachers are more important than ever.

Allow Interaction with Adults

A third-grade child loves to listen in on adult conversations even to the point of seeming nosy. He or she is highly influenced by the opinions of respected adults. Like a sponge, a third grader picks up the beliefs of his or her parents and teachers. At family gatherings your child will want to sit at the adult table and listen to family conversation, especially family stories about Dad, Mom, Grandma, and Grandpa. It's beneficial to include your third grader in these interactions instead of sending him or her back to the children's table.

Honor the Need to Be Heard

Third graders are talkers, and they talk to be heard. They often talk loud and fast, exaggerate what they say, and dramatize everything using facial and arm gestures for emphasis. A third-grade child will specialize in exclamations such as "That was the longest movie ever!" or "I could die from this!" and "I am never going to another game again!" Your third-grade child will want to share everything with you, and it may be hurtful for him or her if you don't make time to listen or fail to pay adequate attention.

Your third grader may also become very possessive and needy with his or her primary caregiver, perhaps more solicitous and needy than at any other time. Your child will seek your undivided attention and may even want to be around you constantly. Not only does your third grader want you to pay attention, he or she also needs to feel that you want to pay attention. Simply going through the motions will be perceived as a slight and may cause anxiety or acting out.

If the demands on your time and energy become overwhelming, you might designate specific slots of time each day when your third grader knows he or she will receive your undivided attention. Be clear about these boundaries. You may also consider giving your third grader a secret memento to hold during times that you have to be away from each other. Your child will then be able to hold the memento while you are gone and know that you're thinking especially of him or her.

Be careful not to underestimate the importance of meeting your child's developmental needs for acknowledgment. If your third grader is allowed to satiate himself or herself with your attention and caring during this stage, once it's complete he or she will move on with a solid foundation for later relationships.

Give Praise Authentically

You third grader is constantly assessing everything and everyone, including himself or herself. A third grader's acute awareness of mistakes can make him or her very self-critical. Acknowledgement and praise are eagerly sought after. Your child may make statements such as "I did a terrible job on that project" or "I'm not good at anything" in hopes that you will disagree and offer reassurance. This is normal for this growth stage, and it's okay to give a third grader the praise he or she is indirectly seeking. However, when your third grader is fishing for praise, try not to overexaggerate. Third graders have an understanding of the actual level of their achievements, and it's better to find the smallest thing to praise with heartfelt sincerity than to overly praise mediocre work.

Recognize Changing Physiology

A third-grade child begins to look physically more mature. Your child is truly growing up, and you may begin to see hints of his or her future physique and body type. Third graders become more physically coordinated and develop their own unique gestures and mannerisms. They also tend to be healthier and tire less easily than they did as second graders. Eating improves and your child may enjoy more types of food or be less rigid in food preferences. Your third grader may be more independent when getting ready in the morning and at bedtime, but he or she may still be very much in need of the emotional connection of being tucked in at night or having a story read before bed.

Third graders are aware of sexual differences at a new level, and some children may avoid or resist being near the opposite sex. Many third graders become more interested in learning more about how babies actually get into their mothers as well as how they get out. Honest answers to these types of questions will be most appreciated by children of this age. While some boys and girls stick to the "cooties" philosophy about the opposite sex, others may demonstrate the first signs of sexual feelings and begin to take interest in each other in small ways. Boys may point out the girls they think are pretty, and girls may begin playing chasing games with the boys. Some write notes back and forth or even talk about a girlfriend or boyfriend, although the behavior associated with "going steady" in older children is usually absent.

Embrace Expanding Intellect

Your third grader is expanding intellectually. Third-grade minds understand cause and effect and are acutely aware of similarities and differences. Thinking is more imaginative and original, and you may see a new awareness of three-dimensional representation in your third grader's artwork. Your third-grade child also is accepting reality on a new level.

A child at this stage is aware of the forces of nature and develops an interest in the life cycles of plants and animals. Your child's spatial perception also is expanding. He or she is more comfortable going farther from home on foot in your neighborhood. A third grader can conceptualize the four directions on a map and is interested in taking trips to the zoo or museums. He or she also likes to visit new cities and learn about the geography of other places. *Making the Grade* includes several lessons that give your child the opportunity to develop and practice map and directional skills in your community.

Similarly, you may find that your third grader has become more responsible in the area of punctuality and awareness of time. Although known to lose or break watches, third graders regularly look at the clock, ask others for the time, and maintain a sense of time passing throughout the day.

Structure Learning

Since having your undivided attention is so important for third graders, teaching your third-grade child one-on-one at home can be a wonderful experience, provided it's done in a focused manner. Third graders are just beginning to make the learning transition from an elementary level to a middle grade level and can still require a good deal of hands-on projects and field trips to balance book learning. *Making the Grade* is a good resource for engaging activities and learning projects. Structuring devices such as to-do folders and designated storage areas for different projects and subjects can be very helpful for the ambitious and scattered third grader.

Maintain Perspective and Enjoy!

Though demanding and self-critical at times, the third-grade child still seems to enjoy the growth experience and have reasonably good self-esteem at this stage. The greatest challenge for a parent or teacher is to listen attentively and from the heart. The zest for life, silliness, and untempered braggadocio can be a wonderful source of enjoyment for you both when your child has the understanding, structure, and help to set limits that he or she needs so much during this time.

Promoting Literacy

Promoting Literacy

Key Topics

Fiction
Pages 3–10

Writing Sentences and Supporting Details
Pages 11–18

Dialogue and Contractions
Pages 19–26

Writing Dates and Time
Pages 27–30

Science Fiction
Pages 31–38

Folktales and Poetry
Pages 39–48

Biographies and Nonfiction
Pages 49–60

Taking Notes and Writing Directions
Pages 61–72

Thank You's
Pages 73–76

Reading Fiction

*Fiction provides a place for imaginations to expand and soar.
Begin your exploration today!*

OBJECTIVE	BACKGROUND	MATERIALS
To help your student identify and understand elements of fiction	This lesson draws upon your student's knowledge of stories to teach fiction. Fiction is a type of literature in which the story is invented by the author. A fictional story has three main elements of literature—setting, characters, and plot. In this lesson, your student will read a fictional story, identify the elements of the story, and understand how these elements bring meaning to the story.	■ Student Learning Pages 1.A–1.C ■ 1 copy Sequence Chain, page 354 ■ 1 copy Web, page 354

VOCABULARY

FICTION   a story that is not true
SETTING   where a story takes place
CHARACTERS   who or what the story is about (such as people, animals, objects)
PLOT   the action in a story
THEME   the overall meaning of a story
MONARCH   a person who rules over a kingdom
SUMMONING   commanding someone to come forward

Let's Begin

1   **INTRODUCE** Invite your student to skim the story "The King's Toys" on Student Learning Page 1.A. Have your student look at the pictures and read the title of the story. Together with your student discuss his or her predictions for what will happen in the story. Challenge your student to think about reasons for his or her predictions.

Tell your student that "The King's Toys" is **fiction.** Reveal that a fictional story is not true. The author makes it up. Fictional stories include a **setting** or settings, **characters,** and a **plot.** Help your student understand the meanings of these words.

2   **REVIEW VOCABULARY WORDS** Give your student a list of the vocabulary words from this section. Ask your student to say each word aloud. Encourage your student to figure out the

ENRICH THE EXPERIENCE

Discuss your student's favorite toy. Have him or her ask peers, grandparents, or other close adults to discuss their favorite toys.

unknown word by dividing it into syllables or units of sounds. Challenge your student to use the words verbally in sentences.

3 **READ** Give your student a copy of the Sequence Chain found on page 354. Have him or her read aloud "The King's Toys." After he or she has finished reading, have him or her write the sequence of the plot on the chart.

4 **DISCUSS** Consider with your student the characters in the story. Ask your student, *Who is the main character of the story?* [the king] *How do you know this?* [he is mentioned the most; he gets the toys; he learns the lesson] *Who are the other characters in the story?* [librarian, butler, footman, page boy, Jack] *How are they important?* [they help the king get the toys; Jack teaches the king how to play with toys]

5 **DIRECT** Give your student a copy of the Web found on page 354. Ask him or her to write the word **theme** in the center. Remind your student that the theme is the overall meaning of a story. Brainstorm with your student possible themes for "The King's Toys." [don't grow up too fast; people give meaning to objects; ask others for help] Assist him or her in thinking about the meaning behind the story and prompt him or her to come up with possible ideas.

6 **REVISIT** Together with your student review the predictions that you discussed earlier. Ask your student which predictions were accurate. Ask your student what surprises he or she found in the story.

7 **DISTRIBUTE** Distribute Student Learning Page 1.B. Inform your student that he or she will practice writing fiction. Monitor your student as he or she completes Student Learning Page 1.B. Discuss how dialogue helps to tell the plot of a story.

Branching Out

TEACHING TIP

If you have a struggling or reluctant reader, you may want to first read the story aloud to your student and then ask him or her to read it aloud to you. You may also alternate reading sections of the story with your student.

CHECKING IN

Check if your student can generalize the skills learned in this lesson and apply them to a story of his or her choice. Have your student write the words *setting, characters, plot,* and *theme* on a sheet of paper. Ask your student to select a story and share it with you aloud. When he or she is finished reading, invite him or her to identify the setting, characters, plot, and theme of his or her story.

ENRICH THE EXPERIENCE

Explain to your student that some fictional stories are made into movies. Check with your local library for information on some fictional stories that have been made into movies. Read the story. Then view the movie. Discuss how the two are alike and different and why.

ENRICH THE EXPERIENCE

Together read *The Velveteen Rabbit.* Then ask your student if the queen's "no toy" rule was wise?

FOR FURTHER READING

Guided Reading: A How-To for All Grades, by Bonnie Burns (Skylight, 2001).

Reaching Readers: Flexible and Innovative Strategies for Guiding Reading, by Michael F. Opitz (Heinemann, 2001).

Read-Alouds with Young Children, by Robin Campbell (International Reading Association, 2001).

Explore Fiction

The King's Toys
from *Tick Tock Tales*
by Margaret Mahy

When the king was just a little king, his mother, who was very strict, would not let him have any toys at all.

"You are a king," she said. "You must take life seriously. You must learn to spell."

His mother, the queen, thought that knowing how to spell was most important for a king. She had a room specially designed for him in which to practice his spelling.

When he was nearly a grown-up king, his mother left for a few days to visit her aunt who lived on top of a glass mountain. While his mother was away, the king decided to give himself a treat: He would buy a toy. By now he was the best speller of any **monarch** in the world, but in his entire life he had never had a single toy.

Summoning the royal librarian, the king asked him: "Librarians are meant to know everything. What toy would you suggest I buy?"

"Well, when I was small," said the librarian, "I used to be very fond of my teddy bear."

"Right!" said the king. So he sent his butler out to buy a teddy bear.

(CONTINUED)

But the butler, who did not wish to be seen buying a toy, sent for a footman and told him to go instead.

But the footman did not want to be seen buying a teddy bear. So he sent for the page boy and told him to go in his place.

But the page boy, who was almost thirteen and very grown-up, did not want anyone to see him buying a teddy bear either. So he sent for the kitchen boy, Jack—the youngest of the king's staff.

He ran to the toy shop across the road from the palace and bought a beautiful, large, golden teddy bear.

"I like this bear," he said. "I like it so much that perhaps I should get another one. It will be rather lonely by itself."

(CONTINUED)

"Why not try a rocking horse next?" suggested the librarian.

The king's royal spelling room gradually became a royal toy room. Soon it was so full of toys that there wasn't room for any more.

"Right!" exclaimed the king. "That's enough. Now let's see what happens next."

He looked at his huge collection of toys, waiting for them to do something. At last, the king sent for the butler.

"I certainly have a lot of toys," he said.

"You do have a lovely collection, Your Majesty," agreed the butler.

"Yes, but when are they going to *do* something?" the king asked.

But the butler seemed to have forgotten exactly what toys were supposed to do.

"One moment," he said, and shot off through the maze of palace corridors to find the footman. "Just remind me," the butler said, "for it's a long time since I had any toys myself . . . what are the king's toys supposed to *do*?"

"Just remind me," the footman said, hurrying to the page boy. "What are those toys supposed to *do*?"

The page boy ran to the kitchen and found Jack scrubbing soup off a royal saucepan.

"His Majesty wishes to know when the toys are going to *do* something," the butler said

(CONTINUED) ▶

sternly to Jack. Jack looked at the king. He looked at the toys.

"Your Majesty, *you* are the one who has to do something," Jack cried. "Toys are meant to be *played* with. They are waiting for you to *play* with them."

"Play?" cried the king. He spelled the word. "P-L-A-Y! But how do I P-L-A-Y?"

"I'll show you!" cried Jack. Grabbing the teddy bear, he leaped on to the rocking horse. Then he rocked until the horse nearly came off its elegant rockers. He made the dollhouse dolls ask the hero dolls and robot dolls to tea, and they all had a slice of pink cake, and yet there was plenty left over.

Finish the Story

"The King's Toys" ends with Jack showing the king how to play with toys. Now it's your turn to write what happens next in the story. What do you think will happen when the king's mother returns from visiting her aunt? Include the answer to this question and any other information you want to add in your story. Use quotation marks to show who is talking in your writing. Look back at "The King's Toys" if you need help with placing your quotation marks. Draw a picture in the blank box to illustrate your part of the story. Share the entire story, including the part that you wrote, with others. You may want to put on a puppet show of your story, or read it into a cassette recorder.

I think that he x is going to be playing with the toy and his mother will see him Playing with them. Then one year later the King is going to want some different toys. And give the old ones to the CHEILF JACKs. Ant

What's Next? You Decide!

Now it's your turn to choose what to do next in the lesson. Read the activities and decide which one you want to do—you may even want to try them both!

Build Your Kingdom

MATERIALS

❏ 1 sheet posterboard
❏ 6–10 colored pencils or crayons

STEPS

Hello your majesty! It's your turn to rule the kingdom.

❏ Imagine you are the ruler of a kingdom. Describe what your kingdom looks like and who lives in your kingdom.

❏ Create a posterboard to show your kingdom. On the posterboard include a map of your kingdom, a drawing of the people who live in your kingdom, and a list of rules for your kingdom. Don't forget to name your kingdom.

❏ When you're finished, hang your posterboard so everyone can see your kingdom!

Create a Word Wall

MATERIALS

❏ 5 sheets unlined paper
❏ 6–10 markers or colored pencils

STEPS

Reading stories helps you learn new words. You learned many new words in "The King's Toys."

❏ Divide each sheet of paper into four boxes. Draw lines separating the boxes.

❏ Write each new word you learned in one of the boxes with a marker. Color and decorate the box to make it stand out.

❏ In the other boxes write antonyms (words with opposite meanings) for the words in the story.

❏ As you read more stories, make more boxes on paper and write new words.

❏ Share your word boxes with your friends and family and invite them to add a new word to a box!

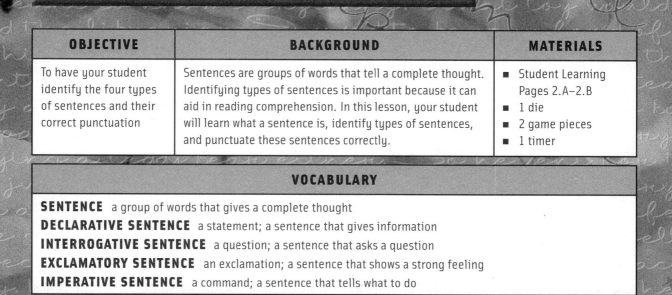

PROMOTING LITERACY

Learning Sentences

Words make up sentences, sentences make up paragraphs, and paragraphs make up stories!

OBJECTIVE	BACKGROUND	MATERIALS
To have your student identify the four types of sentences and their correct punctuation	Sentences are groups of words that tell a complete thought. Identifying types of sentences is important because it can aid in reading comprehension. In this lesson, your student will learn what a sentence is, identify types of sentences, and punctuate these sentences correctly.	■ Student Learning Pages 2.A–2.B ■ 1 die ■ 2 game pieces ■ 1 timer

VOCABULARY
SENTENCE a group of words that gives a complete thought **DECLARATIVE SENTENCE** a statement; a sentence that gives information **INTERROGATIVE SENTENCE** a question; a sentence that asks a question **EXCLAMATORY SENTENCE** an exclamation; a sentence that shows a strong feeling **IMPERATIVE SENTENCE** a command; a sentence that tells what to do

Let's Begin

1 **INTRODUCE** Begin this lesson by showing your student the following groups of words. Invite your student to read each group of words aloud.

- The girl sees the dog. (sentence)
- Ate peanut butter. (not a sentence)
- Can read the story. (not a sentence)
- A pen is used for writing. (sentence)
- You and your friend. (not a sentence)
- Jim swims in the lake. (sentence)

2 **REVEAL** Share with your student that the first, fourth, and sixth group of words are sentences. Ask your student why he or she thinks the others aren't sentences. Together go over each and talk about how they're different or the same. Then reveal that a **sentence** tells a complete thought. Sentences begin with a capital letter and end with a period, an exclamation point, or a question mark.

3 **SHARE** Tell your student that there are four kinds of sentences. Together walk through each one on the next page.

A BRIGHT IDEA

Use coins or buttons for handy game pieces.

- A sentence that makes a statement, or declares something. Here is an example: Basketball is fun. This type of sentence is called a **declarative sentence.** These types of sentences always end with a period.
- A sentence that asks a question. Here is an example: Do you like to play soccer? This type of sentence is called an **interrogative sentence.** Interrogate means to ask questions. These types of sentences have a question mark at the end.
- A sentence that has a lot of feeling or excitement. Here is an example: This ball is heavy! This type of sentence is called an **exclamatory sentence.** *Exclaim* means "to speak loudly." These types of sentences always end with an exclamation point.
- A sentence that tells or commands someone or something to do something. Here is an example: Take your backpack. This type of sentence is called an **imperative sentence.** If something is imperative, that means it's something necessary.

4   **MODEL AND PRACTICE** On a separate sheet of paper write an example of each type of sentence, including end punctuation. Then tell your student what type of sentence each is. Then write four more examples and have your student tell you what type each is. You may have to guide him or her through this exercise. If you feel your student needs more practice, write more sentences and have him or her tell you what types they are.

5   **DISTRIBUTE AND PRACTICE** Distribute Student Learning Page 2.A. Be sure to give your student enough time to complete the activities.

Branching Out

TEACHING TIP

Take three index cards. On one have your student write a question mark. On another one have him or her write an exclamation point. On the third have him or her write a period. Then say simple sentences aloud to your student. After each one have your student hold up the card that has the correct punctuation for that sentence. Then switch and have your student say sentences aloud while you hold up the cards with the correct punctuation.

CHECKING IN

Check if your student can demonstrate the skills learned in this lesson with a story of his or her choice. Ask your student to select a story. Then have him or her read a few pages of it to you aloud. Periodically stop your child's reading and ask him or her what type of sentence he or she just read. Have your student share how he or she knew it was a particular type of sentence.

FOR FURTHER READING

How to Write a Sentence, by Kathleen Christopher Null (Teacher Created Materials, 1998).

Silly Sentences: Grammar Skills Practice for the First Three Years of School (DK Publishing, Inc., 2000).

Build a Sentence

Read each sentence. Write the correct punctuation at the end of each sentence. Choose from a period (.), a question mark (?), and an exclamation point (!).

1. What did you see today _____

2. This pumpkin is so big _____

3. Tanya likes math _____

4. Take your books with you _____

Read each sentence. Put the words and punctuation in order. Then write each sentence in order.

5. The watch children game. the

_____

6. love I apples! to eat

_____

7. buy Save your a money to bike.

_____

8. big is balloon? How the

_____

Write an example of each of the four types of sentences.

9. _____

10. _____

11. _____

12. _____

Play Make a Sentence

Put your game pieces at start. Player 1 rolls the die. Then he or she moves his or her piece that number of places on the board. Player 2 sets the timer to 10 seconds. Player 1 has 10 seconds to say out loud a sentence that uses the type of punctuation on that space. When saying the sentence, use a different body movement for that type of punctuation: jump up for exclamation point, sit down for period, throw hands up for question mark. If Player 1 says the right type of sentence, he or she rolls again. If Player 1 doesn't, Player 2 takes a turn. The first player to get to the finish line wins.

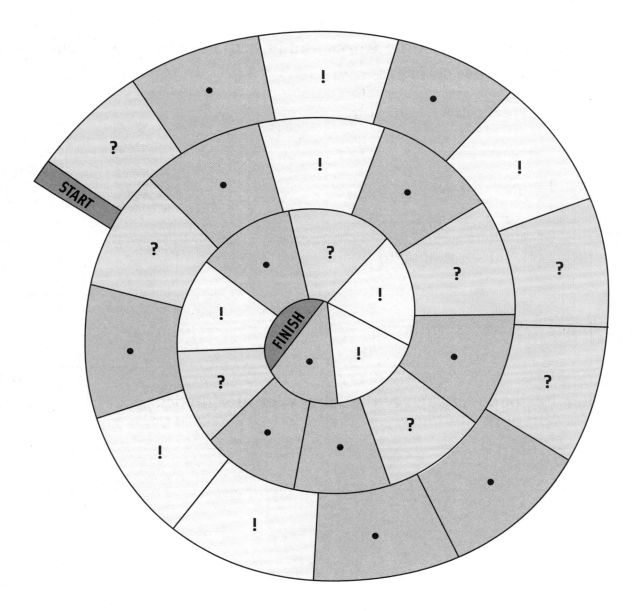

PROMOTING
LITERACY

LESSON
1.3

Finding Topic Sentences and Supporting Details

*Words within sentences are like bricks in a sturdy house:
Building strong sentences leads to strong writing.*

OBJECTIVE	BACKGROUND	MATERIALS
To have your student learn how to identify topic sentences and supporting details	Sentences are groups of words that tell a complete thought. Topic sentences state what an entire paragraph is about and usually appear at the beginning of the paragraph. Each sentence within a paragraph should support and connect with the topic sentence. The details expand the paragraph and help the reader understand the topic sentence further. In this lesson, your student will read and analyze a paragraph and write a paragraph with a topic sentence and supporting details.	<ul><li>Student Learning Pages 3.A–3.B</li><li>1 copy Web, page 354</li><li>1 copy Writing Lines, page 355</li></ul>

VOCABULARY

PARAGRAPH a group of sentences about one main topic
TOPIC SENTENCE a sentence that explains what an entire paragraph is about
SUPPORTING DETAILS sentences that give details about the topic sentence

Let's Begin

1 **READ** Invite your student to read aloud this **paragraph:**

Yesterday, I won first place in a drawing contest. I drew a picture of the forest in a nearby park. My drawing had squirrels, birds, bees, and even ants. These are things I see when I go to the park. My teacher gave me first prize because I added so many colors and details to my picture. He said it looked very real.

2 **ASK** Ask your student what the paragraph is about. Walk your student through these questions and guide as necessary. Ask, *What is the main idea or main point of the paragraph?* [the writer won first place] *What are the reasons in the paragraph that help tell you what the main idea is?* [the writer drew a picture of a forest; it had many colors and details; the drawing looked very real]

3 **REVEAL** Share with your student that these sentences are grouped into a paragraph, and that every paragraph has a main idea that is often written in a **topic sentence.** Tell your student that a topic sentence is a sentence that explains what an entire paragraph is about. This sentence is often the first sentence of a paragraph.

4 **ASK** Now ask your student, *What is the topic sentence of the paragraph you just read?* ["Yesterday, I won first place in a drawing contest."] Tell your student that the rest of the sentences in a paragraph give more ideas or details about the topic sentence. These are called **supporting details.**

5 **PRACTICE** Make a copy of the Web found on page 354. Have your student think of his or her favorite food and write that food in the center. Then have him or her write details about this food, such as why it's a favorite, what color it is, what it tastes like, and so on, in the surrounding circles.

6 **CONNECT** Have a conversation about your student's favorite food and narrow down what a possible topic sentence might be if he or she were to write a paragraph about the favorite food. Have him or her write this topic sentence in his or her notebook. Then brainstorm with your student and come up with supporting details for the topic sentence. Encourage him or her to refer to the Web. If it helps, have your student think of a table with four legs. The legs are the details that support the table top.

7 **DISTRIBUTE** Distribute Student Learning Page 3.A. Be sure to give your student enough time to complete it. Make a copy of the Writing Lines found on page 355. Have him or her write a paragraph using the topic sentence and three supporting details from Student Learning Page 3.A. Then give your student enough time to write a paragraph. Encourage him or her to write more details!

GET ORGANIZED

If you'd like, plan ahead and have that food ready for him or her prior to beginning the Web to give an appealing twist to the activity.

Branching Out

FOR FURTHER READING

Marvelous Month-by-Month Writing Prompts, by Justin McCory Martin (Scholastic Professional Books, 2001).

Third Grade Reading Level (Modern Curriculum Press, 2000).

TEACHING TIP

Have your student think about a favorite vacation spot, a recent visit to a relative's house, or a favorite trip to a museum or park. Have him or her use this topic sentence: Going to vacation spot/relative's house/museum or park was a favorite trip I took. Then ask him or her to give you details about the trip—why it's the favorite.

CHECKING IN

Assess your student's understanding of topic sentences and supporting details by having him or her read a paragraph from a book. Ask your student to share the paragraph with you aloud. Then have him or her identify the topic sentence and supporting details.

Write the Details

Read the topic sentence in the water faucet. Then write three supporting details about it in the water drops.

Water is important.

What's Next? You Decide!

Now it's your turn to choose what to do next in the lesson. Read the activities and decide which one you want to do—you may even want to try them both!

Guess What Object

STEPS

Play this game with friends.

❏ Choose an object.

❏ Tell your friends one detail about the object, such as its color.

❏ Each friend gets to guess what it might be.

❏ If they can't guess it, tell them one more detail at a time until someone guesses the object.

❏ Then have someone else choose an object, and you guess what it is.

Write About You

MATERIALS

❏ 4 sheets $8\frac{1}{2}$-by-11-inch paper

❏ markers or crayons

❏ 1 stapler

STEPS

You are a great topic for a paragraph. There are many details about you that are interesting. Create an All About Me book!

❏ Put four sheets of paper in a stack. Fold the paper in half.

❏ Ask an adult to staple it together in the center. This is your book!

❏ Write your name on the cover because you're the topic.

❏ Write and draw one supporting detail about you on each page of the book. You could write about your hobbies, your favorite food, your hair color, your favorite book, or anything else.

❏ Share your book with an adult.

Writing Dialogue

Good conversation brings our thoughts and feelings to life!

OBJECTIVE	BACKGROUND	MATERIALS
To help your student learn to read and write dialogue using correct capitalization and punctuation	Learning how to identify and punctuate dialogue is an important writing skill. In this lesson, your student will examine examples of dialogue in stories and learn to use correct punctuation and capitalization in writing original dialogue.	■ Student Learning Pages 4.A–4.B ■ colored pencils

Let's Begin

1 **EXPLAIN** Explain to your student that dialogue is the written version of conversation between two or more people. Ask your student to think of reasons that a writer may include dialogue in his or her writing. Help the student understand that dialogue makes characters "come to life" for the reader by allowing the reader to hear the actual words that were exchanged.

2 **MODEL** Show your student that, to separate what characters in a story are saying from the rest of the story, special punctuation is used. Have your student write the following sentences in his or her notebook:

> It is getting late Jack said.
> Sally asked what time is it?

Help your student see that these sentences are confusing because they don't have proper punctuation. Ask your student to determine which words are being spoken. Have your student add quotation marks, comma, and capitalization to make the sentences read:

> "It is getting late," Jack said.
> Sally asked, "What time is it?"

3 **EXPLAIN AND REVIEW** Explain that quotation marks are written around the words that were actually said. Also point out that the first letter of the quotation is always capitalized, and a comma is used to separate the quotation from the rest of the sentence. Finally, mention that end punctuation should be placed inside the final quotation marks. For a review of types of sentences, together with your student go to Lesson 1.2.

4   **WRITE**   Have your student write theses sentences in his or her notebook.

> Where are you going my mother called after me.
> I said I'm going to Miguel's house.
> Be back at five for dinner she answered.
> Okay, I will I said.

5   **IDENTIFY**   Have your student use a colored pencil to underline what's being said in each sentence. [Where are you going; I'm going to Miguel's house; Be back at five for dinner; Okay, I will] Then ask your student to use a different colored pencil and add quotation marks. Then have him or her use another color of pencil and add the commas and end punctuation. Finally, have him or her capitalize any letters. Refer him or her to the dialogue that he or she wrote in Step 2 for help. If you'd like, you can have your student check his or her own work:

> "Where are you going?" my mother called after me.
> I said, "I'm going to Miguel's house."
> "Be back at five for dinner," she answered.
> "Okay, I will," I said.

6   **PRACTICE**   Distribute Student Learning Page 4.A. Together read each sentence. Have your student insert correct punctuation and use correct capitalization.

Branching Out

TEACHING TIP

Remind your student that dialogue should sound like two people really talking to each other. For extra reinforcement, direct your student to books that he or she has read and point out the dialogue in them.

CHECKING IN

Assess your student's understanding of writing dialogue by reading the original dialogue that he or she writes on Student Learning Page 4.A or other sentences that you give him or her to practice. Be sure that the student:

- Writes dialogue that sounds like real people speaking.
- Places quotation marks around the words being spoken.
- Capitalizes the first letter of the quotation.
- Places end punctuation inside the quotation marks.
- Uses proper punctuation.
- Uses a comma to set the quotation apart from the rest of the sentence.

FOR FURTHER READING

Building Grammar Homework Booklet— Grade 3 & 4, by Meredith Van Zomeran, Wendy Roh Jenks, and Jane Harodine, eds. (McGraw-Hill Children's Publishing, 2001).

Write Dialogue

Max just moved into your neighborhood. Read what Max says. Use quotation marks, commas, periods, and question marks to complete his dialogue. Don't forget to capitalize the right letters!

Hi, the boy said. My name is Max. what's your name?

Well, it's nice to meet you. Are there a lot of kids that live in this neighborhood Max asked.

I think I'm really going to like it here Max said. It seems like a really nice place to live. What do you do for fun around here?

Max said I'm glad that we moved in next to you. I hope that we can be friends!

Oh, there's my brother. I think he needs help bringing boxes in the house, Max said quickly.

Now write two more sentences about what you would say. Don't forget to use correct punctuation and capitalization.

What's Next? You Decide!

Now it's your turn to choose what to do next in the lesson. Read the activities and decide which one you want to do—you may want to try them both!

Write a Conversation

STEPS

Dialogue is all around you every day. Every time you hear two or more people talking to each other, you're listening to dialogue!

- ❑ Listen to your own conversations and others around you. (Make sure they're conversations that you're meant to hear!)
- ❑ Then think about what kind of conversation you'd have with a space alien that has just landed or a talking pet.
- ❑ Choose who or what you'd have a conversation with.
- ❑ Write the conversation.
- ❑ Share your conversation with another person and take turns reading the dialogue.

Make a Comic Strip

MATERIALS

- ❑ your favorite book
- ❑ 1–2 clean sheets paper
- ❑ 1 page newspaper comics
- ❑ colored pencils

STEPS

Make your own comic strip!

- ❑ Look over a page of newspaper comics. See how the words are put into "cartoon bubbles" as a way to show who's speaking what.
- ❑ Now read some pages from your favorite book. Turn your book into a comic or make up your own dialogue.
- ❑ Look at what the people and things in your book are saying. Then draw them saying those words like a newspaper comic.
- ❑ Use colored pencils to color your comic.
- ❑ Ask to display your comic for everyone in your family to see.

Exploring Contractions

When taking a walk, one often takes the shortest route. Contractions are the shortest route to expressing yourself through words.

OBJECTIVE	BACKGROUND	MATERIALS
To help your student learn to use contractions properly in speaking and writing	Contractions are an important part of everyday language. People often use contractions without even thinking about them. In this lesson, your student will learn to decode contractions and to recognize common contractions.	■ Student Learning Pages 5.A–5.B ■ 21 index cards ■ 1 copy Writing Lines, page 355

Let's Begin

1 INTRODUCE Ask your student to think of a time that he or she has taken a shortcut. Invite him or her to think about why that route was chosen. Help the student to see that shortcuts save time and can be easier than another, longer route. Explain that speakers and writers take shortcuts for the same reasons. When we speak and write, we often use contractions, which provide a shorter, easier version of two words. Ask your student if he or she knows what a contraction is.

2 DISCUSS Say this sentence to your student, *I don't know where my shoes are.* Then write it on a sheet of paper for your student or have him or her write it in his or her notebook. Ask him or her if she can identify the contraction in the sentence. Point out that the contraction is the word with the apostrophe, *don't.* Then say this sentence to your student, *I do not know where my shoes are.* Have him or her write it next to the other sentence. Point out the words *do not.* Ask your student if he or she sees the difference between the two sentences. Discuss.

3 EXPLAIN AND PRACTICE Go back to the first sentence with the contraction and cover *do* with your fingers and have your student look at the end of the word, *n't.* Encourage the student to think about what *n't* might stand for. Explain that the apostrophe takes the place of a letter or letters. Assist him or her until he or she understands that the *n't* replaces *not*, so *don't* is a short version, or contraction, of *do not.* Ask your student to use the method just modeled of finding a familiar word and examining the remaining part of the word to determine the meaning of the words *can't* and *you'll.*

4 **PREPARE AND DISTRIBUTE** Before distributing Student Learning Page 5.A, prepare the 21 index cards. On one side of each card, write these contractions—one contraction per card:

can't	isn't	you'll
we're	I'll	that's
they've	don't	she's
I've	they're	we've
won't	you're	here's
doesn't	he'll	we'll
she'll	they'll	wasn't

On the opposite side of each card, write the words that make up the contraction. For example, *is not* for *isn't*.

5 **SORT** Together with your student follow the directions for 1–5. Give him or her enough time to sort the contractions by ending. Help him or her to see the patterns in these contractions; *n't* is short for *not* and so on.

6 **SAY** Help your student complete questions 6–10. You may have to provide assistance if he or she is having trouble determining what words make up the contraction. Encourage your student to check his or her answers by turning over the cards. Than have him or her complete the rest of the page.

7 **CONTINUE** Tell your student that contractions are common in everyday language. If you'd like, have your student watch a TV program or movie of your choosing and have him or her count the number of contractions that are used during it.

ENRICH THE EXPERIENCE

Explain to your student that although contractions generally are formed by simply replacing a letter or letters with an apostrophe, there are some exceptions. The most common of these is *won't,* which is a shortened form of *will not.*

Branching Out

TEACHING TIPS

❏ If you find that your student is having trouble recognizing contractions and the words that make them up, give your student a copy of the Writing Lines found on page 355 and randomly call out contractions. Have him or her write the words that make up the contractions. Or randomly call out words, such as *does not,* and have him or her write the corresponding contractions.

❏ To help your student recognize how often contractions are used, listen to how many times he or she uses contractions in the next hour or so. Keep it lively and make a buzzer sound each time he or she does so.

CHECKING IN

Assess your student's understanding of contractions by randomly choosing a few of the index cards and asking him or her to say the contraction out loud, tell you what words make up the contraction, and then use it in a sentence.

FOR FURTHER READING

Building Grammar Homework Booklet— Grade 3 & 4, by Meredith Van Zomeran, Wendy Roh Jenks, and Jane Harodine, eds. (McGraw-Hill Children's Publishing, 2001).

Categorize Contractions

Spread the index cards on a flat surface. Put them in five piles: *n't*, *'s*, *'ll*, *'ve*, and *'re*. Write what those letters stand for.

1. *n't* means <u>not</u>

2. *'s* means _____

3. *'ll* means _____

4. *'ve* means _____

5. *'re* means _____

Say each contraction out loud. Then say the words that make up each contraction. Turn the index card over to check your answer. Then answer the questions.

6. *we've* means <u>we have</u>

7. *she'll* means _____

8. *doesn't* means _____

9. *here's* means _____

Write a sentence using at least one contraction.

10. _____

_____

_____

Jimmy **doesn't** have his two front teeth!

What's Next? You Decide!

Now it's your turn to choose what to do next in the lesson. Read the activities and decide which one you want to do—you may want to try them both!

Make a Match

▪ MATERIALS

❑ 42 index cards

▪ STEPS

Use index cards to create a contraction matching game.

❑ Write a contraction on one index card. Then write the two words that make up the contraction on another card.

❑ Keep doing this using the same contractions you used for Student Learning Page 5.A.

❑ Mix up the cards and put them all facedown on a flat surface.

❑ With a friend, take turns turning over two cards at a time. If the cards turned over are a contraction and its matching words, pick them up and take another turn. If not, turn them back over and have the other person take a turn.

❑ Keep playing until all of the cards have been picked up. The winner is the one with the most pairs of index cards.

Graph Contractions

▪ MATERIALS

❑ graph paper
❑ 1 ruler or straight edge
❑ markers

▪ STEPS

People use contractions a lot! For one day, count how many times you hear the words *can't, don't, doesn't, wasn't,* and *won't.*

❑ At the end of the day, add up how many times each contraction was used.

❑ Make a bar graph on a sheet of graph paper like this one.

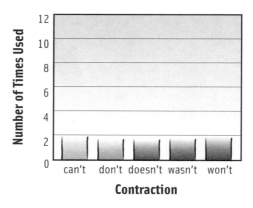

❑ Which contractions were used the most? Which ones were used the least?

Writing Correct Dates and Times

Learning how to indicate time correctly helps a writer be more specific.

OBJECTIVE	BACKGROUND	MATERIALS
To have your student learn appropriate punctuation and capitalization for dates and verb tenses that accompany time	Understanding and using dates and times are useful not only in reading and writing but in other parts of life. In this lesson, your student will learn how to correctly capitalize and punctuate dates. He or she also will learn verb tenses that accompany time.	▪ Student Learning Pages 6.A–6.B ▪ 1 current calendar

Let's Begin

1 **INTRODUCE DATES** Show your student a calendar. Ask, *What month is it? What day of the week is it? What is the date? What is the year?* Walk your student through each of the answers if he or she is struggling.

2 **EXPLAIN** Distribute Student Learning Page 6.A. Explain that there is a correct way to write dates. Then read with your student the bulleted list at the top of the page. Offer an example of each point. Then ask, *How would you write today's date?* Then have him or her complete the top part of Student Learning Page 6.A.

December 2004

S	M	T	W	T	F	S

3 **ORAL PRACTICE** For additional practice, point to random dates on the calendar. Then ask your student to say what date you are pointing to.

4 **INTRODUCE VERB TENSES** Explain that sometimes when referring to yesterday, today, and tomorrow (and other days), certain words can be used to make it clear to the listener what day you're talking about. Say, *Yesterday, the date was _____. Today, the date is _____. Tomorrow, the date will be _____.* Point out how the verb tenses changed in the sentences. Explain that *was, is,* and *will be* tell about the past, present, and future.

5 **EXPLAIN: PAST TENSE** Explain to your student that a verb in the past tense shows something that has already happened, or that already was. Point out that usually the past tense of a verb is formed by adding *–ed*. If the verb ends with an *e*, drop the final *e* before adding *–ed*. For example, *change* becomes *changed*. The past tense of the verb *be* is *was* or *were*. Say the following sentences to provide examples: *The girl went to the store yesterday. It rained last night. I touched a frog.* To encourage your student to use past tense verbs, ask, *What did you do last weekend? Where did you go yesterday?*

6 **EXPLAIN: PRESENT TENSE** Tell your student that a verb in the present tells that something is happening right now. Provide the following examples: *The man fixes the car. Maria calls her friend. The food is hot.* Prompt your student to create sentences using present tense verbs by asking *How is the weather today? What do you see in the room?*

7 **EXPLAIN: FUTURE TENSE** Explain that a verb in the future tells that something is going to happen. It is usually formed with the helping verb *shall* or *will.* To provide your student with practice using future tense verbs, ask questions such as *What will you do next week? Will it rain tomorrow?*

8 **PRACTICE** Distribute Student Learning Page 6.B. Then have your student complete the exercises. Read the directions for each exercise with your student to make sure that she or he understands them.

Branching Out

TEACHING TIP

Point out to your student that sentences sometimes have clue words that tell when an action happens. For example, the words *yesterday, last year,* and *a while ago* are clues that an action took place in the past. The words *soon, tomorrow,* and *next week* are clues that an action will happen in the future. Make a list of time words to look for when reading.

CHECKING IN

Assess your student's understanding of the correct way to write dates and verb tenses by asking him or her to write the responses to questions such as *What did you do last night? What will you do next week? What are you doing today?* Look for correct capitalization, punctuation, and your student's ability to identify different verb tenses, how to form them, and how to use them correctly.

ENRICH THE EXPERIENCE

Have your student read aloud a paragraph from his or her favorite book. After he or she reads each sentence, have him or her call out whether the verb is in the past, present, or future. Or have your student look at a newspaper or magazine article and highlight the different tenses in different colors.

FOR FURTHER READING

25 Great Grammar Poems and Activities, by Bobbi Katz and Karen Kellaher (Scholastic, Inc., 1999).

Kites Sail High: A Book About Verbs, by Ruth Heller (Putnam Publishing Group, 1998).

Write Dates

Read the rules for writing dates. Then read the dates. Each date has at least one mistake. Write the date correctly.

- ❏ Capitalize names of days.
- ❏ Capitalize names of months.
- ❏ Use a comma between the day and the year.
- ❏ Use a comma between the day and the month.

1. february 22, 1988

_____

2. June 26 1951

_____

3. 2003 14 March

_____

4. tuesday december 2004 21

_____

Read each sentence. Circle the mistakes in each sentence. Then write the sentence correctly.

5. Labor Day is the first monday in september.

_____

6. The mall first opened on april 5 2000.

_____

7. My aunt visited us last Tuesday, July 4, 1996.

_____

8. My birthday is Friday, August 12, 1999.

_____

Write Verb Tenses

Read each word. Then write the past and the future tense of each verb.

1. add   past: _____   future: _____

2. invite   past: _____   future: _____

3. paint   past: _____   future: _____

4. clean   past: _____   future: _____

Read each sentence. Then write the correct form of the word in parentheses that completes the sentence.

5. Last month, Marie _____ some seeds.
   (plant/planted/will plant)

6. Her garden _____ so beautiful now. (looks/looked/will look)

7. Soon, her roses _____. (bloom/bloomed/will bloom)

8. I _____ the roses grow next year.
   (watch/watched/will watch)

Exploring Science Fiction

Science fiction allows settings, characters, and plots to push your imagination's limits!

OBJECTIVE	BACKGROUND	MATERIALS
To have your student read and learn about the nature of science fiction	Science fiction is a popular type of literature found in today's movies, TV shows, and books. In this lesson, your student will read a science fiction story, identify the elements of the story, and understand how the elements bring meaning to the story. Your student also will have the opportunity to write his or her own science fiction story.	■ Student Learning Pages 7.A–7.C ■ 1 copy Writing Lines, page 355 ■ 1 copy Web, page 354

VOCABULARY

SCIENCE FICTION a fantasy story where science concepts are used to create a fantasy character, setting, or plot

WAVERING fluttering or wavy

ILLUMINED to be lightened; illuminated

DELICATE easily broken

PECULIAR different or unusual

ATMOSPHERE air

RESEMBLE to look like

FASCINATION full of wonder

PRIMITIVE-LOOKING simple

SETTING when and where a story takes place

PLOT the action of a story

Let's Begin

1   **INTRODUCE** Begin this lesson by telling your student that the name of the story he or she is going to read is *The Wonderful Flight to the Mushroom Planet*. Share with your student that he or she will be reading a part of a **science fiction** book. Reveal that science fiction stories aren't true—science fiction stories are made up by the author. Explain that science fiction often incorporates ideas from science, such as unusual inventions or different kinds of planets. Together with your student think of science fiction books he or she has read and talk about them. Let your student make predictions about what the story is about.

A BRIGHT IDEA

The study of science fiction can be enhanced by a trip to a museum, which can help spur creative ideas. Take a trip to a planetarium, an oceanarium, or a science museum near you. Invite your student to use what he or she sees to begin a science fiction story.

ENRICH THE EXPERIENCE

Save a few "new discoveries in science" type of articles from newspapers or magazines. Together you and your student can use the ideas from the articles and convert them into a fictional story about the future.

2   **DISTRIBUTE AND REVIEW**   Make a copy of the Writing Lines from page 355. Have your student write these words from the story onto the Writing Lines sheet: **wavering, illumined, delicate, peculiar, atmosphere, resemble, fascination,** and **primitive-looking.** Have your student say each word aloud. You may have to guide him or her at times with pronunciation. Now walk your student through the definition of each word. Challenge your student to use each word in a sentence. Remind your student that there may be other words in the story that he or she doesn't understand. Tell your student to add these new words to the list of vocabulary words as he or she reads.

3   **DISTRIBUTE AND READ**   Distribute Student Learning Page 7.A. Have your student read aloud the story. Be prepared to guide as necessary through difficult passages. You may want to read it aloud to him or her first. Also, allow him or her time to read silently as well.

4   **DISCOVER**   Talk with your student about the story's **setting.** Explain that the setting is where and when a story takes place. To help your student understand setting, give him or her a copy of the Web from page 354. In the center of the Web have him or her write "planet." Then ask your student for words and phrases to describe the planet, such as green, covered with mushrooms, and outer space. Have him or her write these words and others in the Web's smaller circles. Or perhaps have him or her draw a picture of the planet, including details mentioned in the story.

5   **DISCUSS AND CONNECT**   Discuss with your student the characters in the story. Ask, *Who are the characters in the story?* [David, Chuck, Mr. Bass] *What do you know about David?* [David also goes by Dave and his full name is David Topman; his voice sounded funny; he was fascinated with the planet] *What do you know about Mr. Bass?* [he was a Basidiumite] Then help your student connect to the characters and ask how he or she would feel if he or she landed on a planet like that. Discuss.

6   **INVESTIGATE**   Ask your student what the story he or she just read is about. You may want to guide your student by asking what happened first, next, and so on. Then tell him or her that what he or she just told you was the **plot.** The plot is the action of the story. Offer a twist on the plot and help your student explore what would've happened if David and Chuck had landed on a different planet.

7   **PREDICT**   Ask your student what he or she thinks might happen next. If your student is having difficulty, you may want to offer

suggestions such as *Will David and Chuck run into aliens? Will they see other things besides mushrooms?*

8   **DISTRIBUTE**   Share with your student that he or she will write the next chapter of the story! Ask your student to think about what David and Chuck will see, hear, do, and feel. Perhaps you also may want to talk about what they would eat, where they might sleep, and who they might meet. Then distribute Student Learning Page 7.B. Give your student enough time to work through the page.

9   **CONCLUDE**   When your student is done writing, have him or her read what he or she wrote out loud. If your student encounters errors in his or her work as he or she reads, work with your student to make any corrections of errors, such as misspellings.

Branching Out

TEACHING TIPS

❑ Allowing enough time for your student to respond to your questions is an important teaching strategy. After you ask your student a question, provide 10 to 15 seconds of wait time before you rephrase a question or guide your student to the answer. Thinking takes time and your student will need to pause to formulate his or her answer.

❑ If your student shows an interest in this story, encourage him or her to read the rest of the book. This is the first book in the Mushroom Planet series.

CHECKING IN

Check if your student can generalize the skills learned in this lesson and apply them to a story of his or her choice. Ask your student to select a science fiction story and share it with you aloud. When he or she is finished reading, invite him or her to explain why the story is science fiction. Ask him or her to identify the characters, plot, and setting in the story. You also can have your student listen to a science fiction book on cassette tape and then identify the parts of the story.

FOR FURTHER READING

Reading Grade 3, by Vincent F. Douglas (McGraw-Hill Children's Publishing, 2001).

Summer Scholar Grade 3, by M. C. Hall (School Zone Publishing Company, 2000).

Enjoy Science Fiction

The Wonderful Flight to the Mushroom Planet
by Eleanor Cameron

The Pale Planet

David could not think what had happened to him or where he was. He sat up and rubbed his eyes, and the first thing that struck him was the color of the light. It was green—a real green—**wavering,** misty. It was like clouded sea water **illumined** by sun. But if it was light, then it must mean they were near something that was reflecting light.

David caught his breath and leaned to look out. There, a great way below them but dimly visible through the winding mists, hung a small planet, so small that he could see how the edge of it curved, far, far rounder than he had seen the dimly lighted edge of the earth curve against space.

Already, while they had slept, their space ship had turned so that its tail pointed toward Basidium. Now it was in free fall—falling into a landing on the little planet instead of blasting toward it nose-first as it had been doing when they were awake.

"Chuck!" he cried eagerly. "Wake up, Chuck, wake up! We're almost there!" Ah, but how strange his words sounded to him, and how strange his voice—high and **delicate** and far away like the tinkle of wind chimes. Chuck stirred, then raised his head and blinked.

"Where—wha—what is it?" he asked in confusion. Then he sat up. "Why, it's all green. The light—"

Yes, and Chuck's voice too sounded **peculiar,** the voice of another being entirely than the Chuck David knew. And then his

(CONTINUED)

words—what could be the matter with them? Chuck started forward and pressed his face to the window and looked straight down. "Dave!" he cried. "It's Basidium—we're there, Dave! We're there!" Then he turned, a startled look on his face.

"Yes," said David, and he knew how it felt to have his heart leap in his throat. "It's the little planet just our size." But Chuck was staring at him.

"Dave," he whispered. Then he tried it out loud *"David Topman!"* He put his hand to his mouth. "We sound different," he got out at last.

"I know," Dave answered quietly. "Perhaps it's the **atmosphere.**" But all the same, he had a feeling it wasn't the atmosphere at all. And then, as the small world below them swung up nearer, he had an awful moment of uncertainty. "There it is, Chuck. But what if the people aren't people? What if they're—?" He couldn't even begin to imagine what impossible sort of being they might be. Of course, as Mr. Bass was a Basidiumite, though of a race that had lived long on earth, surely they would **resemble** him in some way or other.

Neither of them spoke any more, but stared down in silent **fascination** as they came nearer and nearer to the pale green surface of Basidium. Now the ship came to rest with a slight thud and David turned off the motor.

With huge eyes the boys peered out at what lay about them.

Through the wavering green light they made out that this entire world was pale. Over its surface grew what seemed to be spongy moss, and from it sprang **primitive-looking** growths that were like fern trees, with feathery fronds and trunks as smooth as bamboo. Yet these trunks were not the color of tree trunks at all, but as pale green as the rest of the plants. And there were mushrooms—hundreds and hundreds of mushrooms wherever you looked!

Create a Chapter

Think about what might happen in the next chapter of the book. Read each question. Then write your answers.

1. David and Chuck will see and hear this: _____

   _____

2. David and Chuck will do this: _____

   _____

3. David and Chuck will feel: _____

   _____

Now use your answers above for ideas. Choose how you want to "write" the next chapter in the book. You can write the chapter below or choose another idea: You can draw it in the form of a comic strip and use words and drawings to show the story.

What's Next? You Decide!

Now it's your turn to choose what to do next in the lesson. Read the activities and decide which one you want to do—you may even want to try them both!

Show the Planet

MATERIALS

- ❏ 1 piece hard foam, 12 inches by 12 inches
- ❏ 1 sheet green construction paper, 12 inches by 12 inches
- ❏ glue
- ❏ 20 toothpicks
- ❏ 20 small marshmallows
- ❏ pipe cleaners, buttons, yarn

STEPS

Make the planet Basidium come to life!

- ❏ Glue the green paper onto the foam. This is the planet's surface.
- ❏ Put each toothpick into a marshmallow. These are your mushrooms.
- ❏ Stick the toothpicks into the foam.
- ❏ Now use pipe cleaners, yarn, buttons, or anything else you want and add what else you think the planet has.
- ❏ Show your planet to a friend!

Make a Spaceship

MATERIALS

- ❏ 1 cardboard toilet paper tube
- ❏ aluminum foil
- ❏ 1 pair scissors
- ❏ 1 plastic grocery store bag
- ❏ 1 marker
- ❏ 1 ruler
- ❏ tape
- ❏ 4 pieces 10-inch string

STEPS

- ❏ Cover the tube in aluminum foil.
- ❏ Draw a square on the plastic bag that's 10 inches by 10 inches. Then cut out the square.
- ❏ Tie each piece of string to each corner of the plastic.
- ❏ Tape the ends of the string to the inside of the tube.
- ❏ Toss the spaceship in the air.

Reading Folktales

Watch these folktale characters come to life as you and your student explore similar feelings and experiences.

OBJECTIVE	BACKGROUND	MATERIALS
To help your student read and learn about folktales	Folktales offer glimpses into the lives of other cultures, including our own. In this lesson, your student will read and learn about folktales and retell stories of his or her own.	■ Student Learning Pages 8.A–8.C

VOCABULARY

FOLKTALE an often timeless tale with a universal theme, usually passed along orally through generations of a people

WARRIOR a person involved in warfare; a soldier

BRAGGED talked in a boastful or an arrogant manner

PROUD having or showing pride, or reasonable self-esteem; also, having or showing conceit

WIGWAM a type of hut, or home, built and used by Native Americans, usually made of wood and animal skins, or hide

MAPLE SUGAR sugar made from the syrup, or sap, of maple trees

DISOBEYED did not obey; did not follow commands

MEDICINE BAG a container used to carry medicines for healing; often used to carry herbs, powders, or other natural healing items

HEADDRESS a covering for the head, often used by Native Americans and made of feathers, animal skins, shells, or other items found in nature

Let's Begin

1 **EXPLAIN AND EXPLORE** Explain to your student that *Why the Baby Says "Goo"* is a Native American **folktale.** Ask your student if he or she knows what a folktale is. Mention that a folktale is an often timeless tale with a universal theme, usually passed along orally through generations of a people. Build background for the story and ask, *What facts do you know about Native Americans?* Then discuss.

2 **EXPLAIN AND PREVIEW** Explain that this tale is about a Native American **warrior** and a baby. Ask the student if he or she knows what a warrior is and, if not, explain that a warrior is like a soldier. Then preview the challenging or unfamiliar vocabulary terms that will be encountered in the story. Read the

DID YOU KNOW?

During World War I and World War II, the U.S. armed forces used a special code to communicate radio messages that the enemy could not understand. This special code came from the Navajo language and parts of other Native American languages.

definitions and use them in a sentence to assist in reading comprehension. For example, **bragged** means talked in a boastful or an arrogant manner. An example sentence: *She bragged about her shiny new bike.* For another example, **proud** means having or showing pride, or reasonable self-esteem; also, having or showing conceit. An example sentence: *He was proud to be on the winning team.*

3 **READ TOGETHER** Distribute Student Learning Page 8.A. Have your student read this passage aloud as you follow along. You may have to help him or her read the more difficult words or passages.

4 **EXPLORE** Explore the meanings of the folktale with your student. Ask your student what makes Grandmother wise. Then ask, *What does the baby's war cry, "Goo, goo, goo," mean?* [possible answer: it means the baby is happy]

5 **DISTRIBUTE** Distribute Student Learning Page 8.B. Assist your student in getting started with the retelling. You may want to have your student retell the story to you or another person first before completing the activity.

6 **CONNECT** Remind your student that folktales are passed down orally. Help your student to think of some family or neighborhood stories that have been told over and over again.

Branching Out

TEACHING TIP

You may wish to connect this folktale to Lesson 4.7, which discusses Native Americans.

CHECKING IN

To assess your student's learning, have him or her choose a few folktales for both of you to read together. Then have him or her retell one of them back to you and discuss it.

FOR FURTHER READING

Creatures: A Book of Rhymes About Emotions and Experience for Children and Parents to Read, Talk About and Enjoy Together, by Teresa M. Assenzo and William C. Schirado (TW Publishing, 1998).

Heroes and Heroines, Monsters and Magic: Native American Legends and Folktales, by Joseph Bruchac and Daniel Burgevin, ill. (Crossing Press, Inc., 1998).

Why the Baby Says "Goo"

In a village near the mountains, there lived a chief. He was a brave man who had fought in many battles. No one in the tribe had killed more enemies than he.

The chief feared no one. He fought the ice giants who came out of the North and carried away the women and children. He made them go back to their home in the North. He killed some of the evil people that lived in the caves, and he drove the others out of the land. Everybody loved the chief. He was so brave and good that the villagers thought there was no one like him anywhere.

But after he drove the giants out of the land, the chief began to think that he was the greatest **warrior** in the world.

"I can conquer anyone," he **bragged.**

Now a wise old woman lived in the village. When she heard what the great chief bragged, she smiled.

"Our chief is wonderful," she said, "but there is one who is more powerful than he."

The villagers told the chief what the wise woman had said. He came to visit her **wigwam.**

"Grandmother, who is this wonderful one?" he asked.

"His name is Wasis," answered the wise woman.

"And where is he, Grandmother?" asked the chief.

"He is there," said the wise woman, and she pointed to a place in the wigwam.

The chief looked. What do you think Wasis was? He was a fat little baby. He sat in the middle of the floor, talking to himself and sucking a piece of **maple sugar.** He looked so sweet and seemed very happy with himself.

The chief had no wife and knew nothing about babies. But he was very **proud** of himself, and he thought he knew everything.

(CONTINUED)

He was sure that the baby would obey him. He smiled to little Wasis and said, "Baby, come to me!" But the baby smiled and continued sucking his maple sugar.

The chief was surprised. The villagers always did everything he asked. He could not understand why the baby did not obey him. So he smiled and again said to little Wasis, "Baby, come to me!"

The baby smiled back and continued sucking his maple sugar.

The chief was surprised. No one had ever **disobeyed** him before. He grew angry. He gave little Wasis a mean look and shouted at him, "Baby, come to me!"

Little Wasis opened his mouth and began crying and screaming. The chief had never heard such awful sounds. Even the ice giants did not scream so terribly. The chief was more and more surprised. He could not think why such a little baby would not obey him.

"Amazing!" he said. "All other men fear me. But this baby shouts back war cries. Perhaps I can control him with my magic."

He took out his **medicine bag.** He danced magic dances and sang wonderful songs.

Little Wasis smiled and watched the chief with big round eyes. He thought it was all very funny. But he continued to suck his maple sugar.

The chief danced until he was tired out. Sweat ran down his face. Red paint ran down his face and neck. The feathers on his **headdress** fell down. At last, he sat down. He was too tired to dance any longer.

"Didn't I tell you that Wasis is stronger than you?" said the wise old woman. "No one is stronger than the baby. He always controls the wigwam. Everyone loves him and obeys him."

"So it is," said the chief sadly as he went out of the wigwam. As he went out, he could hear little Wasis talking to himself.

"Goo, goo, goo!" the baby said as he sucked his maple sugar. Now when you hear a baby saying "Goo, goo, goo," you will know what it means. It is the baby's war cry. The baby is happy because he remembers the time when he won the battle with the chief in the wigwam of the wise old woman.

Retell the Story

Retell the story from Grandmother's point of view. Read each question. Then write the answer.

1. How does the Grandmother describe the chief? Look for words that describe what he is like.

   _____

   _____

   _____

2. Who did Grandmother say was the wonderful one?

   _____

   _____

   _____

3. Who did Grandmother say was stronger than the baby?

   _____

   _____

   _____

4. Who did Grandmother say loves and obeys the baby?

   _____

   _____

   _____

5. Why do you think Grandmother is called a wise old woman?

   _____

   _____

   _____

What's Next? You Decide!

Now it's your turn to choose what to do next in the lesson. Read the activities and decide which one you want to do—you may want to try them both!

Make a Plaque

MATERIALS

❑ 1 12-inch piece yarn
❑ 1 10-inch by 10-inch piece cardboard
❑ colored markers
❑ glue

STEPS

Think about the type of strength in the folktale you just read.

❑ Look up the word *strength* in the dictionary.

❑ Then think of what it means to you to have strength; for example, be courageous, do things that are important to you.

❑ Then, with an adult's help, search in books or on the Internet for a quote or proverb (important saying) that reminds you of the word *strength*. For example: There is no one else like me. Or, you could make up your own!

❑ Write your saying on the cardboard. Then glue one end of the string to each corner of the cardboard.

Discover Your Area's Native Americans

MATERIALS

❑ colored construction paper
❑ 1 pair scissors
❑ glue

STEPS

❑ With an adult's help, go to your library and ask for books on Native Americans in your area. You may also want to go to your local museum.

❑ Learn what type of houses they lived in, what they wore, and anything else.

❑ Use the construction paper and glue to make the type of house they lived in and the type of clothing they wore.

Discovering Poetry

Poets use words to paint pictures. See, hear, smell, taste, and feel the world around you—you can paint with words, too!

OBJECTIVE	BACKGROUND	MATERIALS
To have your student read and understand the uniqueness of poetry	Poetry is a very unique form of literature. Poets use details to help paint a picture in the reader's imagination. Just as there are many different types of poems, there are many different poets. In this lesson, your student will learn the characteristics of poetry and interpret a poem.	■ Student Learning Pages 9.A–9.B ■ your favorite poem ■ 1 copy Web, page 354

VOCABULARY
ACROSTIC POEM a poem in which one word has other words extending from each letter of the word

Let's Begin

1 **INTRODUCE** Begin this lesson by helping your student find a favorite poem of his or hers. Invite your student to listen to you read it aloud. Ask your student to close his or her eyes while you read. Read the poem aloud twice. Have your student draw a picture of what came into his or her mind as you read the poem. Then have him or her describe the picture to you.

2 **REVEAL** Share with your student that what you just read was a poem. Tell him or her that poetry is unique, or different. Poets use words to create an image in the reader's mind. Poems don't have to be written in sentences. Poets choose their words carefully to paint the best picture. Remind your student of the picture he or she created as you read the poem to start the lesson. Ask him or her what he or she thought of the poem you just read. Discuss.

3 **DISTRIBUTE** Distribute Student Learning Page 9.A. Direct your student to the poem "Pull Hitter" by R. Gerry Fabian. Ask, *What do you notice about the poem without reading the words?* [there aren't many words written, the words are spread out, one word angles downward, one word is in all capital letters, the words don't run across the page like writing in a book does]

Rhyming is a fun way to introduce young learners to poetry. Give your student an example of words that rhyme (small/tall, cake/snake, run/fun, sing/king) and then ask your student to create his or her own list of words that rhyme. Have him or her use the words in sentences to create a silly rhyming poem.

FOR FURTHER READING

I Asked a Tiger to Tea: And Other Poems, by Ivy O. Eastwick, Walter Burke Barbe, and Melanie W. Hall, ill. (Boyds Mills Press, 2002).

Sea Dream: Poems from Under the Waves, by Nikki Siegen-Smith, Joel Stewart, ill., and Nikki Siegen-Smith, comp. (Barefoot Books, Inc., 2002).

Under the Moon and Over the Sea: A Collection of Caribbean Poems, John Agard, ed.; Sara Fanelli and Jane Ray, ills. (Candlewick Press, 2003).

Where the Sidewalk Ends, by Shel Silverstein (HarperCollins Children's Books, 2000).

4 **READ** Have your student read the poem aloud. Tell your student that reading poems takes practice. Often a poem needs to be read two or three times before you're able to say it clearly or with the right effect. Challenge your student to imagine his or her own picture for the poem as he or she reads it aloud again.

5 **DISCUSS** Discuss with your student why the poet chose to write the poem the way he did. Ask, *What do you think the poet was trying to show through arranging the words in this way?* [to show the action of the poem; the words look like what's happening in the scene]

6 **GUIDE** Guide your student through the details in the poem that help the reader create this image. Explain that the word *crack* is spelled with all capital letters to represent the loud sound of the ball hitting the bat. *Long* has spaces between the letters to create the sense of waiting as the ball goes through the air. *Curving* is slanting down to show the action of the ball as it goes foul.

7 **READ** Invite your student to read aloud the poem "Butterfly" on Student Learning Page 9.A. Share with your student that this is an **acrostic poem.** Ask, *What word does the poem spell out?* [butterfly] Invite your student to make an acrostic poem using his or her first name.

8 **REVIEW** Distribute to your student a copy of the Web found on page 354. Ask him or her to write "butterfly" in the center. Then have him or her fill in the surrounding circles with ideas or images detailed in the poem "Butterfly." Words that he or she could be writing are *bobbing, twinkling, gentle, roaming, flowers, landing, light.* Discuss with your student why these words work well for creating an image of a butterfly.

Branching Out

TEACHING TIP

Listening to poetry read aloud is a wonderful way to enjoy and learn about poetry. Read several children's poems aloud to your student. Tell your student that he or she can be an active listener by picturing the words as you say them and by listening for rhyming words or repeating sentences.

CHECKING IN

Tell your student to suppose that he or she is the teacher and you are the student. Invite him or her to teach you about poetry and how one can actively listen to it.

Discover Poetry

Pull Hitter
by R. Gerry Fabian

At
the
CRACK
of the bat
a   l o n g drive

                c
                u
              r
            v
          i
         n
       g

Foul!

Butterfly
from *Silver Seeds* by Paul Paolilli and Dan Brewer

Bobbing
Up and down;
Twinkling
Through the air
Ever so gently,
Roaming among the
Flowers,
Landing lightly on
Your shoulder.

What's Next? You Decide!

Now it's your turn to choose what to do next in the lesson. Read the activities and decide which one you want to do. You may even want to try them both!

Plan a Poetry Party

MATERIALS

❑ 1–2 children's poetry books

STEPS

Invite family and friends to share their favorite poem with you at a poetry party!

❑ Look through the different poems in books. Find a poem that you want to share with others.

❑ Practice reading it aloud. Keep practicing until you feel good about reading it in front of a group.

❑ Ask other family members and friends to bring their poems to the poetry party.

❑ You can even make invitations!

❑ At the poetry party take turns reading the poems aloud.

❑ Ask an adult to help you organize drinks and snacks for your party.

Paint a Poem

MATERIALS

❑ washable paints

❑ 1 paintbrush

❑ 3–4 sheets paper

❑ 1 smock

STEPS

Poets paint pictures using words.

❑ Choose a poem that you like or use one from this lesson.

❑ Read it aloud many times, and let the words paint a picture in your head.

❑ Use the paint and paintbrush to make the picture in your mind come to life. Don't forget to ask permission first!

❑ Ask an adult where to hang your painting.

Reading Biographies

In each person, there is a story to be told!

OBJECTIVE	BACKGROUND	MATERIALS
To have your student read and explore the elements of biographies	For ages stories have been told about people, the problems they encounter, and the actions they take to solve those problems. Your student will read stories about people throughout his or her life. In this lesson, your student will use various reading skills to read and understand a biography and learn parts of a biography.	■ Student Learning Pages 10.A–10.C ■ 1 copy Web, page 354

VOCABULARY

BIOGRAPHIES true stories about people written by other people
INVENTION something new that is created to do a specific task
CLEVERNESS mentally quick
RECREATIONAL exercise or sporting

Let's Begin

1 **INTRODUCE** Begin this lesson by asking your student to list names of people he or she is interested in learning more about. Share with your student some people you look up to or find interesting. Tell your student that he or she can read more about the people he or she is interested in through reading **biographies.** Ask him or her who the people are that he or she looks up to.

2 **REVEAL** Share with your student what a biography is. Then tell your student that he or she will read the biography of a scientist named Stephanie Kwolek. Explain that biographies include information about the person's birth and death (if applicable), childhood and adulthood, and contributions that the person has been involved with.

3 **PREVIEW** Preview the challenging words that your student might encounter in this biography. Together with your student walk through each vocabulary word and discuss its meaning.

4 **DISTRIBUTE** Distribute Student Learning Page 10.A. Tell him or her that the biography he or she is going to read involves an

invention and an inventor. Have him or her read the biography excerpt. Guide as necessary as your student reads the passage.

5   **DISCUSS** Discuss with your student how this story may be different from other things he or she has read. Encourage your student to see that they're like some of the stories or books he or she has read. However, a biography has no plot, setting, or characters. Help him or her to understand that this is a true story about a real woman's life and accomplishments. Ask your student how this is different from other stories he or she has read. Then discuss.

6   **DIRECT** Make a copy of the Web found on page 354 and distribute to your student. Ask him or her to write *Stephanie Kwolek* in the center. Ask your student to fill in the surrounding circles with details about Kwolek from the passage, such as when and where she was born. Then, using the details he or she wrote, invite your student to draw a picture of Kwolek working to create her invention.

7   **DISTRIBUTE** Distribute Student Learning Page 10.B. Have your student read the directions out loud. Before he or she begins the activity, review with him or her what cause and effect are. Explain that when something happens, like an event, that is the *cause*. What happens next because of that event is the *effect*. Share with your student this example: A boy is holding an apple in his hand. Another person bumps his arm. Accidentally, this bump makes the apple fall out of his hand and onto the floor. Explain that the cause is the bumping of the arm and the effect is that the apple falls on the floor.

Branching Out

TEACHING TIPS

❑   If your student has shown an interest in chemistry at this young age, this might be an opportunity to talk more about what chemists do today. Help your student find names of other important chemists or scientists and see if you and your student can learn more about them.

❑   If your student has shown an interest in learning more about women inventors, have him or her read the rest of the book that the passage is from: *Women Inventors* by Jean F. Blashfield.

CHECKING IN

Teaching is one of the best ways to learn. Invite your student to become the teacher. Have him or her summarize what he or she has learned about biographies. Have your student teach you the lesson.

FOR FURTHER READING

Amelia Earhart, by Jane Sutcliffe (Lerner Publishing Group, 2003).

Christopher Columbus, by Susan Bivin Aller (Lerner Publishing Group, 2003).

One Giant Leap: The Story of Neil Armstrong, by Don Brown (Houghton Mifflin Company, 1998).

Explore a Biography

Stephanie Kwolek
1923–
Mightier Than a Speeding Bullet
by Jean F. Blashfield

"**Invention** is invention," says chemist Stephanie Kwolek. Creativity, or the ability to look at things in a new way, is what is important. It does not matter whether a woman invents for the home or for industry. The same **cleverness** is needed.

While working at a chemical company, E.I. du Pont de Nemours and Company, she invented a new fiber, called Kevlar®. It is extraordinarily strong, five times as strong as steel. It is used on **recreational** boats, in outer space, and in vests worn by police confronting dangerous, armed criminals.

Police officers often wear Kevlar vests for protection.

(CONTINUED)

PROMOTING LITERACY 10.A

Putting Cold to Work

Stephanie Louise Kwolek was born in New Kensington, Pennsylvania, in 1923. She earned a college degree in chemistry and then went to work for Du Pont in 1946. She planned to stay just long enough to earn money to go to medical school. But new processes in chemistry captured her interest and she never went on to medical school.

When Kwolek started to work, chemists were just beginning to discover the many things that can be done with the chemical compounds of petroleum. Most plastics have been developed from petroleum.

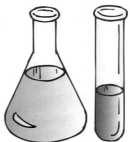

Kwolek worked with chemicals at very cold temperatures, which led to important discoveries.

Kwolek continued to study this process for the next 40 years. Sometimes her co-workers laughed at the amount of time she spent working on these chemicals. But she became one of the most important chemists in the nation.

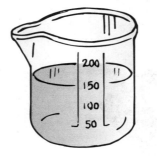

Stephanie Kwolek has said that women have as much ability as men to be inventors. "You must develop the ability to notice the unusual," she says. "You must repeat and repeat and repeat until you have the problem solved."

Explore Cause and Effect

When something happens, that is the cause. What happens after is the effect. Read the sentences. Complete the chart with the cause or effect from Stephanie Kwolek's biography. You may need to reread the story.

CAUSE

1. New processes in chemistry captured her interest.

2.

3. Kwolek studied chemical processes for 40 years.

4.

EFFECT

Recreational boats and vests worn by police use Kevlar.

You can solve the problem encountered.

What's Next? You Decide!

Now it's your turn to choose what to do next in the lesson. Read the activities and decide which one you want to do. You may even want to try them both!

Be an Inventor

STEPS

Have you ever wished for something that doesn't exist? Well, it's time for you to invent it!

❑ Just as Stephanie Kwolek invented a new fiber that people use for a lot of things, you can make something new for people to use.

❑ You can invent something that can help people or it can be for just plain fun.

❑ First choose what you want to invent and draw it.

❑ Then explain in writing what you want to invent.

❑ Include details about what your invention looks like and what it does.

❑ Next show your invention to your family. Is it something they would need or want?

Write a Biography

STEPS

A person who writes biographies is called a biographer. Become a biographer by writing someone else's story.

❑ Ask a family member or friend if you can write a biography about him or her.

❑ First ask questions to find out more about his or her life. Here are some questions you can ask:
  - Where was the person born?
  - How old is the person?
  - What does the person like to do?

Come up with your own questions too!

❑ Write the person's story. Remember to check your writing for correct spelling and punctuation.

❑ Write in pen and make a final copy of the person's story to share with the person.

Reading Nonfiction

True stories can be as interesting as those that are created.

OBJECTIVE	BACKGROUND	MATERIALS
To help your student identify and understand nonfiction literature	Reading nonfiction literature is an opportunity to learn new and interesting information. In this lesson, your student will read nonfiction literature and identify its elements.	■ Student Learning Pages 11.A–11.C ■ 1 copy Venn Diagram, page 353

VOCABULARY

MAIN CHARACTERS people who the story is largely about
THIRD-PERSON POINT OF VIEW a narrator outside of a story who explains the events
SUBJECT names what someone or something is in a sentence
PREDICATE tells what the subject is or does in a sentence
AMPUTATED removed through a surgical operation
PROSTHESIS a device that replaces a missing body part

Let's Begin

1 **IDENTIFY NONFICTION** Invite your student to think of stories or books that they have read. Ask, *Were these stories told about real people, things, places, and events?* Explain to your student that stories about real people, things, places, and events are nonfiction literature.

2 **DISCUSS** Explain to your student that he or she will be reading a true story about a boy who invented a device to help another boy play baseball. Before beginning, ask your student to think of things that a person does when playing baseball. [throw, catch, bat] Ask your student to think about playing baseball with no hands. Discuss problems that he or she might encounter.

3 **READ THE SELECTION** Before reading, review the vocabulary words with your student. Then distribute Student Learning Page 11.A and have him or her begin reading the selection. Pause often to be sure that your student understands what was read. When your student has completed the reading, ask him or her for an initial reaction to the selection. Ask, *How does the selection make you feel? What does the selection make you think about?* Discuss these answers.

DID YOU KNOW?

Many organizations hold contests for young inventors, and some inventions are even patented by children! For more information, visit the kids pages of the United States Patent and Trademark Office Web site at http://www.uspto.gov.

4   **DISCUSS THE CHARACTERS** Ask your student to name the **main characters** in the story. Help him or her to see that although Josh's dad is mentioned in the story, Josh and David are the main characters because they are the people who we learn the most about. Give your student a copy of the Venn Diagram found on page 353 and ask him or her to label the circles "Josh" and "David." In the overlapping section, have your student write down the similarities between Josh and David. In the outside sections, have him or her write down the differences between Josh and David. Discuss with your student the similarities and differences in their characters.

5   **EXPLORE POINT OF VIEW** Explain to your student that this selection is written in the **third-person point of view,** which means that a narrator outside the story explains the events. Talk about how point of view would change the story. Discuss what would be different and what would be the same.

6   **OBSERVE SEQUENCE OF EVENTS** Remind your student that there are several words that tell the order of events in a story, such as *first, next,* and *then.* Invite your student to find these words within the reading. Ask your student to explain the order of events, or steps, that these words represent.

7   **DISTRIBUTE AND PRACTICE** Remind your student that when answering questions, a single word is usually not enough. To answer a question clearly, it is often helpful to use part of the question in the answer. Distribute Student Learning Page 11.B. Explain that this page will help the student practice answering questions correctly and completely.

Branching Out

TEACHING TIP

Research other things invented by children or adults. Some children's museums have invention rooms where children are encouraged to use their imaginations. You can also visit the National Inventors' Hall of Fame Web site at http://www.invent.org. This Web site includes information on how to apply for a patent and many other interesting and useful items.

CHECKING IN

To assess student understanding of the story, ask your student to summarize the story. To further explore student understanding, ask him or her to draw conclusions about how the characters in the story felt when the prosthetic device worked.

FOR FURTHER READING

Imaginative Inventions: The Who, What, Where, When, and Why of Roller Skates, Potato Chips, Marbles, and Pie (and More!), by Charise Mericle Harper, M. Tingley, ed., and Charice Mericle Harper, ill. (Little, Brown Children's Books, 2001).

The Kids Who Invented the Popsicle and Other Surprising Stories About Inventions, by Don L. Wulffson (Penguin Books, 1999).

Nonfiction Matters: Reading, Writing, and Research in Grades 3–8, by Stephanie Harvey (Paperback/ Stenhouse Publishers, 1998).

Write a Super Sentence, by Jo Ellen Moore and Joy Evans (Evan-Moor Educational Publishers, 1999).

Enjoy Nonfiction

The Prosthetic Catch and Throw Device
by Arlene Erlbach

Josh Parsons wanted to help David Potter play baseball. Both of David's arms had been **amputated** below the elbows because of an accident he had had when he was two years old. Still, David wanted to be on a Little League team. Josh thought he could help David.

Josh's dad is the one who told Josh about David. Mr. Parsons is a Little League director. He judges kids' tryouts for teams. One evening, Mr. Parsons came home and told Josh about a kid without hands who had tried out for a baseball team.

Even without hands, David could catch and bat a ball! He caught the ball in a glove he wore at the end of his left arm. To bat, David held the bat between his left upper arm and chest. He used his right arm to push the bat. The only thing David couldn't do was throw a ball. Josh hoped he could change that.

(CONTINUED)

First Josh thought about all the things David could already do. David was able to use a glove to catch. So maybe a special kind of glove could help him throw.

Josh decided to design a special glove that would replace David's lower right arm and hand. A device that replaces a missing body part is called a **prosthesis** (pross-THEE-sis).

Josh first made a model of the glove out of paper. Next, he sewed a glove from leather. The glove fit onto the end of David's right arm.

Josh hit a ball to David. David caught it in his left glove. Then he dumped the ball into the prosthetic glove and threw the ball into the air!

David started playing right field for the Spring Branch Mustangs. They won first place that season.

Answer Questions Completely

Read the reminders about ways to completely answer
a question.

To completely answer a question:

❏ Read the question carefully.

❏ Look for and underline key words that tell you what the question
is asking for.

❏ Use the key words to form the answer to the question.

❏ Give facts or reasons for your answer.

**Read each question. Then write the answers. Use the reminders to
check your work.**

1. How did *Josh Parsons help David Potter?* Josh Parsons helped David
Potter by inventing a prosthetic catch and throw device.

2. Why were David's arms amputated below the elbows? _____
_____

3. How can David bat without hands? _____

4. How did Josh make the glove for David? _____
_____

5. What did David do when his prosthetic glove worked? _____
_____

What's Next? You Decide!

Now it's your turn to choose what to do next in the lesson. Read the activities and decide which one you want to do—you may want to try them both!

Make an Invention

MATERIALS

❏ materials to build an invention

STEPS

Many useful devices are invented to make people's lives easier.

❏ Make a list of things that you like to do or that you have to do. Then think of ways to make doing those things easier.

❏ Now choose one of those things that you think can be made easier with an invention.

❏ Now make your invention!

Choose Your Own Nonfiction

MATERIALS

❏ access to books or the Internet

STEPS

❏ Look at the list of topics that interest you that you created in this unit.

❏ Choose one of these (or another area of interest) to research and learn more about.

❏ Ask an adult to help you search for appropriate books or articles on the topic. In this way, you will be getting more experience reading nonfiction and learning more about an interesting topic at the same time!

Taking Notes and Writing Research Reports

Reading and writing are the keys to unlocking the world.

OBJECTIVE	BACKGROUND	MATERIALS
To help your student learn how to take notes and write a research report	Notetaking is a skill that is used when doing research. As your student gets older, he or she will be doing more and more research. In this lesson, your student will learn how to take notes and use them to write a research report.	■ Student Learning Pages 12.A–12.B ■ 20 index cards ■ 1 copy Venn Diagram, page 353 ■ 1 copy Web, page 354

VOCABULARY

MAIN IDEA the most important fact, or point, of a reading

HEADINGS these tell what selections are about

SUBHEADINGS these tell what specific sections are about

BOLDFACE TEXTS special words in selections that are darkened in order to stand out

SOURCE any place where information is gathered

PREWRITING brainstorming topic ideas, choosing a topic, gathering research sources, reading, and taking notes

DRAFTING using notes to write the first copy of a research report

REVISING reading over carefully and making changes to make sure a report makes sense and is complete

EDITING checking spelling, grammar, and punctuation in a report

PUBLISHING writing and presenting a final report

Let's Begin

1   **EXPLAIN** Explain to your student that taking notes will help him or her to write a good research report. Tell your student that taking notes will help to organize and summarize information he or she reads and use it in a written report. Explain that the process of notetaking will help him or her understand the **main idea** and important details from a reading. Have your student practice taking notes on a short newspaper or magazine article. You also can have your student highlight the important words or sections, using a highlighting marker.

2   **THINK AND CHOOSE** Ask your student to choose a topic he or she would like to learn more about. Help your student choose a

topic by brainstorming a list of things that are important and interesting to him or her. Ask your student to choose the topic he or she likes best for further research.

3 **EXPLORE AND RESEARCH** Take your student to a local library to find articles from books, encyclopedias, magazines, and the Internet on his or her topic. Have your student obtain at least three appropriate sources on his or her topic.

Have you ever been to the Library of Congress? The Thomas Jefferson Building is one of the buildings that make up the Library of Congress.

4 **EXPLORE** Explain to your student that taking notes when reading helps people to organize and summarize main ideas and important details. Explain that authors organize their writings by using **headings, subheadings, boldface texts,** and paragraphs. Use library books and research materials on your student's topic to explore how authors organize their writings. Ask, *How is the text organized?* Challenge your student to find three ways the text is organized.

5 **ASK AND DISTRIBUTE** Ask your student to choose one book or reference source about his or her topic. Have him or her read one section of the text aloud to you. After each heading, subheading, boldface text, or paragraph, stop and ask your student to find the main idea and supporting details of the section. Explain that the main idea is the most important fact or point of the reading. Then, distribute Student Learning Page 12.A. Have your student write the main idea from each paragraph and three supporting details.

6 **EXPLAIN AND DISCUSS** Explain that notes can be written on notebook papers, index cards, or graphic organizers. Explain that notes can be organized by subheads to tell what the specific section is about. Discuss with your student important information to include when taking notes.

7 **MODEL AND REVIEW** Ask your student to choose one book on his or her topic. Give him or her 10 index cards. Write the title and the author of the book on the first index card. Label this set *A*. Each card that contains notes from this specific book will be labeled *A* followed by a number. *[A1, A2, A3]* Then together, read the book aloud. Help your student take notes on the main ideas and supporting details from each section. Use a different index card for each section. Review and discuss each index card after reading.

8 **EXPLAIN AND PRACTICE** Explain to your student that when he or she is doing research, it is important to compare the facts and information from each **source** (any place where information is gathered). Tell your student that good research relies on many sources for information on a specific topic. Encourage your student to compare information from more than one source.

9 **EXPLORE** Have your student review his or her notes and look for similar facts and ideas between different sources. Have your student use a Venn Diagram to compare and contrast the two sources he or she used. Have your student fill in the Venn Diagram with facts and ideas from the notes made on the index cards. Encourage your student to find as many similarities and differences between the two sources as possible.

10 **RESEARCH AND EVALUATE** Have your student create a fact or an idea web for his or her research report. This web should have the topic in the center bubble and the important facts and ideas in each extension bubble. Ask your student to use the Web graphic organizer to help.

ENRICH THE EXPERIENCE

Remind your student that some sources can come from real people. Encourage your student to interview someone who is an expert on the topic that he or she is researching.

11 **PROCESS** Explain that there are five steps in the writing process: prewriting, drafting, revising, editing, and publishing. Explain that **prewriting** is brainstorming topic ideas, choosing a topic, gathering research sources from the library, reading, and taking notes. **Drafting** is using notes to write the first copy of a research report. **Revising** is reading over carefully and making changes to make sure the report makes sense and is complete. **Editing** is checking spelling, grammar, and punctuation in a report. **Publishing** is writing and presenting a final report.

12 **WRITE AND EDIT** Now have your student use his or her notes to write a research report. Guide your student through the writing process of prewriting, drafting, revising, editing, and publishing. Emphasize editing in the writing process. Explain that it is important to present a final report that has been edited. Ask your student to check his or her report for grammar, punctuation, and spelling. Review his or her report and make additional corrections. Finally, have your student write a final paper. Emphasize that the final published draft should always represent his or her best effort!

Branching Out

TEACHING TIP

Encourage your student to use details and interesting words when writing research reports. Explain that a good research report is both interesting and informative. Suggest that your student use a variety of sentence types to make his or her report more interesting. Also suggest that he or she focus his or her attention on the opening sentence in each paragraph. Explain that the topic sentence should tell the main idea of each paragraph and should be interesting because it needs to grab the attention of the reader and make him or her want to read the report.

CHECKING IN

Assess your student's understanding of notetaking and writing research reports by walking through these steps with your student.

- ❏ Choose a topic.
- ❏ Explore the library and various publications to find information.
- ❏ Read three to five different sources.
- ❏ Take notes on each source, extracting the main ideas and supporting details.
- ❏ Compare information from various sources.
- ❏ Write a first draft.
- ❏ Revise and edit.
- ❏ Publish and present research.
- ❏ Have your student talk about the important components of taking notes and doing research, by asking the questions below.

> **Reminders for You and Your Student**
> ✓ Did you choose a topic that interests you?
> ✓ Did you find books that were appropriate to your topic?
> ✓ Did you take notes on the main ideas and details?
> ✓ Did you organize your notes?
> ✓ Did you use your notes to write your report?
> ✓ Did you revise and edit your report?

FOR FURTHER READING

Handy Homework Helper: How to Write School Reports, by Helen H. Moore (Publications International, Ltd., 2002).

I Search, You Search, We All Learn to Research: A How-to-Do-It Manual for Teaching Elementary School Students to Solve Information Problems, by Donna Duncan and Laura Lockhart (Neal-Schuman Publishers, Inc., 2000).

Wake Up, Brain!!, by Michelle Ball and Barbara Morris (ECS Learning Systems, Inc., 2000).

Main Ideas and Details

Choose a section of your research. Read and take notes on the section.

Main Idea

Supporting Detail 1

Supporting Detail 2

Supporting Detail 3

What's Next? You Decide!

Now it's your turn to choose what to do next in the lesson. Read the activities and decide which one you want to do—you may want to try them both!

Pass Notes

MATERIALS

- ❑ 1–2 newspapers or magazines
- ❑ 20 index cards

STEPS

- ❑ Get together with a friend or family member.
- ❑ Choose an informational article from a newspaper or magazine for each of you to read.
- ❑ Take notes on index cards as you read. When you both have finished reading, pass your index cards to one another.
- ❑ Read and review your partner's index cards.
- ❑ Using the notes your partner wrote, retell the story to your partner.
- ❑ Check and see if your notes were accurate.
- ❑ Did your partner understand what happened in the story? If so, you took good notes!

Make a Newscast

MATERIALS

- ❑ 5 index cards
- ❑ 1–2 newspapers or magazines

STEPS

- ❑ Research a current event that is interesting to you.
- ❑ Take notes on this topic using index cards.
- ❑ Try to answer the 5 *W*s on this topic: who, what, when, why, and where. Use one card for each question.
- ❑ Use these index cards as cue cards for your newscast.
- ❑ Present your news report to your family and friends.

Following and Giving Directions

Directions are a part of daily life, whether it's how to do something or how to get somewhere.

OBJECTIVE	BACKGROUND	MATERIALS
To have your student learn how to follow and give directions, both orally and in writing	Giving and following directions are crucial forms of communication that your student will use throughout his or her life. It's important to be able to give them, as well as to follow them, correctly. In this lesson, your student will learn the steps to take when giving and following directions.	■ Student Learning Pages 13.A–13.D ■ 1 copy Writing Lines, page 355

Let's Begin

1 **INTRODUCE DIRECTIONS** Prompt a discussion about directions. Ask, *Have you ever had to follow directions? When? What were the directions for?* [responses may include playing a game, making something, getting to a place] Ask, *How were the directions helpful? What happens when you don't follow directions carefully?*

2 **DISTRIBUTE** Distribute Student Learning Page 13.A. Review the numbered steps in Part A for following directions. Discuss the importance of each numbered item.

3 **FOLLOW DIRECTIONS** Together with your student read the directions for making the sandwich in Part B of Student Learning Page 13.A. Explain that directions can be written in a paragraph or in numbered steps. Then have your student answer the questions. Review your student's responses. Ask your student why it's important to understand each step before going on to the next. Then ask him or her why it's important to follow the steps in order. Ask, *What words help you know the order of steps?* [first, next, then, finally] Now make a copy of the Writing Lines found on page 355, and have your student rewrite the paragraph into a numbered list. Then ask him or her which is easier to understand.

4 **EXPLAIN AND DISTRIBUTE** Ask your student, *Have you ever given anyone directions about how to do something or how to get*

somewhere? What were the directions for? Generate a discussion with your student about what to keep in mind when giving directions. Then distribute Student Learning Page 13.B. Review with your student all the things to keep in mind when giving directions. Ask questions such as *Why is it important to give a list of the things that are needed? What happens if you leave out a step? What if you don't put all the steps in the right order?* Then have your student complete the page.

5 **REVIEW** Review your student's responses on Student Learning Page 13.B. Help clarify any confusion your student may have about the map. Now have your student take another look at the map on Student Learning Page 13.B. Choose a scenario from the map, such as having the student give you directions orally that explain how Shea would get to the park. Guide as necessary.

6 **ASSIGN** Distribute Student Learning Page 13.C. Have your student complete the page. Review it to make sure all the steps are in order. If they aren't in order, work with him or her to get them in order. Then ask how he or she knew what order to put them in. Ask, *What clue words told you what the order might be?* [first, after, then, when, last]

Branching Out

TEACHING TIP

The next time you take a trip away from your neighborhood, have your student help you plan the route. Suggest that he or she write the directions and then read them aloud as you take your journey.

CHECKING IN

To assess your student's comprehension of the lesson, take turns with your student giving and receiving oral directions.

FOR FURTHER READING

Expository Writing, by Tara McCarthy (Scholastic Trade, 1999).

Following Directions, by Barbara Allman; Sara Bierling, Debra Olson Pressnall, and Angella Phebus, eds. (Frank Schaffer Publications, 2002).

Follow Directions

Following directions exactly as they are given is important.
Read these steps to help you follow directions.

1. Be sure you understand each step.

2. Notice words that show order, such as *first, then, next,* and *finally.*

3. Follow the steps in order.

4. Finish each step before going to the next one.

Read the directions for how to make a veggie sandwich. Then answer the questions.

You need:
- ❏ 2 slices bread
- ❏ 2 slices cheese
- ❏ 4 cucumber slices
- ❏ 2 tomato slices
- ❏ 1–2 lettuce leaves
- ❏ mayonnaise or other sandwich spread

First, put the two slices of bread side by side. Next, spread mayonnaise on one side of each slice of bread. Then add the cheese slices to one side of one slice of bread. Then add the tomatoes, cucumbers, and leaves of lettuce. Finally, put the other slice of bread on top. Your sandwich is ready to eat!

1. What vegetables do you need?

   _____

2. What is the first thing you should do?

   _____

3. What do you do before you add the vegetables?

   _____

4. What words help you know the order in which to do things?

   _____

Give Directions

Giving clear directions is important. Read these steps to help you give directions.

1. Be brief. Be clear.

2. If you are telling how to make something, give a list of the things you'll need.

3. Make a list of all the steps.

4. Make sure all the steps are in the right order.

5. Use words such as *first, second,* and *next* to help the reader.

6. Use pictures if they might help.

Look at the map. Write the name of the streets to complete the directions.

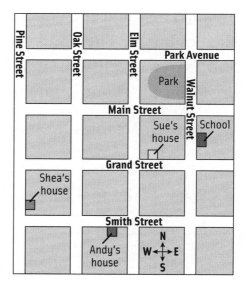

Andy wants to visit Sue. Then they are going to the park with their families. Which way should Andy go first? Andy lives on _____ Street. He should turn right to _____ Street. Turn left onto Elm. Walking down _____ Street, he will get to _____ Street. He should turn right at _____ Street. Then he'll be at Sue's house.

Order the Directions

Read the directions. Put them in order. Write the letter of the step next to the number.

Steps

1. _____   3. _____   5. _____

2. _____   4. _____   6. _____

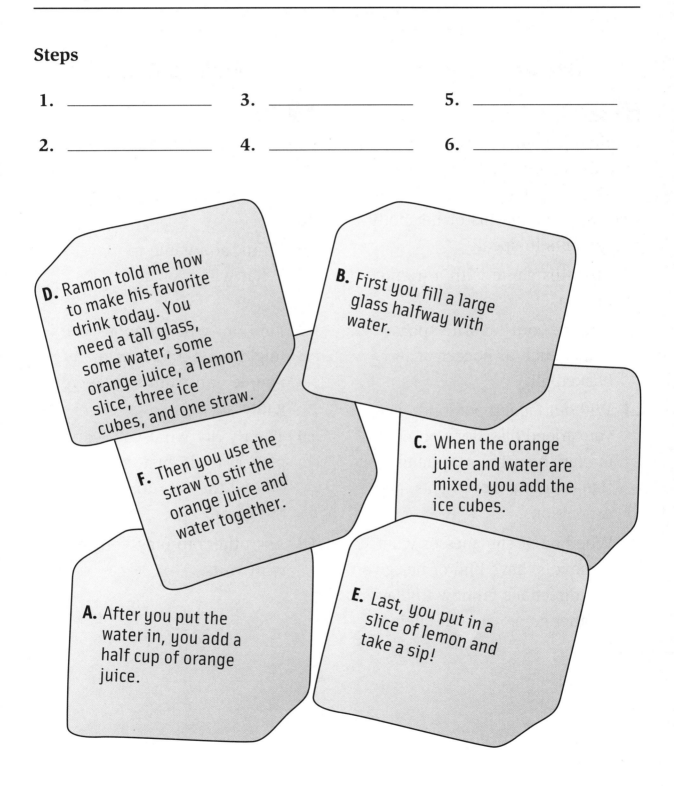

D. Ramon told me how to make his favorite drink today. You need a tall glass, some water, some orange juice, a lemon slice, three ice cubes, and one straw.

B. First you fill a large glass halfway with water.

F. Then you use the straw to stir the orange juice and water together.

C. When the orange juice and water are mixed, you add the ice cubes.

A. After you put the water in, you add a half cup of orange juice.

E. Last, you put in a slice of lemon and take a sip!

Student Learning Page 13.C: Order the Directions **71**

What's Next? You Decide!

Now it's your turn to choose what to do next in the lesson. Read the activities and decide which one you want to do—you may want to try them both!

Become a Mime

STEPS

A mime is someone who tells you about something without speaking out loud. A mime uses hand signals and his or her body movements to speak.

❑ Play this game with a friend or two.

❑ Choose your favorite sports game, such as soccer or basketball.

❑ Without talking out loud, give your friend directions on how to play the game. Use hand signals, body movements, and expressions.

❑ When he or she guesses what game it is, have him or her give you directions on how to play another game without talking.

Make a Game

STEPS

Suppose you're writing this page of this book. Write directions to a game that you want others to play.

❑ Think of a game to play. What will you call your game?

❑ Find out what supplies you might need and how many people you want to play your game.

❑ Then write what you want the players to do first, second, and all the way to the end of the game.

❑ Ask others to play your game with you.

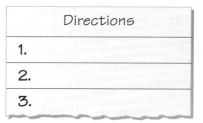

Directions	
1.	
2.	
3.	

Writing Thank-You Notes

It's always nice to thank someone for his or her kindness.

OBJECTIVE	BACKGROUND	MATERIALS
To help your student understand how to write a thank-you note	In many social situations, people are required to show gratitude toward others who have been kind or generous. It has been a tradition to show gratitude by writing thank-you notes. In this lesson, your student will learn to write a thank-you note using proper grammar.	■ Student Learning Pages 14.A–14.B

Let's Begin

1 **INTRODUCE THE CONCEPT** Ask your student if he or she has ever received a very special gift. Invite him or her to describe it to you. Ask, *What did you say to the person who gave you the gift?* Help your student to remember that he or she probably showed thanks in some way, through writing, words, or actions. Explain that these are all acceptable ways to thank someone for doing something kind or giving you something special. Talk about why it is a good idea to say thank-you to someone who has been kind. Explain to your student that people are often encouraged to write thank-you notes or letters to people who give them gifts. Ask your student to think of words that might appear in a thank-you note.

2 **SET A PURPOSE** Explain to your student that a thank-you note has two purposes. First, it should explain why the person is being thanked. Next, it should mention why the gift or action was important.

> Dear Ms. Jones,
>   Thanks for the book, *How to Train Your Dog*. It will really help me when I begin to train my dog, Sam.
>
>   Sincerely,
>   Matt

PROMOTING LITERACY

LESSON 1.14

A TIME-SAVER

Tell your student that it is sometimes a good idea to address envelopes for thank-you notes at the same time as you address invitations to a party, where gifts are expected. This is a great time-saver, since he or she won't have to look up addresses twice!

FOR FURTHER READING

Sentence Composing for Elementary School: A Worktext to Build Better Sentences, by Don Killgallon and Jenny Killgallon (Heinemann, 2000).

The Thank You Book for Kids: Hundreds of Creative, Cool and Clever Ways to Say Thank You!, by Ali Lauren Spizman (Longstreet Press, Inc., 2001).

Thanks, Aunt Zelda!: Thank-You Cards for Kids to Craft, by Cynthia MacGregor and Anouk Perusse-Bell, ill. (Lobster Press, 2002).

3 **EXPLAIN AND ASK** Explain to your student that a thank-you note is a personal letter. To make this letter more personal, the writer might use the reader's name in the introduction and within the body of the letter. Give the following examples.

> *It was very kind of you to come to my party.*
> *It was very kind of you, Alex, to come to my party.*

Ask your student to choose the sentence that is more personal. [the second sentence] Point out the commas before and after the name, *Alex,* which set the name apart from the rest of the sentence. Remind your student that there should be a comma after the greeting phrase in a letter. [Dear Sam,]

4 **PRACTICE** Distribute Student Learning Page 14.A. Explain to your student that this page shows an example of a thank-you note written by a girl to her aunt, thanking her for a gift. Review the instructions with your student; then allow time for him or her to read the letter and make the corrections. When completed, look over his or her work to make sure it is correct.

5 **WRITE** Invite the student to think again about the special gift mentioned in the beginning of the lesson. Have him or her write a thank-you note to the person from whom he or she received the gift. Ask the student to be sure to use commas properly and to form compound sentences when possible. When this is complete, help the student edit his or her work.

Branching Out

TEACHING TIP

Explain to your student that in writing it's important to use words that are clear. For example, ask your student to think of more interesting words to describe how someone is eating. Ask your student to look back at his or her thank-you note and make any possible changes.

CHECKING IN

To assess your student's understanding of the concepts in this lesson, ask him or her to name the purposes of writing thank-you notes.

Proofread a Thank-You Note

Read and follow the directions.

1. Read the thank-you note.

2. Add two commas.

3. Capitalize three letters.

4. Make a contraction from two words.

5. Rewrite the letter correctly on a separate sheet of paper.

> March 13 2002
>
> Dear Aunt katherine
>   Thank you so much for the new pair of skates. I have been hoping to get new skates all year! I am glad you chose purple because it is my favorite color. I cannot wait for spring to come so I can go skating!
>   Maybe the next time you come over, we can go skating together. Now that I am nine, I think that I can keep up. Thanks again for the great gift.
> Love,
> kaelyn

What's Next? You Decide!

Now it's your turn to choose what to do next in the lesson. Read the activities and decide which one you want to do—you may want to try them both!

Make a "Pop Up" Card

MATERIALS

- ❑ 2 sheets construction paper
- ❑ 1 pair scissors
- ❑ glue

STEPS

- ❑ Fold two sheets of construction paper in half, the short way. One of these will be the outside of your card.
- ❑ On the other card, cut three sets of two slits, each between one and two inches long and about a half-inch apart, on the fold.

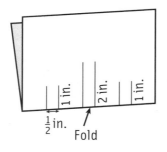

1 in.   2 in.   1 in.
½ in.
Fold

- ❑ Unfold the card, pushing the cut-out slits through.

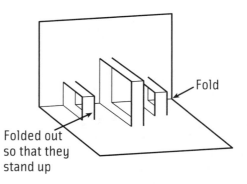

Fold

Folded out
so that they
stand up

- ❑ On these slits glue words or pictures that you cut out of construction paper. These will "pop out" when you open the card. Decorate your card.

Write a Thank-You

MATERIALS

- ❑ stationery
- ❑ stamps

STEPS

- ❑ Think of someone who has done something nice for you or who has just been a good friend to you.
- ❑ Write a thank-you letter thanking that person.
- ❑ Send the letter in the mail. Ask an adult for a stamp and help to mail the letter.

In Your Community

To reinforce the skills and concepts taught in this section,
try one or more of these activities!

Listen to Storytelling

Check your library or community center for storytelling. Some places have a regular weekly or monthly story hour. Encourage your child to listen to not just what the storyteller says, but also how he or she says it and what bodily movements or facial expressions he or she uses. At the end of the story, discuss these things with your student. If the storyteller read from a book that's age- and reading-level appropriate, you may want to encourage your student to read the same book and then present his or her version of the story to you and your family.

Do You Know Your Librarian?

You may make regular visits to your library and even ask the librarian questions, but how well do you know him or her? Have your student become a reporter and interview your librarian. Help your student prepare a list of about five questions that he or she would want to ask, such as "How did you become a librarian?" Arrange to have your student talk with the librarian. If you'd like, have your student write a profile of the librarian. See if it can be published in the library's newsletter or in your local newspaper.

Tour Your Newspaper Plant

Watching hundreds of sheets of paper being printed in a short amount of time can be fascinating to a child. Arrange to have a tour of your local newspaper's printing plant. See if you can meet with an editor or a writer and have him or her show your student the process of how an article makes it from the writer's computer to the printed page. If your student has shown an interest in writing, he or she may be especially interested in this activity.

Your Town's Own Biographer

Help your student find someone in your community about whom he or she would like to learn more. Would it be the mayor? A police officer? You and your student may want to spend some time together looking through the newspaper for people your student would like to talk to. Arrange to have you and your student meet with him or her to ask questions. Assist your student in preparing topics for the interview, such as information about childhood, what he or she wants to do in the future, and so on. If you'd like, bring a cassette tape recorder to the interview, but be sure to get permission first before using it. Then have your student write a biography of the person. He or she can add drawings and anything else to the biography. You also can have your student make a videotape of the interview or perhaps make a timeline of the person's life. Then help your student figure out a way that he or she would like to present it to the person. Your student also can make a certificate of appreciation to the person.

We Have Learned

Use this checklist to summarize what you and your student
have accomplished in the Promoting Literacy section.

❏ **Fiction and Science Fiction**
❏ reading fiction
❏ reading science fiction
❏ characteristics of fiction
❏ characteristics of science fiction

❏ **Identifying Sentences**
❏ identifying four types of sentences
❏ using four types of sentences
❏ correct punctuation of four types
   of sentences

❏ **Writing Dialogue**
❏ identifying dialogue
❏ using correct punctuation and
   correct capitalization

❏ **Folktale**
❏ reading folktale
❏ characteristics of folktale
❏ listening to oral narrative
❏ delivering oral narrative

❏ **Notetaking**
❏ learning notetaking process
❏ looking for main-idea clues:
   subheads, heads, boldfaced text
❏ recognizing important facts, details,
   definitions

❏ **Biography**
❏ reading biography
❏ characteristics of biography

❏ learning past tense, present tense,
   future tense

❏ **Topic Sentence and Supporting
   Details**
❏ identifying, writing topic sentence
❏ identifying, writing supporting
   details

❏ **Writing a Thank You**
❏ using commas in direct address,
   introductory phrases
❏ using correct format

❏ **Writing Correct Dates and Times**
❏ using correct punctuation,
   capitalization
❏ using correct order of days, months,
   years

❏ **Following and Giving Directions**
❏ understanding importance of ordering steps
❏ following order of steps/directions
❏ giving order of steps/directions

❏ **Poetry**
❏ reading poetry
❏ characteristics of poetry

We have also learned:

_____

_____

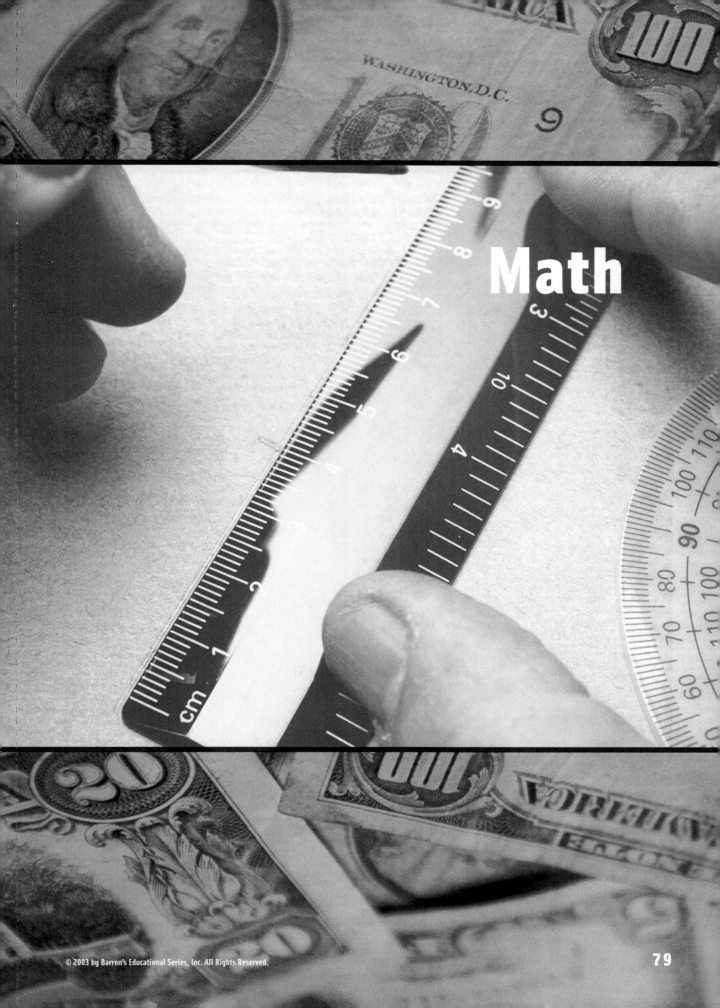

Math

Math

Key Topics

Place Value

Addition and Subtraction

Money

Time and Measurement

Multiplication

Division

Fractions and Decimals

Data and Graphs

Geometry

MATH

LESSON
2.1

Understanding Large Numbers

Understanding large numbers builds a strong foundation for math in the years to come.

OBJECTIVE	BACKGROUND	MATERIALS
To help your student identify number order, placement, and the value of each digit in a number with four or more digits	Large numbers may not be as common in your student's everyday life as small numbers, but soon he or she will begin to encounter them regularly. Working with the concept of place value, this lesson uses simple tables and explanations to help the student understand large numbers. Your student will learn how to order large numbers, round up and round down, and solve problems by estimating.	■ Student Learning Pages 1.A–1.B

VOCABULARY

DIGIT any one of the ten numerals 0, 1, 2, 3, 4, 5, 6, 7, 8, or 9 used to write numbers

PLACE-VALUE CHART a type of chart that shows the value of each digit in a number

Let's Begin

FOUR-DIGIT NUMBERS

1 **EXPLAIN** Explain that large numbers are based on the same system as small numbers. Reveal that, in fact, a large number is simply a combination of the same **digits** that make up a small number. Help your student picture large numbers by having him or her think of them as being made up of digits in the same way that words are made up of letters. Each digit has a special value based on its place in the number—whether in the thousands, hundreds, tens, or ones position. Ask your student, *What are some large numbers that you know?* [possible answers: the year, the amount of people in your town]

2 **EXPLORE** Ask your student where he or she might find large numbers. Brainstorm with your student to come up with ideas. For example, look at the number of pages in a large book or a telephone directory, prices of cars listed in the newspaper, or street addresses. You also can have your student search on the Internet by typing in *studying four-digit numbers*. Have your student tell you how many matches result.

DID YOU KNOW?

The highest mountain in the United States is Mt. McKinley, in Alaska, at 20,320 feet. The lowest point is Death Valley, California, which is actually 282 feet *below* sea level!

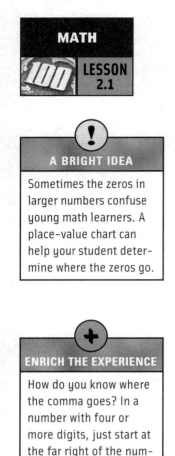

3 **GUIDE** Distribute Student Learning Page 1.A. Refer your student to Chart A. Use this **place-value chart** to demonstrate how to pronounce the four-digit number 1,439. Start with the tens and ones, which are pronounced together (thirty-nine), and work back to the thousands, as in *one thousand, four hundred thirty-nine*.

4 **DEMONSTRATE** Show your student that in Chart A, the number 1,439 (one thousand, four hundred thirty-nine) is made up of the digits 1, 4, 3, and 9. There are three ways to write the number:

Standard Form: 1,439
Expanded Form: 1000
                                   400
                                    30
                        +   9
                        ‾‾‾‾‾‾‾‾‾‾
Word Form: one thousand, four hundred thirty-nine

5 **PRACTICE** Ask your student to rewrite the other four-digit numbers in Chart A. In his or her notebook have him or her write each number in the three ways. Then have your student read the answers aloud (*hint:* both the standard form and word form are pronounced the same). Verify that your student wrote this in his or her notebook:

Standard Form:	594	1,058	4,604
Expanded Form:	500	1000	4000
	90	50	600
	+ 4	+ 8	+ 4
Word Form:	five hundred ninety-four	one thousand, fifty-eight	four thousand, six hundred four

ORDERING

1 **EXPLAIN AND DEMONSTRATE** Explain to your student that to put large numbers in order from smallest to largest and vice versa, look at the quantity of digits first. Then look at the value of the digits, starting from the left. Now ask your student to compare the numbers in Chart A. Present your student with this math problem, *Place the numbers in order from the smallest to largest.* Remind him or her to look at the quantity of digits first, and then start at the left to look at the value of the digits. [594; 1,058; 1,439; 4,604]

If your student **solved the problem** correctly ask, *How did you solve this problem?* Encourage your student to tell you how he or she used the value of the digits in the thousands and hundreds columns to determine the value of the number as a whole.

If your student **didn't solve the problem,** ask, *How did you solve it?* Explain what went wrong. Then work with him or her to determine the value of the digits in the thousands and hundreds categories to decide the value of the number.

The number 594 has no thousands, so it's the smallest. The number 4 is bigger than 1 so 4,604 is the biggest number of the four. There are two 1s in the thousands place, so your student should look to the next number to determine which is the smaller of the two; because 0 is less than 4, 1,439 is the larger number of the two, and 1,058 the smaller of the two. Therefore, the order of the numbers from smallest to largest is: 594; 1,058; 1,439; 4,604.

2 **EXPAND THE CONCEPT** Reveal that place value works the same way for any whole number, no matter how big it is! Have your student look at Chart B on Student Learning Page 1.B. Show your student that this chart includes ten thousands. When writing the word form of a five-digit number, explain that the ten thousands and thousands are hyphenated. Show your student that, for example, the word form for the number 85,392 is eighty-five thousand, three hundred ninety-two.

3 **PRACTICE** Now go to Student Learning Page 1.B for more practice.

ROUNDING AND ESTIMATING LARGE NUMBERS

1 **EXPLAIN** Share with your student that numbers are rounded up or down to give an approximate value of the number. In this case, for example, 5,448 was rounded up to 5,450. Together with your student walk through these rounding rules:

- To round a number to the nearest 10, look at the ones, or last digit, in the number.
- If it's greater than or equal to 5, round up. So, 6,475 becomes 6,**480**. If it's less than 5, round down. So, 6,474 becomes 6,**470**.
- To round a number to the nearest 100, look at the tens, or second-to-last digit, in the number:
- If it's greater than or equal to 5, round up. So, 3,574 becomes 3,**600**. If it's less than 5, round down. So, 3,534 becomes 3,**500**.

2 **REVIEW** Review with your student the rounding rules. Have your student write these numbers in his or her notebook: 5,523; 4,001; 7,010. Then tell your student, *Round these numbers to the nearest 10.* [5,520; 4,000; 7,010] Have your student write these numbers in his or her notebook: 8,427; 9,910; 3,246. Then tell your student, *Round these numbers to the nearest 100.* [8,500; 9,900; 3,200]

If your student answered **correctly** ask, *How did you find the answer?* Encourage your student to tell you how he or she looked at the value of the number in the ones place (for rounding to the nearest 10) and looked at the value of the number in the tens place (for rounding to the nearest 100). Then go to Step 3.

If your student **didn't answer correctly,** have him or her write another set of numbers of your choosing in his or her notebook. Walk through each step with him or her. You may even want to have him or her "teach" the rounding rules back to you for greater comprehension. Remind your student that rounding up or down takes you to the nearest ten, hundred, and so on to give the approximate number.

3 **EXPAND THE CONCEPT** Explain that rounding up or down works the same for rounding to the nearest thousand. Together with your student walk through these rounding rules:

- To round to the nearest 1,000, look at the hundreds when deciding to round up or down.
- To round to the nearest 10,000, look at the thousands when deciding to round up or down.

If you feel your student is ready to move on to rounding these larger numbers, have him or her write down a few numbers of your choosing and then round up or down.

4 **EXPLAIN ESTIMATES** Reveal that when a number of items is too large to count, or when you don't need to know the exact number of things, you can estimate the total. Offer examples of the types of things that might be estimated: the number of coins in a jar of pennies, the distance between two cities, or the number of books on a bookshelf. Ask, *What are some things that you might estimate?* [possible answers: the number of rubber bands or paper clips in a box, the number of cars in a parking lot]

5 **DESCRIBE** Describe this scenario to your student: *Two weeks ago you bought a box of 500 paper clips. You took out five last week, and you think you may have taken out three to five clips this week.* Ask your student to estimate how many clips are still in the box. Explain that because only a few were taken out, and we're not sure how many, a safe estimate might be 490 clips.

Branching Out

TEACHING TIP

If working with large numbers gets confusing for your student, it may help to attach the numbers to real items, such as the quantity of apples your family eats in a month or the number of plates in your house.

FOR FURTHER READING

Developing Number Concepts: Place Value, Multiplication, and Division, by Kathy Richardson (Dale Seymour Publications, 1998).

CHECKING IN

You can assess the ability of your student to determine place value by using a calculator. Place random four- or five-digit numbers in the calculator and ask the student to tell which of the digits is in the tens place, the thousands, and so on. Then ask the student to round the same number up or down to the nearest 10, 100, and 1,000.

Understand Value and Number Order

Chart A

	Thousands	Hundreds	Tens	Ones
A.	1,	4	3	9
B.		5	9	4
C.	1,	0	5	8
D.	4,	6	0	4

Chart B

	Ten Thousands	Thousands	Hundreds	Tens	Ones
A.	8	5,	3	9	2
B.	3	0,	4	3	9
C.	5	9,	3	0	0
D.	2	2,	0	9	6

Read the numbers in Chart B. Then put the numbers in order from smallest to largest. Write the letter of the number in order from smallest to largest.

1. _____

2. _____

3. _____

4. _____

Write each number in Chart B in standard form. Then write each number in word form.

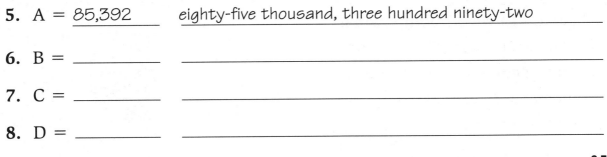

5. A = _85,392_   _eighty-five thousand, three hundred ninety-two_

6. B = _____   _____

7. C = _____   _____

8. D = _____   _____

What's Next? You Decide

Now it's your turn to choose what to do next in the lesson. Read the activities and decide which you want to do—you may want to try them both!

Create Your Own Game

MATERIALS

❏ 10 index cards, each with a number 0–9

STEPS

Play this game with a friend.

❏ Shuffle the cards and turn them with the numbers facing down so you can't see them.

❏ Have a friend choose four cards. Turn the cards over.

❏ Combine all four cards into one large number. Write the four-digit number on paper.

❏ Put the cards back into the pile and shuffle them again.

❏ Now you choose four cards and turn them over.

❏ Combine them into one large number. Write this number.

❏ Whoever has the larger number gets a point. The first person to get 10 points wins!

❏ You can play this game with more people or choose more index cards to make larger numbers!

Guess the Buttons

MATERIALS

❏ 1 glass jar
❏ buttons to fill the jar
❏ 1 crayon

STEPS

❏ Place enough buttons in the jar to fill it halfway.

❏ Take these buttons out and count them. Write this number down.

❏ Put the buttons back in the jar.

❏ Make a mark on the jar with a crayon at the place where the buttons fill the jar.

❏ Now fill the jar full with the rest of the buttons.

❏ Estimate how many items are now in the container.

❏ Take out the buttons from the jar and count them. How close was your estimate?

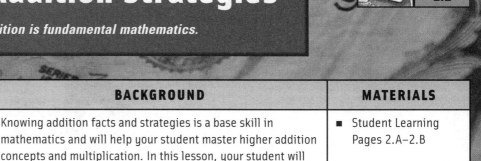

Using Addition Strategies

Addition is fundamental mathematics.

MATH

100 LESSON 2.2

OBJECTIVE	BACKGROUND	MATERIALS
To show your student strategies for adding and estimating numbers	Knowing addition facts and strategies is a base skill in mathematics and will help your student master higher addition concepts and multiplication. In this lesson, your student will add three or more numbers, use estimation strategies, and practice adding two- and three-digit numbers.	■ Student Learning Pages 2.A–2.B

Let's Begin

1 **EXPLAIN** Point out that football games are divided into four quarters. A team's final score is the sum of the scores from each of the four quarters. Have your student copy the score chart into his or her notebook.

Quarters	1	2	3	4
Home	7	3	9	6
Visitors	0	14	21	7

2 **ASK** Ask, *Would you add or subtract to find the total number of points scored by the home team in the first three quarters?* [add] *How many points did they score?* [19] Observe what method the student uses to set up and solve this problem. Point out that the first two numbers add up to 10 (7 + 3), which makes the rest of the addition problem easier.

3 **DISCUSS** Have your student estimate the total scores of the two teams. Ask, *Just by looking at their scores, can you tell who won the game? How?* [the visiting team's scores have two larger two-digit numbers, while the home team's are all single digits; the visiting team probably had a higher total score] *How else can we quickly find out the winner?* [round each quarter's score to the nearest 5 and then add] Have your student round the scores from each quarter and add to find which team scored the most points. Then have the student compare the result with his or her initial conclusion.

4 **DETERMINE** Have your student determine if his or her predictions were correct by adding both team's scores. Watch as your student sets up the two addition problems. Ask, *What was the total score of the game?* [home team: 25; visitors: 42]

If your student **didn't solve the problems** correctly, ask, *How did you set up your addition problems?* Be sure the student lined up the problems correctly.

5 **PRACTICE** Have your student write the following addition problems in his or her notebook.

$$\begin{array}{r} 24 \\ + 12 \\ \hline \end{array} \qquad \begin{array}{r} 261 \\ + 589 \\ \hline \end{array}$$

Check to make sure your student has lined up the numbers correctly. Lining the problems up on graph paper can be helpful. Ask your student to point out the ones, tens, and hundreds place in the problems. Then observe his or her methods of solving the problems. Review regrouping as needed (making ones into tens, tens into hundreds). Have your student complete Student Learning Page 2.A for more practice.

Branching Out

TEACHING TIP

Look in your local paper for other sports scores and determine the winner by following the same steps as above.

CHECKING IN

Have your student weigh himself or herself and everyone else who lives in your home. Then ask your student to add all of the weights together to get a total weight for the household! Another option is to have your student estimate the total number of doorknobs in his or her home, then have him or her count them to check the estimate.

FOR FURTHER READING

Addition, Subtraction, Place Value, Other Numeration Systems: Reproducible Skill Builders and Higher Order Thinking Activities Based on NCTM Standards, by Brenda Opie with Lory Jackson (Incentive Publications, Inc., 1999).

A Collection for Kate (Math Matters), by Barbara deRubertis and Gioia Fiammenghi (Kane Press, 1999).

Solve the Addition Problems

Add.

1.
```
   6
   2
 + 2
```

2.
```
   1
   8
 + 5
```

3.
```
  64
+ 28
```

4.
```
  47
+ 21
```

5.
```
  891
+  75
```

6.
```
  203
+  44
```

7.
```
  125
+ 257
```

8.
```
  345
+ 161
```

9.
```
  369
+ 432
```

10.
```
  599
+ 188
```

Student Learning Page 2.A: Solve the Addition Problems   **89**

What's Next? You Decide!

Now it's your turn to choose what to do next in the lesson. Read the activities and decide which one you want to do—you may want to try them both!

Keep It Low

MATERIALS

❑ 1 die

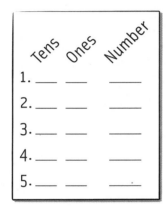

STEPS

❑ Each player copies the above drawing into his or her notebook.

❑ Each player takes turns rolling the die twice. After each roll, the player chooses whether to write the number in the Ones or Tens place.

❑ Then write this two-digit number under Number.

❑ For each round, the player with the lowest two-digit number gets 1 point. If there is a tie, both players get 1

point. Keep track of points on a separate sheet of paper.

❑ At the end of five rounds, add the total points. The player with the most points is the winner.

Add the Ages

STEPS

❑ Write down the names and ages of at least eight friends and family members.

❑ Add all the ages together and write the sum.

❑ Now divide the people on your list into two groups. Try to make the sum of the ages of the people in each group and the number of people in each group as close to equal as possible.

❑ Now choose the oldest person on your list. Begin adding the ages of the younger people on your list until the sum is equal to the oldest person. How many younger people did it take?

MATH

LESSON
2.3

Subtracting Whole Numbers

The curriculum is essential, but warmth and feeling are the heart of teaching.

OBJECTIVE	BACKGROUND	MATERIALS
To teach your student to use fact families and other strategies to subtract whole numbers	Mastering the basic addition facts builds a strong foundation for subtraction. Linking the two skills will help your student strengthen both. In this lesson, your student will review subtraction strategies and apply subtraction skills to larger numbers.	■ Student Learning Pages 3.A–3.B ■ 13 buttons

Let's Begin

SUBTRACTION STRATEGIES

1 **EXPLAIN** There are different methods your student can apply when subtracting numbers. Counting forward or backward to find an answer are two common methods. Give your student the following two subtraction problems: $11 - 8 =$ _____ and $13 - 2 =$ _____. Have him or her decide which method works best. Ask, *Which strategy would you use to solve $11 - 8$ and why?* [since 11 and 8 are close on a number line, count up from the eight to find the answer; 3] *What about $13 - 2$?* [it would be easiest to count back 2 from 13 to find the answer; 11] Have your student write the fact family for each problem. [$11 - 8 = 3$, $11 - 3 = 8$, $8 + 3 = 11$, $3 + 8 = 11$; $13 - 2 = 11$, $13 - 11 = 2$, $11 + 2 = 13$, $2 + 11 = 13$]

2 **DISCUSS** Explain that knowing other quick ways to subtract is helpful if you don't have a pencil and paper available. Another way to add and subtract is to make a 10. Give the student 13 buttons or counters, and tell him or her to make a group of 9 and a group of 4. Then write the following problems on a piece of paper: $9 + 4 =$ _____ and $13 - 9 =$ _____. Ask, *How can you solve the addition problem by making a 10? Demonstrate with your buttons.* [by taking 1 from the group of 4, make the group of 9 a group of 10; now the addition problem becomes easier: $10 + 3 = 13$]

3 **ASK** Ask, *How would you solve $13 - 9$ using a group of 10?* [to make 9 into a 10, add 1; then add 3 to get 13; $1 + 3 = 4$, so $13 - 9 = 4$]

MATH

LESSON 2.3

SUBTRACTION AND REGROUPING

1   **EXPLAIN** Explain that when subtracting two- and three-digit numbers, first the problem must be set up correctly. Then it's easier to see if regrouping will be necessary. Lining up the problem on graph paper is helpful. Your student may also find using the three Bs (bottom, bigger, borrow) helpful. Have your student write $831 - 429$ on graph paper. Point out that the bottom number in the ones place (9) is bigger than the top number in the ones place (1), so your student will need to borrow, or regroup, one group of ten. [$11 - 9 = 2$]

2   **PRESENT AND ASK** Describe this situation to your student: *Clarence has 231 baseball cards in his collection. He also has 115 football cards. How many more baseball cards than football cards does he have?* Have your student write out the problem. Ask, *Will this problem require regrouping?* [yes] Have your student subtract the two numbers. Observe his or her regrouping methods. Check the final answer. [116]

     If your student **solved the problem** correctly, have him or her complete Student Learning Page 3.A for more practice.

3   **MODEL** If your student **didn't solve the problem** correctly, have him or her use a place-value chart to help with regrouping. Write the number 231 in the chart and model for your student the steps to follow for borrowing. Ask, *After you regroup, what new numbers do you have in the place-value chart?* [2 hundreds, 2 tens, 11 ones] *Now when you subtract what is your answer?* [116] If your student still has an incorrect answer, check his or her subtraction.

Hundreds	Tens	Ones
	2	11
2	~~3~~	~~1~~

Branching Out

TEACHING TIP

Whenever possible, encourage work with basic facts by asking your student to write the related facts within a fact family. This reinforces the fact that once your student knows one fact, he or she knows three others.

CHECKING IN

Have your student write $365 - 148$ and then solve the problem with regrouping.

FOR FURTHER READING

Math Coach: A Parent's Guide to Helping Children Succeed in Math, by Wayne and Ingrid Wickelgren (Berkley Books, 2001).

Subtraction, by Sheila Cato and Sami Sweeten (Lerner Publishing Group, 1999).

Practice Subtraction

Follow the road. Solve the problems along the way. Find the number of the final destination.

1. $\boxed{+}\ \boxed{-}$

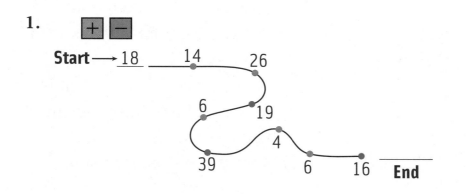

Start → 18 ___ 14 ___ 26

6 ___ 19

39 ___ 4 ___ 6 ___ 16 **End**

Subtract.

2.   804
   − 356

3.   2,379
   − 496

Read the word problem. Then answer the question.

4. Jamie has $200 saved to help buy new school clothes. She buys 2 pairs of pants for $28 each, a new shirt for $14, a sweatshirt for $23, and a new pair of shoes on sale for $18. How much money does she have left after her shopping spree? Show your work.

What's Next? You Decide!

Now it's your turn to choose what to do next in the lesson. Read the activities and decide which one you want to do—you may want to try them both!

Pick a Card

MATERIALS

❏ 10 index cards marked with the numbers 0–9

STEPS

Ask an adult to watch you do this activity and check your work.

❏ Lay the cards out facedown.

❏ Choose two cards. Turn them over and make a two-digit number.

❏ Choose two more cards and do the same.

❏ Use the two numbers to write out a subtraction problem in your notebook with the larger number on the top and the smaller number on the bottom.

❏ First round the numbers to the nearest 5 or 10 to estimate the difference between the two numbers. Write down your estimate.

❏ Then subtract to find the answer. Write down your answer. How far off was your estimate?

❏ Finally, write the fact family for the subtraction problem you solved.

❏ Repeat the exercise using three cards.

Plan a Trip

STEPS

❏ Make your own addition and subtraction road map.

❏ Have someone else take the trip.

❏ Be sure you check to see if he or she gets the correct answer at the end.

❏ If you'd like, have someone else make an addition and subtraction road map for you.

❏ Check your answers at the end of your trip.

Counting Money

Money and math go hand in hand.

OBJECTIVE	BACKGROUND	MATERIALS
To introduce your student to counting coins and bills and solving money problems	Working with money is something every student can relate to. Whether the student receives an allowance or just wants to go to the movies, counting money is relevant to a child's everyday life. In this lesson, your student will practice understanding the value of coins, calculating costs, and reasoning logically with money.	■ Student Learning Pages 4.A–4.B ■ graph paper ■ 4 quarters ■ 4 dimes ■ 10 nickels ■ 20 pennies

Let's Begin

1 **REVIEW** Your student may already be familiar with the values of coins. Complete this simple review to prepare him or her for the lesson. Place one quarter, one dime, and two nickels on a table. Ask, *Which of these coins is worth the most?* [quarter] *Which coin is worth the least?* [nickel] *If you were to add the total value of these coins, which coin would you start with? Why?* [the quarter because it's worth the most] *Have your student line up the coins in order of their worth.* Ask, *How much money is here?* [45 cents]

2 **MODEL AND WRITE** Explain to your student that the four coins are like an addition problem with four addends. Have your student write out the addition problem and solve it on paper. Review his or her work.

$$
\begin{array}{r}
25 \\
10 \\
5 \\
+5 \\
\hline
45
\end{array}
$$

3 **INTRODUCE** Present the following scenario to your student: *Kim is going to the movies and she has $5.00 to spend on snacks. The prices at the theater are as follows.*

> **TAKE A BREAK**
>
> Take your student out for a snack. Have your student choose what he or she wants to eat and tell you how many dollars, quarters, dimes, and nickels he or she needs to buy it. Give your student the currency he or she asks for and remind him or her to count the change!

Popcorn	Drinks
Small: $1.50	Small: $1.25
Medium: $2.25	Medium: $2.50
Large: $3.50	Large: $3.25

Ask, *If Kim wants to buy a large popcorn, can she also buy a large drink?* [no, the total would be $6.75] *If she buys a small popcorn, what sizes of drink can she choose from?* [she can buy any size drink because they would all total under $5.00] *What would the total be for a medium popcorn and a medium drink?* [$4.75] *How much change would she receive?* [25 cents]

If your student **solved the problem** correctly, go to Step 5 and complete Student Learning Page 4.A.

4 **MODEL** If your student **didn't solve the problem** correctly, ask, *How did you solve this problem?* Have him or her set up and solve the problem on graph paper while you observe his or her method. Remind your student that when adding and subtracting money, the decimal points in the problem must be lined up. If Kim buys a medium popcorn and a medium drink, the problem would be written as follows:

$$\begin{array}{r} \$2.25 \\ +2.50 \\ \hline \$4.75 \end{array} \qquad \begin{array}{r} \$5.00 \\ -4.75 \\ \hline \$0.25 \end{array}$$

5 **PRACTICE** Put 4 quarters, 4 dimes, 10 nickels, and 20 pennies into a small bag or box. Have your student use this box to complete exercises 1–4 on Student Learning Page 4.A. Check his or her work and have your student complete the rest of the exercises.

Branching Out

FOR FURTHER READING

25 Math Board Games: Instant Games That Teach Essential Math Skills Including Multiplication, Fractions, Time, Money, and More, by Mary Beth Spann (Scholastic, Inc., 1999).

Secret Code Math, by Bob Hugel (Scholastic, Inc., 1998).

TEACHING TIP

Help your student understand the different ways to make one dollar. Lay out a dollar bill and enough quarters, dimes, nickels, and pennies to make one dollar with each coin. Make a chart listing the coins across the top. Have your student list how many of each coin is needed to make one dollar under each column.

CHECKING IN

Give your student a receipt from the grocery store and have him or her choose four items. Have him or her figure out how much the change would be if he or she had exactly $10, or whether there would not be enough money to buy all the items.

Pull It Out, Add It Up

Reach into a bag of coins. Pull out five coins at a time. Add the total amount of the coins. Do this exercise four times.

1. _____

2. _____

3. _____

4. _____

Count the money. Write the amount.

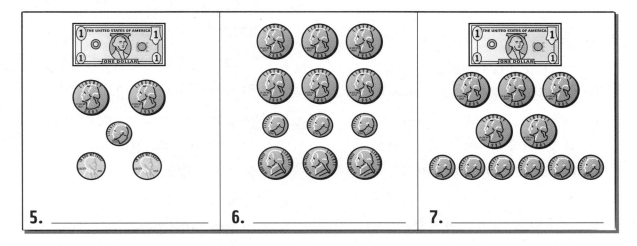

5. _____

6. _____

7. _____

Read the word problem. Then answer the question.

8. Ken has 12 coins in his pocket that total 50 cents. What are the 12 coins?

_____   _____

_____   _____

_____   _____

_____   _____

_____   _____

What's Next? You Decide!

Now it's your turn to choose what to do next in the lesson. Read the activities and decide which one you want to do—you may want to try them both!

Fill Up the Tank

STEPS

Gasoline prices change almost every day. Find out how much a tank of gas would cost for a certain day.

❏ Track the cost of regular unleaded gas over a period of five days. You can check the signs at a gas station near your home, check the Internet, or look in the newspaper. Write the date and price per gallon for each day.

❏ Subtract the lowest price from the highest price to find out how much the prices varied in five days.

❏ Share your work with an adult.

Shop Until You Drop

MATERIALS

❏ store ads or flyers

STEPS

❏ Collect a few advertisement papers from local stores.

❏ Choose five items from the ads that cost between $1 and $10.

❏ Write the price of each item in a column on the left side of a piece of paper.

❏ Suppose that you had only quarters and pennies. Next to the dollar amount for each item, write the amount in quarters and pennies.

❏ Next, do the same thing supposing that you only had dimes and pennies. Write down your answers.

❏ Have an adult check your work.

Telling Time

Time is what you make of it.

OBJECTIVE	BACKGROUND	MATERIALS
To help your student develop the skill of telling time and reading the calendar	Telling time affects everything we do during our day. Whether it's during school or when out to play, being able to tell time and judge elapsed time are skills that your student will use daily. In this lesson, your student will practice telling time to the quarter hour and minute and solving problems that involve elapsed time and calendars.	▪ Student Learning Pages 5.A–5.B ▪ 1 clock with minute and hour hands ▪ 1 year calendar

Let's Begin

TELLING TIME

1 **EXPLAIN** Ask your student to tell you what he or she already knows about telling time. Show your student a clock. Ask him or her to point out the hour hand and the minute hand. Ask, *How many minutes does it take for the minute hand to go around the clock once?* [60 minutes] *How many minutes does it take for the minute hand to go around halfway?* [30 minutes] *How about one quarter?* [15 minutes] Begin at 12:00 and have your student demonstrate the passing of one hour, a half hour, and a quarter hour on the clock.

2 **PRESENT** Ask, *Suppose that your favorite show starts at 8:00 P.M. Can you show me 8:00 on this clock?* Have your student move the hands to 8:00. Explain that the first commercial begins at quarter after eight. Have your student move the hand to 8:15. Ask, *What is another way of reading this time?* [eight fifteen] *If the show ends at 9:00, how many minutes long was it?* [60 minutes] Have your student write "8:15," "quarter after eight," "9:00," and "nine o'clock" in his or her notebook.

3 **REVEAL** Point out the numbers on the clock from 1 to 12. Explain that five minutes pass between each number. Ask, *If your show ended at 9:00 and you spent five minutes brushing your teeth and three minutes changing into your pajamas, what time would it be when you got into bed?* [9:08] Have your student show 9:08 on the clock.

TAKE A BREAK

Have your student complete some simple household tasks, such as running the vacuum or washing some dishes, and time himself or herself. Have your student estimate how long he or she thinks it will take and then compare the estimate to the actual time.

4 **PRESENT** Present this scenario to your student: *You are taking a trip to an amusement park. When you arrive it is 10:00 A.M. The first two rides take 30 minutes and 15 minutes each.* Ask, *What time is it when you are finished with the rides?* [10:45] *Your family is meeting for lunch at 12:00. How much time do you have before you have to meet them?* [1 hour and 15 minutes, or 75 minutes]

5 **MODEL** If your student **didn't solve the problems** in Step 4 correctly, show him or her 10:00 on the clock. Have your student move the clock hands 30 minutes to 10:30. Point out that 10:30 can also be read as half-past ten. Then have your student move the hands of the clock 15 minutes to 10:45. Point out to your student that he or she can count by quarter hours on the clock to calculate the time between 10:45 and 12:00. Have your student complete Student Learning Page 5.A for additional practice.

THE CALENDAR

1 **EXPLAIN** Show your student a calendar of the year. Ask your student to tell you what he or she already knows about the calendar. Point out that the calendar shows the days of the week, the months of the year, and the number, or date, of each day of the month. Point out that there are always 12 months in a year and seven days in a week. Mention that a month has 30 or 31 days except for February, which has 28, or 29 if it's Leap Year. Have your student find today's date on the calendar. Write today's date on paper. [example: Monday, December 9, 2004] Then have your student write tomorrow's date.

2 **WRITE AND PRACTICE** Have your student use the calendar to answer these questions. Ask, *How many days does January have? November? What is the date of the second Sunday in March? What day of the week does the 28th day of August fall on?*

Branching Out

TEACHING TIP

When working with the clock, have your student write times on a sheet of paper. With the abundance of digital clocks available, your student should also recognize how time is shown digitally.

FOR FURTHER READING

Primary Games: Experimental Learning Activities for Teaching Children K–8, by Steve Sugar (Jossey-Bass, 2002).

CHECKING IN

Use your newspaper or the Internet to find starting times for some movies. Write down the times and then have your student show the times by moving the hands on the clock. Look in the listing for the lengths of the movies (or estimate the lengths) and have your student tell at what times the movies will end.

Tell Time

Look at each clock. Then write the time.

1. _____

2. _____

3. _____

4. _____

Look at the clock. Then answer the questions.

5. What time is it? _____

6. Where will the minute hand be 30 minutes from now? _____

7. Where will the hour hand be 60 minutes from now? _____

8. What time will it be 45 minutes later? _____

What's Next? You Decide!

Now it's your turn to choose what to do next in the lesson. Read the activities and decide which one you want to do—you may want to try them both!

Track Waking and Sleeping Time

▦ MATERIALS

❑ 1 clock

▦ STEPS

There are 24 hours in one day. How many of them do you spend awake or asleep?

❑ Put a sheet of paper, a pencil, and a clock next to your bed.

❑ One night, right before you go to bed, look at the clock and write down the exact time on the paper.

❑ The next morning when you wake up, look at the clock and write down the time again.

❑ That night, do the same thing before you go to bed.

❑ The next day, figure out exactly how many hours and minutes you spent asleep and awake. Remember to start counting from one again after 12:00 noon and after 12:00 midnight.

Do a Calendar Countdown

▦ MATERIALS

❑ 1 calendar of year

▦ STEPS

❑ Find your birthday on the calendar. Write the date of your birthday and the day of the week it falls on. For example: Tuesday, August 10, 2004.

❑ Count how many months and days come between your birthday and today's date. Write the number of months and days.

❑ Find your favorite holiday on the calendar. Write its date and day of the week.

❑ Which will be the soonest to arrive, your birthday or your favorite holiday? Write the names of the months that will come between now and then. If they've already passed, figure out how many months and days there are until they're celebrated next year.

Exploring Measurement

Measurement is a skill that can be applied to a variety of everyday activities.

OBJECTIVE	BACKGROUND	MATERIALS
To show your student how to measure with customary units of length, capacity, and weight	Measurement is a practical skill that your student will use every day. In this lesson, your student will learn about the different units of measurement.	■ Student Learning Pages 6.A–6.D ■ 1 customary ruler with half-inch markings ■ 10 items that have weights measured in ounces or pounds ■ 1 Celsius and 1 Fahrenheit thermometer

Let's Begin

UNITS OF LENGTH

1 **DISCUSS** Show your student a customary ruler. Ask, *When you look at a ruler, there are numbers on the inch marks; where are the half-inch marks?* [halfway between the inch marks] Give your student a book. Have him or her use the ruler to measure the book's length, width, and height to the nearest inch and half inch. Ask, *Which would be more accurate, measuring to the nearest inch or to the nearest half inch? Why?* [the nearest half inch; the smaller the measurement, the more accurate]

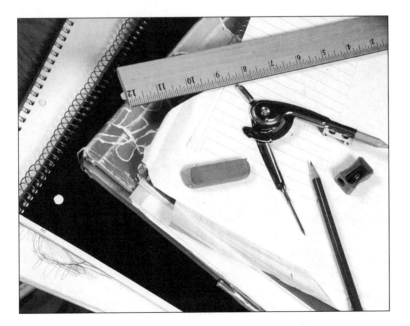

2 **EXPLAIN** Explain that the first thing to decide when measuring an object is what unit of measure to use. When measuring the length of an object, its size will help decide which unit to use. Share with your student a list of units for measuring length (1 foot = 12 inches, 1 yard = 3 feet, 1 mile = 1,760 yards). Ask, *Which of these is the smallest unit of measurement?* [inch] *Which is the largest?* [mile]

3 **APPLY** Have your student consider the following objects and which unit of measure he or she would use to measure each: height of a door (feet); length of a soccer field (yards); length of pencil (inches); distance from your home to the grocery store (miles); and length of a car (feet or yards).

Object	Pencil Length	Door Height	Soccer Field Length	Distance to Store
Unit of Measure	inches	feet	yards	miles

CAPACITY

1 **EXPLAIN** Explain that when measuring in inches, feet, yards, and miles, those are all units of length. When measuring an object's capacity, different units of measure are needed. Measuring capacity helps to find how much liquid an object will hold. Show your student a glass of water and ask, *Can you measure the amount of water in this glass with feet and inches?* [no] Share with your student a list of units for measuring capacity (2 cups = 1 pint, 2 pints = 1 quart, 4 quarts = 1 gallon).

Ask, *Which unit could you use to measure the water?* [cup]

2 **APPLY** Ask, *If you were buying a drink at the county fair, which would be a better deal, one cup for $1.25 or one pint for $1.25? Why?* [one pint for $1.25 is a better deal because you get more drink in one pint than in one cup] *Would you want to purchase nine pints of juice at the store for $3.00 or one gallon for the same price?* [nine pints is a better deal because that is more juice than one gallon; there are eight pints in one gallon]

If your student **solved these problems** correctly, skip Step 3 and go to Student Learning Page 6.A. If your student

didn't solve these problems correctly, have him or her complete Step 3 and then complete Student Learning Page 6.A.

MATH

LESSON 2.6

3 **DISCUSS** Help your student use the information in the chart to compare different measures of capacity. Ask, *Which is the greater amount, four pints or four cups?* [four pints; if needed show student how to use the information in the charts] *If you are making a pot of soup and the recipe says to add five pints of water but you do not have a container that measures pints, what can you do to measure this amount of water?* [use a measuring cup and measure 10 cups of water for the recipe]

4 **EXPLAIN** There are two common metric units used to measure capacity, liter, and milliliter. One liter (L) equals 1,000 milliliters (mL). An eyedropper will hold about one milliliter (mL) of liquid. Some of the large plastic bottles of soda hold one liter of liquid. Ask, *Would you use liters or milliliters to measure medicine in a bottle?* [mL] *Water in a pool?* [L] *A cup of soup?* [mL]

WEIGHT

1 **INTRODUCE** Explain that the units for measuring weight are different than those for measuring capacity. When measuring weight, the units ounces (oz) and pounds (lb) are used. There are 16 ounces in one pound. Give the student items from the kitchen that are measured in ounces or pounds.

2 **ASK** Instruct the student to divide the items into two groups, those best measured in ounces and those best measured in pounds. Ask, *What do you notice?* [student may observe there are more of one type of measurement, a pattern in the size of the containers holding the items, obvious weight difference when holding the items] *Carefully look at the packages; are there any in your ounce group that actually weigh more than one pound?* Help your student find out if any packages weigh more than 16 ounces and recognize that those weigh more than a package that is marked one pound. Have the student make further comparisons with the sizes of the packages. Note that the bigger packages do not always weigh more, as the material inside has an effect on the weight of the package as well.

3 **EXPLAIN** Explain that there are two metric units also used to measure mass. Grams and kilograms measure mass. Mass is a measure of how much matter an object has. Tell your student that 1,000 grams (g) = 1 kilogram (kg). Challenge your student to think of objects that can be measured using grams and kilograms.

TEMPERATURE

1 **EXPLAIN** Have your student examine a Celsius thermometer and a Fahrenheit thermometer. Explain that the customary unit of measure for temperature in the United States is Fahrenheit (°F).

The metric unit of measure is Celsius (°C). Explain that for every 10° change in Celsius, there is an 18° change in Fahrenheit. Have your student note the markings on the thermometers and read the room temperature using each measure.

2 **PRACTICE** Distribute Student Learning Pages 6.B and 6.C to your student to practice using units of measures in capacity and degrees. Give your student Student Learning Page 6.D for additional activities to practice with measurements.

Branching Out

TEACHING TIP

Introduce the idea that ancient civilization based measurements on body parts. Have your student use his or her foot or the span of his or her hand to measure 10 common objects. Keep a chart listing the measurements. Then use a ruler or yardstick to find the item's actual measurements and compare.

FOR FURTHER READING

Measurement Mania: Games and Activities That Make Math Easy and Fun, by Lynette Long (John Wiley & Sons, 2001).

Measuring Penny, by Loreen Leedy (Henry Holt Books for Young Children, 2000).

Sir Cumference and the Great Knight of Angeland, by Cindy Neuschwander and Wayne Geehan (Charlesbridge Publishers, 2001).

CHECKING IN

Measuring things around the house is a good hands-on way to assess your student's understanding of different types of measurement units. Have him or her weigh a large and a small object, measure a short and a long length, and so on. You can make a game out of it by asking questions, such as, *Who has the longest sock in the house? Who wears the heaviest shoe?*

Do You Measure Up?

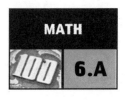

Read each measurement. Then write the letter of the best unit of measurement.

1. Length of a table _____   **a.** 5 feet   **b.** 5 yards

2. Thickness of a book _____   **a.** 2 inches   **b.** 2 feet

3. Distance around a city block _____   **a.** 1 yard   **b.** 1 mile

4. Height of a flagpole _____   **a.** 20 yards   **b.** 20 feet

5. Lemonade in a glass _____   **a.** 2 cups   **b.** 2 quarts

6. Water in a wading pool _____   **a.** 15 quarts   **b.** 15 gallons

7. Milk needed to make pancakes _____   **a.** 1 cup   **b.** 1 gallon

Read each question. Then write the answer.

8. Mary puts 2 quarts of water in the birdbath every day. How many gallons of water does she put in the birdbath in 4 days? _____

9. Joe is 30 inches from Mrs. Smith's desk. Jordan is 2 feet from the desk. Who is closest to Mrs. Smith's desk? _____

10. David bought 3 pieces of rope. The pieces of rope were 12 inches long, 18 inches long, and 42 inches long. If the rope costs 50¢ a foot, how much did David pay for the 3 pieces of rope? _____

Pack for a Hike

Ken and Mark are packing for a hiking trip through the mountains. They want to divide their materials so that both hikers are carrying about the same weight on their backs. On a separate sheet of paper, make a chart with two columns. Divide the materials so that each hiker is carrying almost the same weight. Give a total weight of the materials in each hiker's backpack.

Hiking Materials and Their Weights

Sleeping bag	5 pounds 9 ounces
Tent/fly	6 pounds 5 ounces
Rope	9 pounds 8 ounces
Tent poles/stakes	3 pounds 2 ounces
Pot for cooking	9 ounces
2 bowls	5 ounces
Lantern	5 ounces
Flashlight	4 ounces
First-aid kit	6 ounces
Toiletries	4 ounces
Goggles	3 ounces
2 sets of rain gear	1 pound 4 ounces

Now, what would you pack for an afternoon at the zoo? What about for a trip to Australia or a visit to Mars? Choose a trip you would like to take, and make a list of the things you would pack. Guess how much everything on your list weighs.

How Hot Is It?

The metric unit of measure for temperature is the degree
Celsius (°C). The customary unit of measure for temperature
used in the United States is the degree Fahrenheit (°F).
Look at the thermometer. Read each question. Then write
the answer.

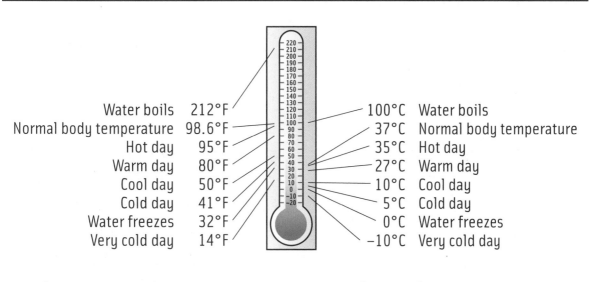

Water boils 212°F	100°C Water boils
Normal body temperature 98.6°F	37°C Normal body temperature
Hot day 95°F	35°C Hot day
Warm day 80°F	27°C Warm day
Cool day 50°F	10°C Cool day
Cold day 41°F	5°C Cold day
Water freezes 32°F	0°C Water freezes
Very cold day 14°F	−10°C Very cold day

1. The temperature was 39°C. It rose 5°. What is the

   temperature now? _____

2. The temperature dropped 5°. It's now 48°F. What was

   the temperature? _____

3. Circle the temperature at which you would want to go swimming:
   95°F or 45°F.

4. Circle the temperature at which you would want to go sledding
   in the snow: 30°F or 80°F.

5. Circle the temperature at which you would want to cut the grass:
   86°C or 20°C.

6. Take the outdoor temperature at 9:00 A.M. every day for a week.

   Write the temperature in your notebook. At the end of the week,

   find the average temperature at 9:00 A.M. What is it? _____

What's Next? You Decide!

Now it's your turn to choose what to do next in the lesson. Read the activities and decide which one you want to do—you may want to try them both!

Research Other Measures

STEPS

❑ Research to find information on other measures such as bushel, peck, hundredweight, long ton, and short ton.

❑ Report your findings.

❑ What are these measurements used for?

Find Different Measurements for the Same Item

MATERIALS

❑ 3 strips tagboard about 1 inch wide and 12 inches long

❑ 1 ruler

❑ 1 copy Comparison Chart, page 353

STEPS

❑ Across the top of your Comparison Chart, label the three columns "inch," "half inch," and "quarter inch."

❑ In each of the four rows, write an item that you will measure.

❑ Use a ruler to mark off inches on the first strip of tagboard.

❑ Use the ruler to measure four items to the nearest inch. Record your findings in the Comparison Chart under the inch column for each item.

❑ Next, on the second piece of tagboard use the ruler to mark off half-inch units.

❑ Remeasure your four items to the half inch and record your findings.

❑ Finally, label the last strip in quarter-inch units.

❑ Remeasure and record your findings.

❑ Look at your chart and write out your findings. Which measurements are the most accurate and why? Is there one item that seemed to vary more than the others when comparing the three measurements?

❑ Share your findings.

Understanding Multiplication

Multiplying makes counting easier.

OBJECTIVE	BACKGROUND	MATERIALS
To teach your student to multiply with the numbers zero to 10	Multiplication helps to add groups of items quicker. In this lesson, your student will learn how to multiply using numbers from zero to 10.	■ Student Learning Pages 7.A–7.B ■ 3 pipe cleaners ■ 25 beads ■ dry cereal pieces

VOCABULARY
ARRAY an arrangement of rows and columns that helps demonstrate multiplication facts **FACTORS** numbers that are multiplied

Let's Begin

MULTIPLICATION

1 **EXPLAIN** Tell your student that he or she is going to use addition and multiplication to learn how many beads are on a pipe cleaner. Give your student the 3 pipe cleaners and 12 beads. Instruct him or her to put 4 beads on each pipe cleaner. Ask, *What is one way you could find the number of beads here?* [addition; if student says multiplication first, just reverse these steps] Have him or her write a number sentence to show how to use addition to find the answer. [4 + 4 + 4 = 12] Tell your student that he or she could use a multiplication problem to count the beads. Show your student a multiplication problem that represents the set of beads (3 × 4 = 12). Have your student explain the groups in the multiplication problem. [there are 3 groups of 4 beads]

DRAW A PICTURE

1 **EXPLAIN** Tell your student that another way to show the meaning of multiplication is to draw an **array** (an arrangement of rows and columns that helps demonstrate multiplication facts). Your student can also use pieces of breakfast cereal or other household items to show an array. Describe the following

scenario to your student: *The teacher set up 6 rows of chairs. If there are 30 chairs, how many chairs should be in each row?* Have your student draw an array to show the problem. [check that there are 6 chairs in 5 rows]

2 **APPLY** Instruct your student to draw a picture to show the fact 7 × 10. [drawing should have 10 rows of 7 items] Have your student use this drawing to find seven multiplication facts (7 × 1, 7 × 2, 7 × 3, 7 × 4, 7 × 5, 7 × 6, 7 × 7, 7 × 8, 7 × 9, and 7 × 10). Have your student write out each problem to demonstrate how each product is 7 more than the previous one. Have your student perform the same exercise using eight facts.

3 **EXPLAIN** Explain that when given three **factors** to multiply, the large multiplication problem can be broken down into two smaller multiplication problems. Give the following example: *There are 2 shelves in the closet. Each shelf has 4 pairs of shoes on it.* Instruct the student to draw an array to show the problem. Help him or her to write the number sentence to find how many pairs of shoes are in the closet. [2 × 4 = 8 pairs; 8 × 2 = 16 shoes] Challenge your student to think of a three-factor multiplication problem on his or her own.

USING A TABLE

1 **EXPLAIN** Copy the chart onto a sheet of paper for your student. Explain that information can be gathered from a chart. Have your student study the chart. Ask, *How many cherry trees were planted?* [20] *What is the fewest number of trees planted? Which tree is it?* [5; peach tree] *What is the greatest number of trees planted? Which tree is it?* [35; apple tree] Have your student write a number sentence to show how many pear trees were planted. [3 × 5 = 15]

Trees Planted

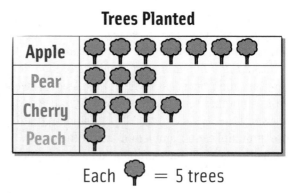

Each = 5 trees

If your student **solved the problems** correctly, have him or her skip Steps 2 and 3 and complete Student Learning Page 7.A for additional practice. If your student **didn't solve the problems** correctly, go to Step 2.

2 **MODEL** Explain the problem to your student. Say, *Using a table requires paying close attention to the information being presented. In this table, the key states that each tree in the table*

represents 5 trees planted. For each row, help the student see that he or she must multiply the number of trees by 5 to find the total number planted. Help your student multiply the trees by 5 to get the correct answer.

3 **MODEL AND ASK** Ask, *To find how many apple trees were planted, what two pieces of information are needed?* [How many trees are in the apple row, 7, and how many trees each picture represents, 5] Say, *Write a number sentence to show what you found.* [$7 \times 5 = 35$] Have your student follow the steps for each tree.

4 **PRACTICE** Assign Student Learning Page 7.A for additional practice.

5 **EXPLAIN** Explain that there are many strategies that can be used to find a missing factor. Tell your student that some strategies will work better than others, depending on the type of problem. Have your student listen to this problem: *I am greater than 30 but less than 40. One of my factors is 5. What number am I?*

Work with your student to decide how making a list will solve this problem. Have your student list the numbers that are greater than 30, but less than 40. [31–39] After he or she lists the numbers, ask, *Which number in your list has a factor of five?* [35] *Does 35 answer the question?* [yes; help your student see that the answer must meet three criteria: greater than 30, less than 40, and has 5 as a factor]

6 **PRACTICE** Have your student complete Student Learning Page 7.B for additional practice.

PATTERNS IN MULTIPLICATION

1 **DESCRIBE** Show your student 2, 3, and 4 groups of 9 beads. Ask, *What did you find when you counted the beads in each group?* [they each had nine beads] Help your student write out multiplication problems using the factor 9.

2 **EXPLAIN** Ask your student to count by 10s. Ask, *What do you notice about all of those numbers?* [they are all two-digit numbers that end in zero] Explain that when he or she counts by 10, he or she is also listing the products of the 10 multiplication table. When multiplying by 10, the answer is a two-digit number made of the factor you multiply by and a zero. Demonstrate with 7×10 and 5×10.

3 **DESCRIBE** Explain that multiplying by larger numbers requires different strategies. When learning multiplication facts through 10, memorization is one of the best ways to learn the facts. Learning to multiply by 11 and 12 may require a different strategy, although memorization is still a useful tool. Work with your student to make a list of the 11 multiplication facts through 9.

MATH

LESSON 2.7

4 **ASK** Ask, *Do you see a pattern in these problems that would help you learn your times 11 table?* [help your student understand that when multiplying by 11, the answer is a double-digit number; the two digits are the same number: the number you multiplied by 11]

5 **DISCUSS** Explain that multiplying by 12 is another math skill that is helpful in higher mathematics. Work with your student to make a list of the 12 multiplication facts through 9.

6 **ASK** Ask, *What patterns to you see in this multiplication table?* [if your student is having a hard time seeing a pattern, have him or her focus on the factors 1 through 4 first] Explain that if he or she looks at the factors through 4, a pattern can be found. Explain that the factor being multiplied by 12 is the first digit in the answer. Tell your student that, if he or she multiplies that number by 2, he or she will get the second digit. Have your student solve the problem 12 × 3 using this method.

7 **EXPAND** Explain that for the factors 5 through 9, the pattern is a little more difficult to see. Since 12 is a two-digit number, the problem can be set up vertically to solve. Show your student the problem 12 × 8 by stacking it vertically. Help your student to solve the problem.

8 **PRACTICE** Distribute Student Learning Page 7.B to your student for additional practice.

Branching Out

FOR FURTHER READING

About Teaching Mathematics: A K–8 Resource, by Marilyn Burns (Pearson Learning, 2000).

Math Made Easy: Third Grade, by Sean McArdle (DK Publishing, 2001).

The Mega Fun Multiplication Facts Activity Book, by Martin Lee and Marcia Miller (Scholastic Trade, 1999).

TEACHING TIP

Have your student correct any mistakes made when multiplying. Correcting errors is an easy way to reinforce the skill and helps with mastering the multiplication tables.

CHECKING IN

Have your student work this multistep problem: *Thomas has 4 bags of carrots, and Gary has 1 bag with carrots inside. Each bag holds 7 carrots. Who has more carrots?* [4 × 7 = 28, so Thomas has 28 carrots, which is more than Gary has] Ask your student to write his or her own multistep problem.

Multiply with 0 to 10

Look at each picture. Write a multiplication sentence for each. Then write the answer.

1.

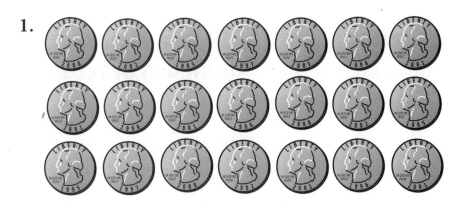

2.

3.

Now come up with your own multiplication sentences.

What's Next? You Decide!

Now it's your turn to choose what to do next in the lesson. Read the activities and decide which one you want to do—you may want to try them both!

Find Groups of Items

 **MATERIALS**

❏ 1 timer

STEPS

❏ Time yourself to see how many groups of items you can find around your home in five minutes.

❏ Challenge yourself to see if you can find a group with 2, 3, 4, 5, 6, 8, 10, and 12 items in it.

❏ Write your items on a sheet of paper as you find them.

Draw a Picture of Hidden Groups

MATERIALS

❏ colored pencils or crayons

❏ drawing paper

STEPS

❏ Draw a picture with hidden groups of objects in it.

❏ Try to have groups of 2 to 12 items in your picture.

❏ Give your picture to a friend or family member.

❏ See if he or she can find your groups!

Multiplying Greater Numbers

Multiplication with greater numbers may seem intimidating at first, but it's really just basic multiplication with some extra place values thrown in.

OBJECTIVE	BACKGROUND	MATERIALS
To help your student learn various strategies for multiplying greater numbers	Multiplying greater numbers will become a daily activity as your student matures and begins managing his or her own finances. In this lesson, your student will use his or her knowledge of place value and the multiplication tables to learn new strategies for multiplying two- and three-digit numbers and for estimating.	■ Student Learning Pages 8.A–8.B

Let's Begin

1 **REVIEW** Before beginning this lesson, review the basic concepts that were covered in Lesson 2.7. Be sure that your student is confident with the basic multiplication concepts and facts.

2 **EXPLAIN** Begin by introducing multiplication patterns of 10. Have your student copy the following three problems into his or her notebook:

$$2 \times 4 = 8$$
$$2 \times 40 = 80$$
$$2 \times 400 = 800$$

3 **REVEAL** Direct your student to notice the one basic math fact in each of the three problems. [$2 \times 4 = 8$] Ask, *What patterns do you see?* [the number of total zeros in the two factors is the same as the number of zeros in the product] *How would you solve $2 \times 4,000$?* [start with the basic fact $2 \times 4 = 8$, and add 3 zeroes; $2 \times 4,000 = 8,000$]

4 **EXPAND** Have your student write out the multiples of the number 9 up to 99. Guide him or her to recognize the pattern of the tens place increasing by one and the ones place decreasing by one for each multiple. [18, 27, 36, 45, and so on] Point out that in every multiple of 9 up to 90, the sum of the number's

two digits is 9. Then help your student to find patterns in the multiples of 8 and 5. Discuss.

5 **INTRODUCE AND PRACTICE** Show your student how to multiply two-digit numbers and how to trade ones for tens. Present the following scenario: *Janet has 19 animal postcards. Susan has 3 times as many cards as Janet. How many cards does Susan have?* Have your student write the problem 19×3 in his or her notebook.

Explain that first the ones are multiplied. [$9 \times 3 = 27$] Show your student how to trade 20 ones for 2 tens by writing the 2 above the tens place in the problem and writing the 7 in the ones place of the answer. Then show your student how to multiply the tens [$1 \times 3 = 3$] and add on the trade. [$3 + 2 = 5$] Write 5 in the tens place of the answer. [$19 \times 3 = 57$] Susan has 57 cards. Have your student complete problems 1–6 on Student Learning Page 8.A for more practice.

6 **EXPAND AND PRACTICE** Explain that three-digit numbers are multiplied the same way, only with one more step for the hundreds place. Present the following scenario: *Every day, 128 people have lunch in the community cafeteria. In 5 days, how many lunches will be served?* Have your student write the problem 128×5 in his or her notebook.

Point out that the answer is a multiple of 5, so it will end in either a zero or a 5. Help your student multiply the ones, [$8 \times 5 = 40$] trade 40 ones for 4 tens, and write the zero in the ones place of the answer. Then multiply the tens and add the trade. [$5 \times 2 = 10; 10 + 4 = 14$] Explain that you need to trade again. Write the 4 in the tens place in the answer and trade 10 tens for 1 hundred. Then multiply the hundreds and add the trade. [$1 \times 5 = 5; 5 + 1 = 6$] The cafeteria will serve 640 lunches in five days. Have your student complete the second section, problems 4–6 on Student Learning Page 8.A, for more practice.

FOR FURTHER READING

Developing Number Concepts: Place Value, Multiplication, and Division, by Kathy Richardson (Dale Seymour Publications, 1998).

Marvelous Multiplication: Games and Activities That Make Math Easy and Fun, by Lynette Long (John Wiley and Sons, Inc., 2000).

Branching Out

TEACHING TIP

Reviewing multiplication flash cards will help your student build confidence with basic math facts.

CHECKING IN

Have your student solve the following problem and observe his or her methods: The school received 217 boxes of crayons. Each box includes 3 shades of brown, 6 reds, 4 blues, and 7 shades of green. How many of each color are there in all? [brown: 651; red: 1,302; blue: 868; green: 1,519]

Multiply and Estimate

Multiply.

1. 46
    × 3

3. 55
    × 9

5. 543
    × 2

2. 81
    × 7

4. 341
    × 8

6. 706
    × 9

Estimate.

7. $17 \times 6 =$

8. $221 \times 4 =$

9. $693 \times 8 =$

10. $403 \times 4 =$

What's Next? You Decide!

Now it's your turn to choose what to do next in the lesson. Read the activities and decide which one you want to do—you may want to try them both!

Play a Multiplication Game

MATERIALS

❑ 9 index cards numbered 1–9
❑ 1 die

STEPS

This game is for two or three players.

❑ Mix up the index cards and spread them out facedown.

❑ Take turns choosing cards until each player has three cards in their hand.

❑ Each player writes a three-digit number using the numbers on the cards, then rolls a die and multiplies the first number by the number on the die.

❑ The player whose multiplication problem has the greatest product gets one point.

❑ Shuffle the cards and repeat.

❑ The first player with five points wins the game!

Compare Corn

MATERIALS

❑ 1 bag popped popcorn
❑ 1 bag unpopped popcorn
❑ the price of each bag
❑ 1 measuring cup

STEPS

Popped popcorn is 38 times bigger than unpopped popcorn.

❑ Measure the total cups in a bag of popped popcorn. If the last cup you measure isn't full, round up or down.

❑ Write the total number of popped cups.

❑ Measure the unpopped popcorn. Round your measurement and write the total number of cups.

❑ Multiply the number of unpopped cups by 38. Compare this number to the number of cups in the bag of popped popcorn and compare the prices of the two bags. Which is a better deal?

Investigating Division

It's wonderful to see how parts can be made into wholes!

OBJECTIVE	BACKGROUND	MATERIALS
To help your student relate division to multiplication and divide facts from 0 through 10	Division is something that can relate to many everyday activities. Being able to divide can help when working with money and finding averages. In this lesson, your student will learn to relate division to multiplication and to divide facts from 0 through 10.	■ Student Learning Pages 9.A–9.B ■ 22 pennies

VOCABULARY

DIVIDEND a number that is divided by another number; how many you have in all (in $12 \div 3 = 4$, 12 is the dividend)

REMAINDER the number that is left over in a division problem that doesn't divide evenly

DIVISOR the number by which another number is divided; the number of groups you want to create (in $12 \div 3 = 4$, 3 is the divisor)

Let's Begin

DIVISION STRATEGIES

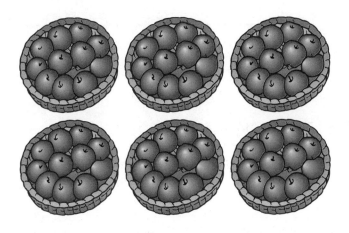

1 **EXPLAIN** Explain that just as it is possible to relate addition and subtraction with fact families, it is possible to relate multiplication and division by using fact families. Each multiplication fact mastered can lead to the answers to one other multiplication problem and two division facts. Show the student the multiplication fact $2 \times 7 = 14$. Say, *Using the Order Property,*

what other multiplication fact can you write with these facts? [7 × 2 = 14] Have your student use these multiplication facts to write two related division facts. Ask, *From the three numbers in the multiplication sentence, which number will become the* **dividend?** [14] Have your student write two division sentences within this fact family using 14 as the dividend. [14 ÷ 2 = 7; 14 ÷ 7 = 2]

2   **EXPLAIN** Explain that using repeated subtraction is another strategy that can be used to solve a division problem. Present this scenario to your student: *The baseball league is passing out equipment to the teams. They open a box of 18 baseballs and want to pass them out to the 6 teams. How many balls will each team receive?*

3   **EXPLORE** Tell your student that he or she can solve this problem by subtracting 6 from the number of balls to find the answer. Share the chart below with your student.

Open Box of 18 Balls	**(18 − 6 = 12)**
⚾ ⚾ ⚾ ⚾ ⚾ ⚾ ⚾ ⚾ ⚾ ⚾ ⚾ ⚾ ⚾ ⚾ ⚾ ⚾ ⚾ ⚾	⚾ ⚾ ⚾ ⚾ ⚾ ⚾ ⚾ ⚾ ⚾ ⚾ ⚾ ⚾
(12 − 6 = 6)	**(6 − 6 = 0)**
⚾ ⚾ ⚾ ⚾ ⚾ ⚾	

Say, *18 minus 6 equals 12. Twelve minus 6 equals 6, and 6 minus 6 equals zero.* Have your student write a subtraction sentence to show how the problem is solved.

4   **DISCUSS AND ASK** Explain that it took three steps to reach zero using subtraction sentences. Ask, *What information did you gather from completing the subtraction problems?* [by writing three subtraction problems, you see that each team would receive 3 baseballs; 18 ÷ 6 = 3]

5   **DISCUSS** Explain that when working to solve a math problem, it is helpful to have more than one strategy available to solve it. The more options to choose from, the better chance of choosing a strategy that best answers the problem. Present this problem to your student: *Kim, Sue, and John are volunteering at the local dog shelter. They have 12 dogs that need to be fed and walked.*

*If they want to divide the work evenly, how many dogs will each
volunteer care for?*

Have your student create a mental picture of the problem in
his or her mind.

6   **ASK** Ask, *What strategies could you use to solve this problem?*
[draw a picture, fact families, and repeated subtraction] Have
your student use two strategies to solve the problem.

7   **MODEL AND ASK** Share the following example that could
have been used to solve the problem. Tell your student that the
first example shows repeated subtraction. Copy the repeated
subtraction example onto a sheet of paper for your student to see.

$$12 - 3 = 9$$
$$9 - 3 = 6$$
$$6 - 3 = 3$$
$$3 - 3 = 0$$

Explain to your student that this models four steps to reach zero, so each volunteer will be in charge of four dogs.

REMAINDERS

1 **DISCUSS** Tell your student that the division problems presented so far have all divided evenly, meaning the dividend could be divided into groups without having any left over. Explain that sometimes a dividend won't divide evenly. When this happens there will be a number left over. This number is called the **remainder.** Ask, *What do we call the number that is left over after we divide?* [remainder]

2 **MODEL** Give your student 22 pennies. Ask him or her to divide them into groups of 4. Ask, *What did you find when you divided pennies into groups of 4?* [student should observe that he or she was able to make 5 groups of 4 with 2 pennies left over] *What do the 2 pennies left over represent?* [the remainder] Have your student write the division sentence that this grouping shows and write the answer. [22 ÷ 4 = 5 R2]

3 **PRACTICE** Have your student complete Student Learning Page 9.A to practice. Check his or her work and review any problems or any concepts that your student is having difficulty with.

4 **EXPLORE** Have your student complete Student Learning Page 9.B for more practice, this time using math word problems.

Branching Out

TEACHING TIPS

☐ Discuss with your student some jobs where division is used daily. Your student may have more interest in a skill if he or she knows it is applicable in the real world. Examples include people working on packaging products on an assembly line; they need to divide the items into boxes. An architect may need to place a specific number of windows on the front of a building and will divide the number of windows by the number of floors in the building. A truck driver who wants to deliver his or her products in three days needs to divide the number of miles he or she will travel by three days to determine how far he or she must drive each day.

☐ There are many opportunities for practicing division skills in the kitchen. Have your student help you make a dish from a recipe. Encourage him or her to divide out the ingredients into portions.

CHECKING IN

Have your student draw a picture to solve the problem 20 ÷ 6.

Divide with 0–10

Divide.

1. $4 \div 1 =$ _____

2. $36 \div 6 =$ _____

3. $32 \div 8 =$ _____

4. $50 \div 10 =$ _____

5. $72 \div 9 =$ _____

6. $14 \div 2 =$ _____

7. $32 \div 5 =$ _____

8. $3 \div 0 =$ _____

Read each problem. Use a calculator or mental math. Write which one you will use. Then write your answer.

9. _____ $28 \div 7 =$ _____

10. _____ $64 \div 4 =$ _____

11. _____ $81 \div 9 =$ _____

12. _____ There are 280 players in the little league baseball league. They are divided among 14 teams. How many players are on each team? _____

Group and Draw to Show Division

Read each word problem. Draw a picture to show the answer. Then write your answer.

1. Mellody wants to give 10 friends the same number of balloons. She has 96 balloons in all. How many balloons will each of Mellody's friends get?

   _____

2. Mrs. Goggins has 36 pencils. She would like to give each student in her class the same number of pencils. She has 12 students in her class. How many pencils will each student get?

   _____

3. There are 72 sandwiches to be arranged equally in 7 trays. How many sandwiches will there be in each tray?

   _____

4. There are 60 flowers to be planted in 10 rows. How many flowers will there be in each row?

   _____

Dividing Greater Numbers

To divide is delightful!

OBJECTIVE	BACKGROUND	MATERIALS
To help your student learn how to divide using two-digit numbers	Dividing by two-digit numbers requires more steps than dividing by a single-digit number. In this lesson, your student will learn how to divide using two-digit numbers with remainders.	■ Student Learning Pages 10.A–10.B

VOCABULARY

REMAINDER the number that is left over in a division problem that doesn't divide evenly

DIVIDEND a number that is divided by another number; how many you have in all (in 12 ÷ 3 = 4, 12 is the dividend)

DIVISOR the number by which another number is divided; the number of groups you want to create (in 12 ÷ 3 = 4, 3 is the divisor)

Let's Begin

REMAINDERS

1 **REVIEW** Before beginning this lesson, review the basic concepts that were covered in Lesson 2.9. Be sure that your student is confident with the basic division concepts and facts.

2 **DISCUSS** Tell your student that by knowing basic facts he or she can determine if a **remainder** will be part of a quotient. Give your student the following problem: 22 ÷ 5. Explain that he or she can look at five facts to decide if there will possibly be a remainder. Tell your student that 5 times 4 equals 20 and that 5 times 5 equals 25, so there isn't a multiple of 5 that equals 22. Therefore, this problem will have a remainder.

3 **ASK** Ask, *It's pizza night in the Johnson house and their pizza is cut into 14 pieces. If there are 4 people eating pizza, how many pieces will each get? Will there be any leftovers?* Instruct your student to think of basic facts to help him or her immediately understand if there will be leftovers—a remainder. The basic facts 4 × 3 = 12 and 4 × 4 = 16 show that there will be a remainder with this problem. 14 ÷ 4 = 3 R2, so each member of the family can eat 3 pieces and there will be 2 pieces of pizza left over.

MULTIPLICATION WITH GREATER NUMBERS

1 **DISCUSS** Tell your student that using division patterns can help when dividing by greater numbers. Explain that when figuring a division problem, you can look for patterns to help divide into the greater numbers. Ask, *How can you tell if a number is divisible by 2?* [if it is an even number, it is divisible by 2] *What about a pattern with numbers divisible by 5 and 10?* [a number ending in 5 or zero is divisible by 5 and a number ending in zero is divisible by 10]

2 **EXPLAIN AND SOLVE** Tell your student that he or she can use these patterns to divide larger numbers. Have your student write the following division problem: $2\overline{)83}$. Ask, *Will 2 divide into 83 evenly or will there be a remainder? How can you tell?* [there will be a remainder because it is not an even number] Encourage your student to use his or her knowledge of number patterns.

3 **CHECK** Ask, *What was your final answer?* [41 R1] If your student **solved the problem** correctly, go to Step 5. If your student **didn't solve the problem** correctly, go to Step 4.

4 **MODEL AND ASK** Help your student work through the steps of the above problem by explaining it in parts. Have your student write out the problem. Tell your student that in order to solve the problem correctly, he or she must first decide if there will be a remainder. [yes] Instruct him or her to decide how many times 2 goes into 8. [4] Instruct him or her to write the 4 over the 2 in the quotient. Ask, *How many times will 2 go into 3?* [1] Instruct your student to write 1 over the 3 and the remainder.

5 **DISCUSS** Tell your student that by finding an estimate of a division problem he or she can determine if his or her final answer is reasonable. Explain that when estimating, it is best to round the **dividend** to the closest number that can easily be divided by the **divisor.** Have your student find an estimate for this problem: 83 ÷ 9. Now have your student go to Student Learning Page 10.A for more practice.

Branching Out

TEACHING TIP

Discuss with your student situations in which an estimate for an answer may be acceptable.

CHECKING IN

Create two-digit division problems in the form of questions for your student to answer. Here is an example: *I'm thinking of a number. When you divide the number by 3, the quotient is 11 R2. What's the number?* [35]

ENRICH THE EXPERIENCE

Reviewing multiplication facts using flash cards is an easy way to remember common factors of numbers.

FOR FURTHER READING

Math Phonics, Multiplication and Division Bonus Book, by Marilyn B. Hein, Judy Mitchell, and Ron Wheeler (Teaching and Learning Company, 2002).

Math Skills Made Fun: Great Graph Art Multiplication and Division, by Cindy Mitchell (Scholastic, Inc., 1999).

Multiplication and Division, by Brenda Opie, Douglas McAvinn, and Nancy Ygnve (Incentive Publishing, Inc., 1999).

Divide with Greater Numbers

Divide.

1. 2)400

6. 7)90

2. 9)720

7. 40)320

3. 3)39

8. 70)630

4. 4)88

9. 39)276

5. 4)78

10. 12)390

11. Bryan made 90 ounces of lemonade. How many 8-ounce glasses can he fill? _____

12. Tim wants to buy 16 potatoes to put in his soup. There are 5 potatoes in a package. How many packages will Tim need to buy? _____

13. How many dimes are in $3.40? _____

What's Next? You Decide!

Now it's your turn to choose what to do next in the lesson. Read the activities and decide which one you want to do—you may want to try them both!

How Much for One?

MATERIALS

❑ grocery store advertisements

STEPS

❑ Find three items in the grocery papers that advertise two or three of the same item for one price.

❑ Divide to find how much it would cost to purchase just one of the items.

Estimate the Quotient

MATERIALS

❑ 2 circles cut from paper or posterboard, one smaller than the other

❑ 1 fastener to attach the two circles

STEPS

❑ Divide the larger circle into eight sections as shown.

❑ Divide the smaller circle into eight sections also, leaving room in the center for the division symbol.

❑ Use the sample below to fill in the numbers.

❑ Attach the two circles with the fastener.

❑ Turn the wheel and estimate the quotient.

❑ You may complete the division to find if your estimate is reasonable.

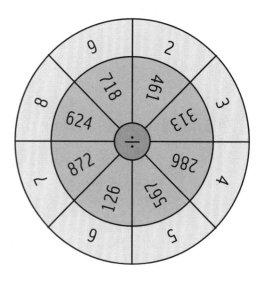

Understanding Fractions

Looking at each part gives you the whole picture.

OBJECTIVE	BACKGROUND	MATERIALS
To help your student learn how to write and order fractions and find equivalent fractions	Fractions are an extension of learning how to divide. In this lesson, your student will learn how to write and order fractions and find equivalent fractions.	■ Student Learning Pages 11.A–11.B ■ 1 nickel and 3 pennies ■ 4 dimes and 7 nickels ■ red, green, and blue crayons ■ 10 red checkers, 10 black checkers

VOCABULARY
DENOMINATOR the number below the fraction bar; tells the total number of parts you have **NUMERATOR** the number above the fraction bar; tells the number of parts you are talking about

Let's Begin

1   **DISCUSS** Tell your student that when looking at a fraction, it is important to realize that the **denominator** is the total number of equal parts. Explain that if the parts are not equal, a fraction can't be written to represent an object. Make a copy of the three squares below for your student to examine.

Instruct your student to write a fraction for the shaded parts if the square is divided into equal parts.

2   **ASK** Ask, *What two fractions did you write?* [$\frac{2}{3}$ and $\frac{1}{2}$] *Why didn't you write $\frac{2}{4}$ for the first square?* [the first square isn't divided into equal parts]

3   **EXPLAIN** Tell you student that the **numerator** is the top number in the fraction. Explain that the numerator shows how many of the equal parts are included in the fraction. Have your student circle the numerator in each of the fractions he or she wrote in Step 1.

4 **PRACTICE** Have your student practice with fractions. Make a copy of the three squares below. One at a time, ask your student to shade the left-hand square to show $\frac{2}{3}$, the middle square to show $\frac{1}{4}$, and the right-hand square to show $\frac{4}{5}$. For each fraction, point out that the square is already divided into 3, 4, or 5 equal parts.

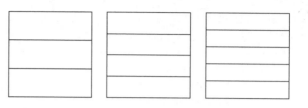

5 **REVIEW** If your student shaded the squares correctly, go on to Step 6. If your student didn't shade the squares correctly, review Step 1 again. Then use one nickel and five pennies to demonstrate in another way. Explain that if five pennies together equal one nickel, then one penny by itself would be $\frac{1}{5}$ of one nickel. Practice having your student select pennies to show $\frac{2}{5}$, $\frac{3}{5}$, and $\frac{4}{5}$ until you are confident he or she has grasped the concepts.

ENRICH THE EXPERIENCE

Reviewing and using the words *numerator* and *denominator* will help your student become familiar with these fraction terms. When they learn other skills in relation to fractions, this will help them further understand these higher concepts.

6 **MODEL** Have your student review the squares he or she shaded in Step 4. Point out that all the boxes are the same size with different amounts shaded. Ask your student to consider which of the fractions is the largest and which is the smallest based on the way they look. Have your student point to the smallest fraction [$\frac{1}{4}$] and the largest fraction. [$\frac{4}{5}$]

7 **EXPLAIN** Point out that when given more than two fractions to compare, your student can list them in order from least to greatest. Copy the pictures of the squares below for your student.

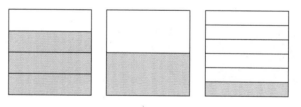

Help him or her write a fraction for each picture and list them from least to greatest.

8 **DISCUSS** Ask, *What three fractions did you write?* [$\frac{3}{4}$, $\frac{1}{2}$, $\frac{1}{6}$] *Which is the smallest fraction?* [$\frac{1}{6}$] *List the three fractions from least to greatest.* [$\frac{1}{6}$, $\frac{1}{2}$, $\frac{3}{4}$] Help your student look at $\frac{1}{6}$ and $\frac{1}{2}$. Both only have one part shaded, but one is smaller than the other. Explain that this shows that sixths are smaller than halves.

9 **EXPLAIN** Tell your student that so far he or she has studied fractions that are part of a whole. This example uses a fraction that is part of a set. Explain that just as he or she can find reasonable estimates with addition, subtraction, multiplication, and division, he or she can do the same with fractions. Finding whether an answer is reasonable helps to predict if an answer may or may not be correct. Present this problem to your student: *Grandma has 7 baskets throughout her kitchen. About $\frac{1}{2}$ of the baskets are filled with flowers. Is it reasonable to think that 6 of the baskets contain flowers?* [no]

10 **EXPLAIN** Tell your student that 6 is close to 7, so a reasonable answer would fall closer to 3 or 4. If there are 7 baskets and 6 have flowers, that is closer to all of the baskets being filled, not just half. If your student **solved the problem** correctly, ask, *What would be a reasonable answer to this problem?* [if 3 or 4 baskets were filled with flowers, that would be about half] If your student **didn't solve the problem** correctly, help him or her draw a picture of the baskets to help demonstrate what half would be and how 6 filled baskets is not a reasonable estimate.

11 **DISCUSS** Explain that the last step looked at a fraction of a set. Tell your student that there are other ways to work with fractions of sets. Have your student draw 9 balloons on a sheet of paper. Then give him or her these directions in regards to the balloons. Say, *Color $\frac{3}{9}$ red, $\frac{2}{9}$ red and blue striped, $\frac{1}{9}$ with green polka dots, and $\frac{2}{9}$ yellow.*

12 **ASK** Ask, *Were there any balloons that did not get decorated?* [yes] *Write a fraction for the balloons that were left plain.* [$\frac{1}{9}$] Use the fractions in Step 11 to see that your student colored the other balloons correctly. Ask, *Are there any fractional parts of this set that are equal? What fractions represent these sets?* [the striped and yellow sets of balloons are both $\frac{2}{9}$ of the balloons; the polka dot balloons and plain balloons are both $\frac{1}{9}$ of the set] *Which set, or fraction, is the largest?* [the red balloons make up the largest set; they are $\frac{3}{9}$ of the balloons]

13 **EXPLAIN** Explain that another way to use fractional parts is to write a fraction for a part of a number. Tell your student that this is a skill that is used quite often in real-life situations. Explain that drawing a picture is the easiest way to apply this skill. Have your student draw 10 circles on a sheet of paper. Have the student divide the circles into 5 equal groups. Have him or her circle groups of 2.

14 **ASK** Ask, *How many groups did you circle?* [5] *How many circles are in each group?* [2] Say, *You have divided your group of 10 circles into fifths.* Tell your student that if he or she wanted to know what $\frac{1}{5}$ of 10 was equal to, he or she would count the number of circles in one of the groups. Ask, *What is $\frac{1}{5}$ of 10?* [2] *Following the same pattern, what is $\frac{3}{5}$ of 10?* [6] *How did you determine that answer?* [three of the groups contain a total of three circles] Stress that drawing a picture is a strategy that can be used to solve a lot of fraction problems.

15 **PRACTICE** Distribute Student Learning Page 11.A for additional practice.

Branching Out

TEACHING TIP

The easiest, and most fun, application of fractions involves food! Take a break and have a snack with your student. Whatever you choose, lay it out and tell your student he or she may have a fraction of the snack. [$\frac{2}{5}$, $\frac{3}{9}$, or another fraction] Have him or her divide the snack using the fraction you give. For extra fun, help him or her see which portion is greater, the snack representing the fraction you gave or the portion remaining. Your student can write a fraction for that remaining portion and easily see which fraction is largest.

CHECKING IN

Lay on the table the 4 dimes and 7 nickels. Ask your student to write a fraction for the number of dimes [$\frac{4}{11}$] and the number of nickels. [$\frac{7}{11}$]

FOR FURTHER READING

Fraction Jugglers, by Ruth Bell Alexander and Tim Robinson, ill. (Workman Publishing Company, Inc., 2001).

Fractions, by Sara Pistoia and Rob Court, ill. (Child's World, Inc., 2002).

Making Fractions, by Andrew King and Tony Kenyon, ill. (Millbrook Press, 1998).

Play Checkers

Put 10 red and 10 black checkers in a bag or box. Then follow the directions for each step. Put the checkers back into their container before moving on to the next step.

1. Pull out a handful of checkers. Write a fraction to represent the red checkers that you pulled from the bag. Use the total number of checkers you pulled from the bag as your denominator. _____

2. Write a fraction to represent the black checkers you pulled from the bag. Use the total number of checkers you pulled from the bag as your denominator. _____

3. Repeat Step 1. Compare the fractions representing the red checkers and the black checkers from both draws. Which is greatest? _____

4. Pull out 4 red and 8 black checkers. Write a fraction for each using 12 as the denominator, or the total number of checkers. _____

5. Using your set of checkers, find $\frac{1}{3}$ of 12. What is $\frac{2}{3}$ of 12? _____ Which is larger, $\frac{1}{3}$ or $\frac{2}{3}$? _____

6. Consider the whole bag of 20 checkers. If you were to give a friend $\frac{1}{3}$ of the bag of checkers, would it be reasonable to estimate that you would give away 15 checkers? Why or why not? How can you check your answer? _____

_____

What's Next? You Decide!

Now it's your turn to choose what to do next in the lesson. Read the activities and decide which one you want to do—you may want to try them all!

Divide Your Snack

MATERIALS

❑ small bag of multicolored candies

STEPS

❑ Dump out the bag of candies and separate the pieces into groups by color.

❑ Count the total number and then write fractions to represent each color.

❑ Eat the candy starting with the smallest fraction, but first write an equivalent fraction to represent this color.

Empty Out Those Drawers

MATERIALS

❑ all spoons and forks in the silverware drawer

STEPS

❑ Empty out all of the spoons and forks from the silverware drawer.

❑ Write fractions to represent the two groups. Which is largest?

Make a Noodle Necklace

MATERIALS

❑ 20 pieces pasta with holes large enough to fit yarn or string through

❑ yarn or string

❑ poster paint or markers

STEPS

❑ Color the pasta using the following fractional parts:

$\frac{1}{5}$ blue

$\frac{2}{5}$ red

$\frac{1}{5}$ yellow

$\frac{1}{5}$ green

❑ Once the pasta is dry, string it on the yarn, making it long enough to fit around your neck.

❑ Tie the ends of the yarn together.

MATH

LESSON
2.12

Working with Data, Graphs, and Probability

Graphs make information easier and quicker to understand.

OBJECTIVE	BACKGROUND	MATERIALS
To teach your student how to work with graphs and probability	Learning to interpret charts and graphs is a necessary skill for comparing and understanding information. During his or her lifetime, your student will encounter many types of graphs. In this lesson, your student will learn to recognize and create different types of graphs and to work with probability.	■ Student Learning Pages 12.A–12.B ■ 1 ruler ■ graph paper

VOCABULARY
BAR GRAPH   a graph that uses bars to organize and compare data **PICTOGRAPH**   a graph that uses pictures to show data **LINE GRAPH**   a graph that uses lines to show change or compare data **ORDERED PAIRS**   two numbers in a specific order that name places on a grid **PROBABILITY**   the chance that something will happen a certain way **TREE DIAGRAM**   a diagram of all the possible outcomes of a situation **PREDICTIONS**   guesses about what might happen in the future

Let's Begin

GRAPHS

1 **INTRODUCE** Explain that one of the most common types of graphs is a **bar graph.** Bar graphs are used to compare many different types of information. Have your student look at the bar graph. Explain the following scenario: *Five people went apple picking. Each person picked the number of apples he or she would eat in one week.*

2 **DISCOVER** Explain that even though this is a small graph, your student can find a lot of information in it. Point out the title of the graph. Ask, *Which person picked the most apples? How many did he or she pick?* [Lilly; 7] *Which two people picked five apples each?* [Grace and Hank] *Did Pat pick more apples than Grace?* [no] *Who picked three more apples than Rick?* [Lilly]

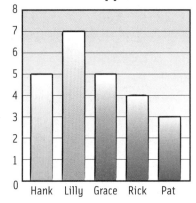

Number of Apples Picked

3   **DISCUSS**   Have your student create a bar graph. Explain that one way to gather data for a bar graph is by taking a survey. Direct your student to survey 10 people about their favorite colors. Then have him or her use a ruler to draw and graph the data. Have your student list the colors along the bottom of the graph and the number of people along the side. Instruct him or her to label the graph appropriately and give it a title. Together analyze the information by looking at which color was chosen the most and which was chosen the least.

4   **EXPLAIN**   Point out that another type of graph is a **pictograph.** Just like the name implies, it uses pictures to chart information. Explain that the data from Step 1 could also be shown in a pictograph. Show your student the pictograph. In this pictograph, each picture of an apple represents one apple. Mention that sometimes pictographs use one picture to represent more than one item when the numbers are larger.

Number of Apples Picked

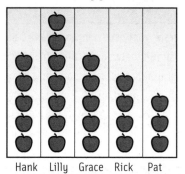

Hank   Lilly   Grace   Rick   Pat

5   **APPLY**   Have your student use the following information to make a pictograph. Assure him or her that the quality of the drawings is not important, as long as the number of drawings accurately represents the data. Present this scenario: *The Wilson family is visiting the zoo. They saw three dolphins, two giraffes, five elephants, and three lions.* Have your student make a pictograph to show how many of each animal the family saw at the zoo.

6   **EXPLAIN**   Tell your student that another type of graph is called a **line graph.** This type of graph is often used with greater numbers and is also useful when showing changes in data over time. Here is a record of average monthly high and low temperatures for New York City from January to June. Have your student copy the data into his or her notebook. Then have your student copy the graph on the next page and use the data to graph a line for the monthly high temperatures.

Average Monthly High and Low Temperatures: New York City

Month	High °F	Low °F
January	40	26
February	40	25
March	49	33
April	58	42
May	69	53
June	78	62

Average High and Low Temperatures: New York City

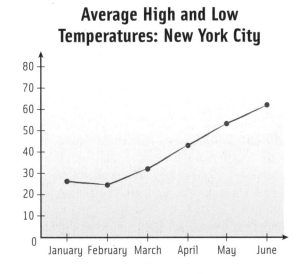

7 **ANALYZE** Have your student analyze the information in the graph. Point out that the line graph is a tool to compare the temperatures side by side and get an idea of how the highs and lows change each month and over time. Ask, *Which month on the chart shows the warmest temperatures?* [June] *Which two months have temperatures that are nearly the same?* [January and February] *From the upward movement of the lines, would you guess that July's temperatures are higher or lower than June's?* [higher]

ENRICH THE EXPERIENCE

If your student seems interested in weather trends, most encyclopedias list the high and low temperatures for each major city. Your student could graph the average temperatures, snowfall, or rainfall for the city closest to you.

8 **DISCUSS** Explain to your student that another type of graph uses a grid and numbers or letters called **ordered pairs.** Ordered pairs have two numbers. The first number always represents the location going across, or column number, and the second represents the location going up, or row number. Many maps are made with ordered-pair grids built in to help map readers find locations. Show you student this grid map of a garden.

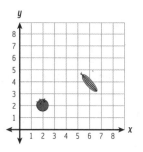

9 **FIND AND CHART** Have your student identify the ordered pairs for the location of the tomatoes and corn in the garden. [tomatoes: (2, 2); corn: (6, 4)] Then have your student copy the graph onto another sheet of grid paper and use the ordered pairs here to finish plotting the locations of the other vegetables in the garden. Your student can draw a small picture to represent the vegetable or write the word. Review your student's graph for accuracy.

Carrots: (1, 5)   Parsley: (6, 8)
Lettuce: (3, 7)   Beans: (5, 1)
Cucumbers: (7, 1)

10 **PRACTICE** Have your student complete problems 1 and 2 on Student Learning Page 12.A for practice with graphs. Help your student organize the data from the word problems as needed.

PROBABILITY

1 **INTRODUCE** Explain that **probability** is a measurement that helps to determine the likelihood that something will happen. Probability can be written as a fraction. The numerator of the fraction is the number of times the event can occur and the denominator is the total number of possible outcomes. For example, to find out the probability that a tossed coin will land on heads, first figure out what the total possible outcomes are. [2: heads or tails] Then figure out how many of the two outcomes could be heads. [1] The probability that a coin toss will land on heads is written as $\frac{1}{2}$. Have your student flip a coin 20 times and keep a tally of heads and tails in his or her notebook. Guide your student to see how the probability of $\frac{1}{2}$ is demonstrated in this exercise.

2 **EXPAND** Have you student consider the probability associated with rolling an odd number on a die. Ask, *How many possible outcomes are there?* [6] *Where does the number 6 go in the fraction?* [in the denominator] *How many odd numbers are on a die?* [3] *What is the probability that you will roll an odd number?* [$\frac{3}{6}$]

3 **EXPLAIN** Explain probabilities of 1 and zero. A probability of 1 means the event will definitely occur and a probability of zero means the event will never occur. For example, the probability that a rolled die will land on a number less than 7 is $\frac{6}{6}$, or 1, since all of the numbers on a die are less than 7. The probability that a rolled die will fall on a 10 is $\frac{0}{6}$, or zero, because there is no 10 on a die. Ask your student to think of other scenarios with probabilities of zero and 1. [the probability that a red checker piece would be drawn out of a bag of black checker pieces is zero, the probability of drawing a black checker piece is 1]

MATH

LESSON 2.12

PREDICTIONS

1 **DISCUSS** Explain that **predictions** can be made about the probability of an event even before doing any calculations. Point out that if there are more red checkers in a bag than black checkers, it's more likely that you will pick a red checker. Ask, *If there are 7 red checkers and 3 black checkers in a bag, are you more likely or less likely to draw a black checker?* [less likely to pull a black checker because there are fewer black checkers]

2 **PRACTICE** Have your student complete problem 3 on Student Learning Page 12.A for practice with probability. Help your student organize the data from the word problems as needed.

Branching Out

TEACHING TIP

Show your student a map of your town, city, or state that has an ordered-pair location key. Give your student several locations that you commonly visit and have him or her use the key and ordered pairs to find them on the map. Point out how helpful it is to know how to use ordered pairs when you're trying to find something small in a large area.

CHECKING IN

Give your student this list of soccer teams and the number of games won during a season. Observe as your student organizes the information in a bar graph and in a pictograph to assess his or her understanding of the concepts.

Panthers: 8
Wildcats: 4
Polar Bears: 7
Cougars: 4
Bulldogs: 2

FOR FURTHER READING

Mathematics for Small Children, by Jean Shaw and Sally Blake (Merril, 1998).

Pigs at Odds: Fun with Math Games, by Amy Axelrod and Shanon McGinley-Nally (Simon and Schuster Children's, 2000).

Tiger Math: Learning to Graph from a Baby Tiger, by Ann Whitehead Nagda and Cindy Bickel (Henry Holt Books for Young Readers, 2000).

Graph and Find Probability

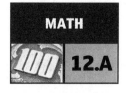

Read each word problem. Then draw the graph or write the answers.

1. Several kids are out planting trees in their community. Joe planted 16 trees, Maria planted 12, Kim planted 6, and Randy planted 10. Draw a bar graph of the data.

2. Now draw a pictograph on another sheet of paper using the tree data. Each tree in your graph should equal two trees planted.

3. Jan is going to the ice-cream shop to get a cone. She has to choose between two kinds of cones: a sugar cone or a waffle cone. She also has to choose between three kinds of ice cream: chocolate, vanilla, or strawberry.

   What is the probability that she will have a sugar cone? _____

   What is the probability that she will have chocolate ice cream? _____

What's Next? You Decide!

Now it's your turn to choose what to do next in the lesson. Read the activities and decide which one you want to do—you may want to try them both!

Watch the Temperature Rise and Fall

MATERIALS

- ❑ newspaper weather report
- ❑ graph paper
- ❑ blue and red markers

STEPS

- ❑ Each day (for five days) record the date and the high and low temperatures from the newspaper in a notebook.
- ❑ Make a line graph on graph paper. Write the dates of five days across the bottom of the graph. Write the temperatures along the side of the graph.
- ❑ Graph the high temperatures for each day with a red dot and the low temperatures with a blue dot. Connect the blue dots together and then connect the red dots together.
- ❑ Write in your notebook about what happened with the temperature over the five days.

Test Probability

MATERIALS

- ❑ 1 paper or cloth sack
- ❑ 3 different colored game pieces (same size and shape)

STEPS

- ❑ Put the three pieces into the sack.
- ❑ Find the probability of reaching in and choosing one of the colors. Write the probability as a fraction in your notebook.
- ❑ Make a tally chart in your notebook for the three colors.
- ❑ Now choose a piece from the bag 15 times without looking and make tally marks of the color that you choose each time. Be sure that all three pieces are in the bag every time you choose.
- ❑ After the 15th time, review your tally marks. Does the total match the probability?

Understanding Geometry

Look up, look down, look all around at the world's interesting shapes.

OBJECTIVE	BACKGROUND	MATERIALS
To help your student recognize and apply geometric terms and shapes	Geometry is a visual learning experience that focuses on shapes. In this lesson, your student will learn to recognize and accurately use geometric terms and shapes.	■ Student Learning Pages 13.A–13.B ■ 1 protractor ■ 1 ball string or yarn

VOCABULARY

PLANE FIGURES flat figures

QUADRILATERAL a polygon with four sides

LINE a straight path that extends in both directions

LINE SEGMENT a part of a line that has two endpoints

RAY a part of a line with only one endpoint

CONGRUENT equal

RIGHT ANGLE an angle that exactly fits into the corner of a square; measures 90°

SYMMETRY an object that has symmetry; it can be folded in half and both sides are the same

PERIMETER the distance around a figure

AREA the number of square units needed to cover an area

VOLUME the number of cubic units that fill an object

Let's Begin

GEOMETRIC FIGURES

1 **DISCUSS** Tell your student that geometry involves studying shapes that are found everywhere. Help your student count how many squares, circles, and triangles he or she can find in his or her environment. Instruct your student to name the object and its shape.

2 **EXPLAIN** Explain that flat figures are called **plane figures.** In a plane figure, the number of sides equals the number of corners. For example, a triangle has three sides and three corners. Explain that a pentagon has five sides and five corners, and a **quadrilateral** has four sides and four corners. Explain that the most common quadrilateral is a square. Give your student objects and have him or her name the plane figure. Challenge

your student to determine how many sides and corners an octagon has. Ask him or her to use a dictionary to look up the meaning of *octagon* if he or she needs help.

3   **EXPLAIN** Tell your student that plane figures that have straight lines all have points, or corners, where these lines meet. Explain that a **line,** a **line segment,** a **ray,** and an angle are often labeled using letters that represent points. Copy the line, line segment, ray, and angle below onto a sheet of paper.

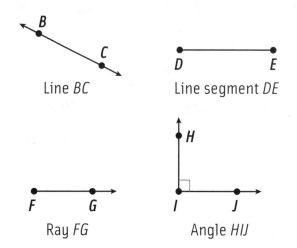

Have your student study how each is labeled. Encourage your student to copy the drawings into his or her notebook.

4   **APPLY** Have your student draw the following: line *MN*; line segment *OP*; ray *QR*; and angle *TUV.* Check to make sure the work is correct.

5   **EXPLAIN** Explain that triangles can be classified by using their sides and angles. Ask, *If two lines are* **congruent,** *what do we know about them?* [the sides have the same length] Tell your student that this definition of congruent is the basis for classifying triangles using sides. Using their sides, there are three classifications of triangles. Share the following classifications of triangles with your student:

- Scalene triangle: a triangle with no congruent sides
- Isosceles triangle: a triangle with at least two congruent sides (may have three)
- Equilateral triangle: a triangle with three congruent sides

Ask, *Which two triangles may look alike? Why?* [the isosceles and the equilateral because both may have three congruent sides] *What else can you call an equilateral triangle?* [isosceles] *Is every equilateral triangle an isosceles triangle?* [yes] *Is every isosceles triangle an equilateral triangle? Explain.* [no, because isosceles triangles also include triangles that have only two congruent sides]

6 **APPLY** Have your student draw a triangle that can fit each of the three classifications. Have him or her use a ruler to verify that the sides are congruent, or in the case of the scalene triangle, to check that none of the sides are congruent.

7 **EXPLAIN AND APPLY** Tell your student that there is a second way to classify triangles: by using their angles. Ask, *What is a right triangle?* [a right triangle measures 90° and fits into the corner of a square] Point out that the corner of this page is a right angle. Tell your student that knowing how to recognize a right angle is essential to understanding these classifications of triangles. Help your student use a protractor to draw a right angle and label it with the appropriate right angle symbol.

Explain that the right angle is the basis of using angles to classify triangles. Share the three classifications of triangles below:

- Acute triangle: a triangle with three acute angles (acute angles are less than 90°)
- Obtuse triangle: a triangle with one obtuse angle (an angle greater than 90°) and two acute angles
- Right triangle: a triangle with one right angle and two acute angles

Help your student use a protractor to draw each one of these three triangles. Tell your student that drawing these triangles will help him or her understand the differences between them. Have your student measure the other angles in the triangle and see what he or she finds.

8 **EXPLAIN** Explain that there are also congruent figures. Tell your student that congruent figures are the same shape and size. Copy the figures below onto a sheet of paper for your student.

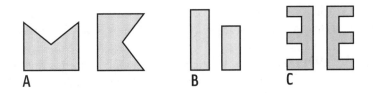

A   B   C

Have him or her look at the figures and tell if they are congruent. Ask, *Of these figures, which are congruent?* [figures in A and C] Explain that by looking at these examples, your student can see that the position of the figure is not important—what matters is that the shape and size of the figure is correct. Ask, *Which of the figures are quadrilaterals?* [figures in B]

9 **DISCUSS** Explain to your student that the figures in C are created using a flip. On the sheet of paper, have your student draw a dotted line between the two figures in C. Explain that the first E is backward, but if it's flipped over the line, the second E is produced. Explain that the two figures are congruent, they are just facing different directions. The line becomes a line of

MATH **LESSON 2.13**

ENRICH THE EXPERIENCE

Have your student find figures that have lines of symmetry in his or her environment.

symmetry. Explain that if the paper is folded along the line, the two sides would match.

Copy the shapes below onto a sheet of paper. Have your student use the shapes to create a second congruent shape for each. The student should create four new shapes, two using flips and two using turns. When showing the flip, have the student draw in the line of symmetry.

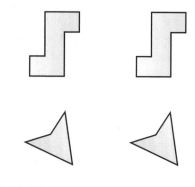

PERIMETER AND AREA

1 **DISCUSS** Explain that measuring the **perimeter** of an object involves finding the distance around the object. Have your student use string or yarn to measure the distance around the desk or tabletop. Have him or her measure the piece of string and record the answer in feet and inches. Tell your student that the perimeter of the table is equal to the length of the string.

2 **APPLY** Have your student draw a rectangle with two sides that are two inches long and two sides that are four inches long. First have him or her find the perimeter. Ask, *How can you find the* **area** *of this same object?* [to find the area, multiply the length of the object by the width] The area of an object is labeled in square units. The area of this rectangle should be labeled in inches squared. Have your student write the problem to find the area of the rectangle and solve. [2 in. × 4 in. = 8 in. sq.]

3 **APPLY** Give your student the following scenarios and ask him or her to give the dimensions of the shapes being described.

Say, *Mary is taking a walk around her block that is shaped like a rectangle. She walks 6 miles in all. How long is each street around the block?* [two are 1 mile and two are 2 miles]

Say, *Ken is building a fence around his property. It is shaped like a pentagon. He needs to order 48 feet of fencing. If there are two sets of fencing that must be the same length, how long are the sides of his property?* [answers will vary; possible answer is two sides are 10 feet, two are 8 feet, and one is 12 feet]

Say, *Patti wants to cover her table with a tablecloth. The table is 57 inches long and 38 inches wide. Would a tablecloth that covers an area of 1,500 square inches be large enough to cover the table? Explain. Here is a helpful hint: try using an estimate.* [no, the area of the table is about 2,400 square inches]

148 *Making the Grade: Everything Your 3rd Grader Needs to Know*

SOLID FIGURES AND VOLUME

1   **DISCUSS** Tell your student that there are six basic types of solid figures. Solid figures differ from polygons because they have length, width, and height. These figures are three-dimensional. Ask your student to help list the six types of solid figures. [cube, rectangular prism, sphere, pyramid, cylinder, cone] Copy the table below.

Name of Figure	Number of Flat Faces	Number of Curved Faces	Number of Edges	Number of Vertices
Cube	6			
Rectangular prism	6			
Sphere	0			
Pyramid	5			
Cylinder	2			
Cone	1			

Have your student think about each figure, and have him or her list what he or she knows about each figure using the table. Anywhere two faces meet on an object, there is an edge. Edges meet at a vertex. Drawing a sketch of each figure may help fill out the chart. Have your student look around the house and find examples of a sphere, a rectangular prism, a cube, and a cylinder.

2   **EXPLAIN** Explain that finding the **volume** of a solid figure is similar to finding the area of a quadrilateral, except there are three different values to multiply. To find the volume of a solid figure, multiply the length by the width by the height. Volume is labeled in cubic units. Copy the rectangular prism below onto a sheet of paper for your student.

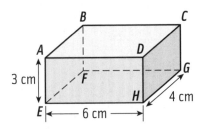

Have your student look at the rectangular prism and answer these questions:

- What is the volume of this rectangular prism? [72 cubic centimeters]

- Name the vertices of this rectangular prism. [*A, B, C, D, E, F, G, H*]
- Name the line segments that make up this rectangular prism. [*AB, BC, CD, AD, EF, FG, GH, EH, AE, DH, BF, CG*]

3 **APPLY** Have your student imagine that he or she has the following shapes in front of him or her. Ask, *Which solid figure can you construct with each set?* Give your student the shapes listed below.

- two squares and four rectangles [rectangular prism]
- four triangles [pyramid]
- two circles and a rectangle [cylinder]
- six squares [cube]

4 **PRACTICE** Distribute Student Learning Pages 13.A–13.B for additional practice.

Branching Out

TEACHING TIP

Show your student two similar boxes, one slightly larger than the other. With your student, make predictions about which box would hold the most material. Take measurements of each box and calculate the volume. Check to see if your predictions were correct.

CHECKING IN

Ask your student to calculate the perimeter and area of a room. Using a tape measure or yardstick, have him or her take and record the room's measurements. Then calculate the perimeter and area using the measurements. Remind the student to correctly label his or her answers.

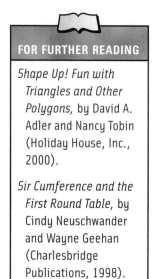

FOR FURTHER READING

Shape Up! Fun with Triangles and Other Polygons, by David A. Adler and Nancy Tobin (Holiday House, Inc., 2000).

Sir Cumference and the First Round Table, by Cindy Neuschwander and Wayne Geehan (Charlesbridge Publications, 1998).

Shape Up!

Read the steps. Then follow the directions to create and move shapes.

1. Draw a hexagon with at least two sides that are larger than the others. Cut out the shape and create a flip. Flip the object and trace it to reproduce the shape. Does your shape have a line of symmetry?

2. Draw two shapes, one shape that has a line of symmetry and one that does not. Draw the line of symmetry where it belongs.

3. Name two capital letters of the alphabet that have one line of symmetry. Name one capital letter that has two lines of symmetry.

4. Fold a piece of paper once. Cut out a shape that starts on the fold. How many lines of symmetry are there? Fold a piece of paper twice and cut a shape on one fold line. Now how many lines of symmetry are there?

5. Draw the following:
   ❑ Line *FG*
   ❑ Line segment *HI*
   ❑ Ray *PQ*
   ❑ Angle *XYZ*
   ❑ Equilateral triangle
   ❑ Obtuse triangle

6. Identify the following shapes. For the triangles, be sure to specify what types of triangles they are.

A.   B.   C.   D.

Take a Walk

Read the paragraph. Then read each question. Write
the answers.

Kerry is planning on starting an exercise program. She
wants to begin by walking around her block. The block
is a quadrilateral with two sides measuring 1 mile and
two sides measuring 1.5 miles. Draw a diagram of Kerry's
city block.

1. What is the perimeter of the block? _____

2. What is the area of the block? _____

3. Which of these measurements will tell us how long
   Kerry will walk if she makes it all the way around
   the block? _____

4. If Kerry makes it halfway around the block and stops
   for juice, how far does she have left to walk?

_____

In Your Community

To reinforce the skills and concepts taught in this section,
try one or more of these activities!

Geometric Architecture

Point out to your student that the structure he or she lives in is a bunch of geometric shapes that fit together nicely. Together with your student meet with a local architect. Have the architect show your student a set of blueprints and reveal the shapes that can be found in them. You also can look in books for examples of blueprints. Then have him or her show you how a house goes from blueprint to construction to final building. Help your student get prepared for the meeting beforehand by having him or her draw a "blueprint" of his or her bedroom. You may have to help him or her measure.

Weighing In at the Post Office

Arrange for you and your student to take a tour of your post office. Go behind the scenes and learn how packages are weighed. Have your student find out how they weigh the really big packages. Then have your student ask what measurements they use to weigh mail (ounces? pounds?).

Tour Your Bank

Your student may have accompanied you to the bank, but does he or she really know what goes on there? Arrange for you and your student to get a tour of your bank. See if you can take a tour of the vault, the money-counting machine, and the safe-deposit box area. If possible, have the tour guide show your student counterfeit money. If your student shows interest in the bank, ask your tour guide to tell you about how he or she came to work at a bank. If you haven't already, you may want to set up a savings account for your student. You can show him or her how you would make deposits at the bank.

"Shape Up" at the Grocery Store

The grocery store is filled with food, but did you ever notice how many shapes are there, too? Go to a grocery store with your student. Supply him or her with a pen or pencil and a clipboard and paper. Have him or her count the different geometric shapes that the food and food packages come in. How many does he or she count? You may want to supply pictures of shapes for reference. Ask your student if he or she thinks certain shapes work better for packaging food. If possible, arrange to have the store manager give you a tour of the store, showing you where food first arrives. What shapes are the packages that food arrives in?

Fractions at a Community Bake Sale

Fractions are used all the time in cooking—especially when making large quantities of food for a bake sale! The next time your community center, religious organization, or other group has a bake sale, encourage your student to help you make the food. Help him or her figure out the correct quantity of ingredients needed, which may be tricky if the batch has to be doubled, tripled, or even quadrupled. Have your student come with you to the bake sale.

We Have Learned

Use this checklist to summarize what you and your student
have accomplished in the Math section.

❑ **Place Value**
❑ reading, writing four-digit numbers
❑ comparing numbers, ordering numbers
❑ problem solving, rounding
❑ exact numbers versus estimates

❑ **Money**
❑ counting, problem solving
❑ using logical reasoning
❑ understanding thousands

❑ **Addition and Subtraction**
❑ fact families, estimating, problem solving
❑ addition strategies, subtraction strategies
❑ adding, subtracting large numbers

❑ **Time**
❑ telling time, elapsed time
❑ using a calendar

❑ **Measurement**
❑ length, capacity, weight
❑ temperature: Celsius, Fahrenheit

❑ **Multiplication**
❑ relating multiplication to addition
❑ patterns, inequalities, estimating
❑ problem solving, multiplying large numbers
❑ expressions with multiplication

❑ **Division**
❑ relating division to multiplication
❑ division as repeated subtraction, dividing by large numbers
❑ fact families, division patterns, estimating
❑ investigating remainders, dividing with remainders

❑ **Geometry**
❑ basic geometry ideas
❑ plane figures, lines, line segments
❑ rays, angles

❑ **Fractions and Decimals**
❑ fractions as part of a whole, fractions as part of a set
❑ finding equivalent fractions, estimating
❑ comparing fractions, ordering fractions

❑ **Data, Graphs, and Probability**
❑ collecting data, organizing data
❑ line graphs, bar graphs, pictographs
❑ understanding probability, outcomes

We have also learned:

_____

_____

_____

_____

_____

Science

Science

Key Topics

Classifying Animals

Stand up straight and show some backbone!

OBJECTIVE	BACKGROUND	MATERIALS
To help your student understand how animals are classified	Understanding the abundant variety of animals on Earth helps us appreciate their similarities and differences. In this lesson, your student will learn about vertebrates and invertebrates, their traits, and where he or she fits within the animal kingdom.	■ Student Learning Pages 1.A–1.B

VOCABULARY

TRAITS   natural qualities or characteristics

VERTEBRATES   a group of animals with backbones

INVERTEBRATES   a group of animals without backbones

WARM-BLOODED   a type of animal that can control its body temperature

COLD-BLOODED   a type of animal whose body temperature matches the temperature around it

Let's Begin

1   **EXPLAIN**   Explain to your student that scientists believe there are more than 1 million kinds of animals living on Earth. Tell him or her that this lesson will focus on how scientists group animals according to their different characteristics. Ask your student to talk about the animals that live in and around your neighborhood. Discuss the characteristics of the animals, where they live, what they eat, how they move, and how they look. Guide your student to consider how the animals are alike and how they are different. Have your student make a chart of the animals in his or her notebook.

ENRICH THE EXPERIENCE

Your student can visit a virtual zoo during this lesson to learn more about different animals he or she finds interesting at http://www.exzooberance.com.

Animal	Where It Lives	What It Eats	How It Moves	How It Looks

A BRIGHT IDEA

Your student can practice classifying animals online on the Cool Science Web site at http://www.hhmi.org/coolscience/critters/critters.html.

FOR FURTHER READING

The Animal Kingdom: A Guide to Vertebrate Classification and Biodiversity, by Kathryn Whyman (Raintree/Steck Vaughn, 1999).

Animals with Backbones, by Elaine Pascoe (PowerKids Press, 2003).

Evolution: The Plant and Animal Kingdoms, by Jackie Ball, Lynn Brunelle, Margaret Carruthers, and Scott Ingram (Gareth Stevens, 2002).

2 **EXPLAIN** Ask your student to think about how scientists might sort animals into groups. Ask, *What makes animals alike and different?* [some are covered with fur and some have scales; some have a backbone and some do not; some eat meat and some do not, and so on] Explain that these similarities and differences are called **traits.** Point out that scientists use these traits to sort animals into groups, or classify them. Have your student write a question about how to group animals in his or her notebook. Encourage him or her to seek to answer it through research during this lesson.

3 **EXPLORE** Remind your student that **vertebrates** are animals with backbones. Point out that humans belong to this group. Ask, *What other animals can you think of that belong to this group?* [cats, dogs, birds, monkeys, whales, and so on] Explain that **invertebrates** are animals without backbones. Ask, *What animals can you think of that belong to this group?* [worms, clams, spiders, jellyfish, snails, and so on] Distribute Student Learning Page 1.A. Have your student research six animals and complete the chart.

4 **DESCRIBE AND ILLUSTRATE** Explain that animals can also be classified as **warm-blooded** and **cold-blooded.** Have your student make a list in his or her notebook of 10 animals he or she thinks are warm-blooded and cold-blooded. Have your student research on the Internet or in life science books to see if he or she was correct. Visit http://sirtf.caltech.edu/EPO/Zoo/coldwarm.html to see infrared photos of different animals. Ask, *Did what you learn surprise you? Why?*

Branching Out

TEACHING TIP

To help your student understand how an animal's traits are important, play a game where you and your student suppose a certain animal had different traits—such as a fish with fur instead of scales—and talk about how that would affect the animal's life and ability to survive.

CHECKING IN

You can assess your student's understanding of how to classify animals by having him or her make a poster that displays vertebrates and invertebrates that live in your region. Encourage your student to accurately portray and describe the traits of the animals.

Identify Vertebrates and Invertebrates

Choose six animals from the list. Write their names in the first column. In the second column, classify them as vertebrate or invertebrate. Write at least three important traits for each animal in the third column.

earthworm	spider	wolf	shark
deer	goat	hawk	gorilla
turtle	slug	whale	toad
lobster	octopus	alligator	tiger

Animal	Vertebrate/ Invertebrate	Traits

What's Next? You Decide!

Now it's your turn to choose what to do next in the lesson. Read the activities and decide which one you want to do—you may want to try them both!

Make a Home for Earthworms

MATERIALS

❑ 1 large glass jar with a lid
❑ moist, fresh soil
❑ 1–2 earthworms
❑ 1 small patch grass

STEPS

❑ Put some fresh, moist soil and a small patch of grass in the bottom of the jar.
❑ Ask an adult to help you poke holes in the jar lid. Sprinkle a few tablespoons of water in the jar.
❑ Collect one or two earthworms from outside. Be very careful with the worms. Since they are invertebrates, their bodies can be easily crushed.
❑ Place the worms in the jar. Keep the jar in a cool, dry place.
❑ Observe the worms and write what you see. Make sure to give them a little water when the soil seems dry, but not too much or they will drown.

❑ After a few days, take the jar to a safe place and let the worms go.

Design a Postcard

MATERIALS

❑ colored pencils or markers
❑ 1 large blank index card

STEPS

❑ Draw a picture of an animal on the front of the card.
❑ Write a sentence on the back of the card in the top left corner that explains what group the animal belongs to.
❑ Fill in the address on the right-hand side and write a note to your friend telling him or her an important fact about the animal.
❑ Put a stamp on your postcard and mail it!

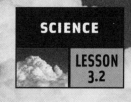

Classifying Plants

*Teach your student about the plant kingdom
and watch his or her knowledge grow!*

OBJECTIVE	BACKGROUND	MATERIALS
To help your student understand how plants are classified	The ability to classify things in the world is an important skill for children to acquire. It's something we do every day that helps us make sense of new things. This lesson introduces your student to the plant kingdom and how scientists classify the many plant species.	<ul><li>Student Learning Pages 2.A–2.B</li><li>variety of plants, flowering (irises, lilies, snapdragons, gladioli, and tulips are best for dissecting) and nonflowering (ivy, shrubs)</li><li>1 lettuce leaf</li><li>1 clump moss (can be found on tree bark, on a rock, or in shady places)</li><li>1 pinecone with seeds</li><li>1 fern with spores on underside of leaf</li></ul>

VOCABULARY

REPRODUCE to make new life

POLLEN powdery material in flowers that's important for plant reproduction

SPORES simple plant cells that are not seeds but can grow into new plants

Let's Begin

1   **REVIEW AND PREVIEW** Discuss with your student what he or she knows about plants, including the parts of plants and their functions. Explain that there are more than 200,000 different species of plants. Just as we classify animals, scientists classify the different plants into groups. Ask your student to look at different plant samples and group them in ways that seem obvious to him or her, such as having flowers and not having flowers. Discuss.

2   **GUIDE AND EXPLORE** Explain that one way scientists classify plants is according to the way they **reproduce,** or make new plants. Some plants have flowers. The flower is where the seeds of the plant form. Before seeds can form, the **pollen** in the flower needs to move from one part to the other. Point out that this is what bees and other insects are doing when they land on a flower, moving the pollen. Some flowers grow into fruit that you can eat, like on an apple tree. The seeds are inside the fruit. Ask, *Can you think of three other plants that have flowers?* [cherry trees, marigolds, roses, and so on]

A BRIGHT IDEA

Check with your local florist, who may have old flowers that he or she will give you free of charge.

3 **EXPLAIN AND OBSERVE** Show your student a pinecone. Explain that it comes from a plant that doesn't use flowers to reproduce, yet it has seeds. Have your student explore the cone and identify the seeds inside. Ask, *Under what types of trees do you usually find cones?* [fir trees, pine trees, spruce trees, evergreens, or trees with needles] Have your student read more about plants with cones in a science book or on the Internet. Have your student go to http://www.aacps.org and search "classifying trees" for a lesson on classifying trees that includes evergreens.

4 **INTRODUCE AND DISCUSS** Point out that still other plants make no seeds at all. These plants reproduce by making **spores.** Spores travel on the wind. When they land on moist soil, they grow new plants. Mosses and ferns are the most common plants that use spores to reproduce. Have your student examine the fern and identify the spores on the underside of the leaf.

5 **PRACTICE** Ask your student to practice classifying plants. Have him or her examine plants in your home as well as outdoors and classify them by whether they have spores or seeds and flowers or cones. Direct him or her to take notes on the plants he or she classifies in a notebook.

6 **APPLY** Distribute Student Learning Page 2.A. Have your student apply his or her new knowledge of plant classification by completing the activity.

Branching Out

TEACHING TIP

Discuss ways flowering plants attract bees and butterflies with their brightly colored petals, odor, and so on. Also discuss how animals that eat the fruit of plants help disperse the seeds so new plants will grow.

CHECKING IN

Discuss with your student the plants he or she found in Step 5 of the lesson and how he or she classified each one. This discussion will allow you to assess whether your student understands the concept of classifying plants.

FOR FURTHER READING

Plant Classification (The Life of Plants), by Louise Spilsbury and Richard Spilsbury (Heinemann Library, 2002).

Trees and Plants in the Rain Forest, by Saviour Pirotta (Steck-Vaughn, 1998).

Classify Plants

Look at each plant. Write "seeds" or "spores" on the first line and "flowers," "cones," or "neither" on the second line.

Pine tree

Fern

1. _____

2. _____

3. _____

4. _____

Moss

Lily

5. _____

6. _____

7. _____

8. _____

What's Next? You Decide!

Now it's your turn to choose what to do next in the lesson. Read the activities and decide which one you want to do—you may want to try them both!

Make a Plant Poster

MATERIALS

❑ 1 large posterboard
❑ 1 pair scissors
❑ glue
❑ old magazines or garden-store flyers
❑ crayons or markers

STEPS

❑ Use a marker or crayon to divide the posterboard into three equal parts.
❑ Write these titles on each of the three parts:
  ▪ Seeds and Flowers
  ▪ Seeds and Cones
  ▪ Spores
❑ Look through old magazines for pictures of plants and cut them out.
❑ Glue the plant pictures onto the poster under the right title for their classification. Write the name of each plant next to the picture. You also can draw pictures of plants to fill in and decorate your poster.

❑ Choose your favorite plant from your poster and read more about it.

Classify Plants You Eat

MATERIALS

❑ plant classification field guide (optional)

STEPS

❑ Write down a list of at least 10 plants or plant fruits that you like to eat. For example, carrots, apples, and so on.
❑ You're going to classify each one. Before you do, make a guess about which type of plant will come up the most from your list. Plants with flowers, cones, or spores?
❑ Now classify each plant. Look in a plant book for help if you need to.
❑ Was your guess right? What did you learn about the plants that you eat?

Exploring Plant and Animal Life

Plants and animals depend on each other.

OBJECTIVE	BACKGROUND	MATERIALS
To help your student understand how plants and animals live, change, and reproduce	The ecosystems in the natural world can teach us about the interrelationship of all living things and the importance of balance and diversity on Earth. In this lesson, your student will learn about food chains, life cycles, and the relationships of plants and animals within ecosystems.	■ Student Learning Pages 3.A–3.B ■ access to a field or garden ■ 1 magnifying glass ■ 1 string ■ craft sticks ■ 1 small spade ■ colored pencils or markers ■ 1 posterboard

VOCABULARY

ADAPTATION something that animals do and characteristics they have to protect themselves against enemies

CAMOUFLAGE the color of animals that keeps them safe by helping them to blend in with their backgrounds

PREDATORS animals that stalk and capture other animals for food

PREY animals that are captured and eaten by predators

FOOD CHAIN a group of living things whose members use other members as food

PRODUCERS things in the food chain that make their own food, such as plants

CONSUMERS animals that consume, or eat, plants or meat

DECOMPOSERS animals that eat other living things or their wastes

PLANT-EATER an animal that eats plants

MEAT-EATER an animal that eats a plant-eater

Let's Begin

1   **EXPLAIN** Explain to your student that all living things, such as plants and animals, use their surroundings to stay alive. Discuss how plants and animals share land, water, food, and shelter. Emphasize that plants and animals depend on each other to survive. Tell your student that he or she will learn about the eating habits of animals, their life cycles, how they adapt to their surroundings, and how they reproduce. Ask your student what he or she knows about these things and then discuss.

SCIENCE

LESSON 3.3

2 **EXPLAIN AND DISCUSS** Explain to your student that all living things have young of their own kind. Talk with your student about animals that usually have multiple births like cats and dogs, and those that usually have one baby at a time, such as a horse. Ask, *How do you think fish reproduce?* [they lay eggs by the thousands] Explain that animals reproduce young in ways that give the babies the best chance to survive. Take your student on a trip to the library to look for books about animal reproduction. Have your student share his or her information.

3 **EXPLAIN** Explain to your student that some animals go through different stages called a life cycle. Talk with your student about the life cycle of a frog. Tell him or her that a frog begins life as an egg, then develops into a tadpole, and later into a frog. Another example is the life cycle of a butterfly. Get a video from the library showing the life cycle of the frog or the butterfly. Encourage your student to record new information that he or she finds out about its life cycle.

4 **DISCUSS AND EXPLAIN** Tell your student that plants and animals in a given environment must adapt, or change, when changes happen where they live. Describe how changes in weather, soil, and water in an area create the need for plants and animals to adapt over time in order to survive. Talk with your student about plants and animals that live in very hot places, such as deserts. Have him or her write a description of a plant or animal of his or her choice that can survive in the desert. Have your student describe how or why the animal survives.

5 **EXPLAIN AND DISCUSS** Explain to your student that plants and animals that have adapted to life in hot places could not live in cold places. Tell your student that some animals have an **adaptation,** called **camouflage,** that lets them hide from predators by blending in with their backgrounds. Continue by discussing how adaptations may be inherited characteristics, such as the hard shell of a tortoise or the needles of a porcupine. Point out that adaptations may be learned from taught characteristics, such as when a mother animal teaches its baby to catch food.

6 **DIRECT** Tell your student to search the Internet to explore more about plant and animal adaptations. Have your student choose a plant or an animal to research. Have him or her write one or two paragraphs about the plant or animal. Encourage him or her to learn enough about it to represent it in a drawing.

7 **DISCUSS AND EXPLAIN** Ask your student to consider how animals living in the wild find their food. Ask, *How do animals that live in the wild differ from pets in how they get their food?* [example responses: some eat plants and berries, some hunt for food] Explain that animals and plants depend on each other to survive and have specific jobs to do. Have your student write down the things he or she wants to know about how plants and animals depend on each other in his or her science notebook.

REVIEW VOCABULARY Explain to your student that **predators** are animals that stalk and capture **prey** for food and are doing what is natural for them to survive. Tell them that a lion is a predator and a zebra is its prey. Share other predators and prey with your student. Ask, *What other predators and prey can you think of?* [example responses: predator—wolf, tiger; prey—gazelle, rabbit]

Wolf   Rabbit

9 **EXPLAIN** Tell your student that a **food chain** is created by animals depending on other animals or plants for survival. Tell your student that food chains are the way that nature shares energy among plants and animals. Tell your student that plants are called **producers** because they make their own food in a food chain. Tell your student that animals that eat plants, or plant-eating animals, are called **consumers** because they use the food in a food chain. Show your student the food chain below and discuss that the wolf eats the rabbit that eats the grass. Have your student look on the Internet or at the library to learn about the importance of the sun in food chains. Have him or her write a description that explains his or her findings.

Wolf   **Rabbit**   **Plant**

Consumer: Consumer: Producer
Meat-Eater   Plant-Eater

10 **DESCRIBE** Tell him or her that worms are known as **decomposers** because they eat dead things, which cause decay. Take a field trip to explore the decomposers around your yard, at a local park, or at the forest preserve with your student. Decomposers are easily spotted in moist places by turning over rocks or rolling logs to one side. You can visit http://www.naturely.com for lesson and activity suggestions for observing and learning about decomposers.

11 **DISTRIBUTE AND DIRECT** Distribute Student Learning Page 3.A. Have your student go to the library and find books or use the Internet to learn more about food chains. Tell your student to classify each animal and plant as a producer, a consumer, a decomposer, a **plant-eater,** or a **meat-eater.**

Branching Out

TEACHING TIP

Talk with your student about scientists who study plants and animals and how plants and animals depend on each other to survive. Encourage your student to conduct research about jobs in ecology by visiting a Web site such as http://www.nceas.ucsb.edu. Click on the link to Kids Do Ecology.

CHECKING IN

You can assess your student's understanding of how plants and animals depend on each other by asking him or her to list several producers and the plant-eating consumers that eat them. Encourage your student to use examples of the plants and animals in your neighborhood. Then you can ask your student to name some examples of meat-eating consumers who might eat the plant-eating consumers.

FOR FURTHER READING

Animal Life Cycles: Growing Up in the Wild, by Tony Hare (Facts on File, Inc., 2001).

Life Cycles, by Holly Wallace and Anita Ganeri (Heinemann Library, 2000).

What Is a Life Cycle?, by Bobbie D. Kalman and Jacqueline Langille (Crabtree Publishing Company, 1998).

Identify Plants and Animals

Write the names of plants and animals that belong to each group.

Producers	Consumers		Decomposers
	Plant-eaters	**Meat-eaters**	

What's Next? You Decide!

Now it's your turn to choose what to do next in the lesson. Read the activities and decide which one you want to do—you may want to try them both!

Check Out Plants and Animals

MATERIALS

❑ access to a field or garden
❑ 1 magnifying glass
❑ string
❑ craft sticks
❑ 1 small spade

STEPS

❑ Go outside to a garden or field with the magnifying glass, string, craft sticks, notebook, and pencil.
❑ Use the craft sticks and string to fence off part of the area.
❑ Find a comfortable spot and watch quietly for a few minutes. The quieter and more patient you are, the more you might see.
❑ Write down the living and nonliving things that you see in your area.
❑ Use your spade to turn over the soil.
❑ Write down the animals and plants that you see the most

of. Then write what you notice about how these plants and animals are depending on each other to survive.
❑ Visit your area each day for a week or more, and write down what you see each day.
❑ Draw a picture of your ecosystem and include pictures of the plants and animals that live there.

Show the Life Cycle of Butterflies

MATERIALS

❑ colored pencils or markers
❑ 1 posterboard

STEPS

Butterflies go through four different stages. They begin life as an egg. Later they hatch into a caterpillar.

❑ Research to find out what they turn into next!
❑ Make a poster to show the four stages of their life cycle.

Examining Living Things

Planet Earth overflows with life.

OBJECTIVE	BACKGROUND	MATERIALS
To help your student understand animals and their habitats	Animals live everywhere on Earth. They occupy all regions in every kind of climate. In this lesson, your student will learn about forest, desert, and water habitats and the living things that inhabit them.	■ Student Learning Pages 4.A–4.B

VOCABULARY

ORGANISMS living things

ENVIRONMENT the surroundings of organisms

HABITAT the place where organisms live and grow

POPULATION a similar group of organisms within a community

ECOSYSTEM groups of organisms and their habitats

Let's Begin

1 **PREVIEW** Tell your student that all living things are called **organisms.** Explain that the area surrounding organisms is called their **environment.** Ask your student to tell about his or her home environment. Ask, *How does the climate and environment affect your home life?* Have your student discuss things his or her family needs to survive, such as food, water, and shelter. Discuss how his or her family might depend on others in his or her community.

2 **EXPLAIN** Point out that the place where an organism lives and grows is its **habitat.** Within a habitat, organisms group to form communities. A similar group of organisms within a community is called a **population.** Plants, animals, and other organisms rely on their habitats and communities for air, water, shelter, and food, just as humans do. Have your student study the habitat and community of one plant and one animal.

3 **EXPLAIN** Explain that an **ecosystem** is a community of living things, such as plants and animals, that depend on each other to survive. The Florida Everglades, for example, is an ecosystem made up of grasslands and all the animals and insects that live there. They all live off the same land, water, food, and shelter.

+

ENRICH THE EXPERIENCE

Your student can
learn about the desert
cottontail, a rabbit
that is well-adapted
to life in the desert, at
http://www.desertusa.
com.

If a plant or an animal species disappears, it affects the other plants and animals in the ecosystem. Encourage your student to find pictures of the Florida Everglades at the library or on the Internet to study its ecosystem.

4 **DISCUSS AND EXPLAIN** Explain that organisms adapt to the conditions of their environments. For example, the environment of a desert is hot, dry, and dusty. Desert plants provide food and water to animals. Large bodies of water have many forms of plant life and rocks to give its organisms food and shelter. Forests get a lot of rain. The rain causes the trees to grow, making the grounds cool and dark for the organisms of the forests. Have your student think about how animals in different habitats survive. Ask, *How do you think forest animals use the trees to help them survive?* Have your student use the library or the Internet to find out how organisms adapt to their environments. Direct your student to summarize his or her findings.

Animals and plants must adapt to the hot and dry environment of the desert.

5 **DISTRIBUTE AND DIRECT** Distribute Student Learning Page 4.A. Direct your student to choose and research a habitat and the organisms that live there. Instruct your student to draw the habitat and organisms that live there and write two or three sentences about his or her drawings.

6 **PRACTICE** Distribute Student Learning Page 4.B for your student to complete additional activities on the lesson.

FOR FURTHER READING

Crinkleroot's Guide to Knowing Animal Habitats, by Jim Arnosky (Aladdin Paperbacks, 2000).

Ecology: The Study of Living Things, by Terry J. Jennings (Gareth Stevens Audio, 2002).

In the Small, Small Pond, by Denise Fleming (Henry Holt and Company, Inc., 1998).

Branching Out

TEACHING TIP

Encourage your student to research two or more ecosystems at http://geography4kids.com.

CHECKING IN

Assess your student's understanding of living things and their environments by creating a nature magazine. Tell him or her to include three sections that show and describe each type of habitat studied in the lesson.

Understand Habitats

Choose a desert, forest, or water habitat to learn about.
Draw a picture of the habitat and organisms that live there.
In your notebook, write one or two paragraphs about the
habitat and its organisms.

What's Next? You Decide!

Now it's your turn to choose what to do next in the lesson. Read the activities and decide which one you want to do—you may want to try them both!

Set Up an Ant Farm

MATERIALS

❑ 1 ant farm

STEPS

Set up an ant farm and watch how the ants survive in their habitat.

❑ Ask an adult to help you locate an ant farm at a toy or science store. An ant farm often comes with directions about where to get ants.

❑ Set up your ant farm.

❑ Now spend time each day watching what the ants do.

❑ Write down what you see.

❑ Notice what the ants are doing to survive in this habitat.

Watch Birds and Animals

MATERIALS

❑ 1 pair binoculars

❑ 1 camp chair, blanket, or seat cushion for each person

STEPS

❑ Ask an adult to help you choose a safe place to watch animals in their habitat. Forest preserves and state parks are good places.

❑ Go to the place with an adult and your binoculars.

❑ Find an area that is quiet.

❑ Choose a comfortable spot to sit where you will blend into the environment. Sit quietly, watch, and listen for at least 20 minutes.

❑ When leaving, move slowly so you don't scare the animals.

❑ Write in your notebook about what you saw and learned.

Learning About People in the Ecosystem

We all have a part to play on Earth.

OBJECTIVE	BACKGROUND	MATERIALS
To help your student understand the role people play in the ecosystem	Ecosystems and habitats are constantly changing. It's important that your student understand the effects of humans, both positive and negative, on the ecosystem. This lesson introduces your student to the interdependence among all living things in ecosystems and to Earth's natural resources.	■ Student Learning Pages 5.A–5.B

VOCABULARY

NATURAL RESOURCES the living things and materials that are naturally found on Earth that people use
RENEW to replace or restore
SOIL the top layer of Earth where plants grow

Let's Begin

1 **DISCUSS** To help your student begin to think about the interdependence in ecosystems, ask, *What do all animals, including humans, need in order to survive?* Guide your student to recognize that all living things need food, water, shelter, and air. Ask your student to think about how humans meet these needs. [go to the grocery store, pour a glass of water, build a home, breathe in air]

2 **EXPLAIN AND QUESTION** Tell your student to consider how animals meet their needs. [hunt for food or eat seeds, drink water from a stream, build nests in trees, breathe air] Point out that we all share the ecosystem with other living creatures. Explain that what humans do has an effect on the ecosystem. Offer this example. Think of a forest with a lot of trees, grass, birds, and other animals. Imagine that many families decide the forest would be a great place for their homes. The people cut down trees and build homes where the trees once stood. Ask, *What has happened to the forest habitat? How has it changed? What effect will it have on the animals that lived there?*

?
DID YOU KNOW?

Some animals store fat or water in their bodies for times when food and water become scarce.

DID YOU KNOW?

Each time a tree is cut down for industry use in the town of Cascade, Idaho, a new one is planted.

3 **DISCUSS** Distribute Student Learning Page 5.A. Discuss the pictures. Ask your student to identify how all the animals are meeting their basic needs. Guide him or her to notice the interdependence, such as the tree using carbon dioxide from the animals while giving off oxygen that the animals need to live. The tree is providing shelter for the owl and food for the squirrel. Have your student complete the page by identifying how the four animals are meeting their needs.

4 **EXPLAIN** Now your student should be aware that habitats are always changing. Explain that another way people change the ecosystem is by using **natural resources.** Point out that some natural resources like the heat and light from the sun can never be used up. Other natural resources like trees, water, and animals are limited in quantity but are able to **renew** themselves over time. Other natural resources like coal, petroleum, and minerals take hundreds or thousands of years to renew themselves. Mention that **soil** is another natural resource that takes a long time to renew itself. Ask, *Why do you think natural resources are important?* [they make our lifestyle possible; they give us food, shelter, power, and so on]

5 **PREDICT AND DESCRIBE** Present a common scenario to your student, such as a factory polluting the air and a nearby river. Ask him or her to predict what could happen to the ecosystem if the problem is not addressed. Describe ways people can help the ecosystem restore its balance, such as using less water or planting trees. Challenge him or her to list three things that can help restore nature.

FOR FURTHER READING

Ecology: Individuals, Populations, and Communities, by Michael Begun, C. R. Townsend, and J. L. Harper (Blackwell Science Inc., 1998).

Environmental Science: Toward a Sustainable Future (8th Edition), by Bernard J. Nebel and Richard T. Wright (Prentice Hall, 2002).

Sharing the World with Animals (Zoobooks Series), by Ann Elwood and Marjoree B. Shaw (Zoobooks/Wildlife Education, 2000).

Branching Out

TEACHING TIP

Explain that even resources that can renew themselves must be used with care. Point out that fish can make more fish, yet in some places people have caught too many fish. Not enough fish were left to reproduce in order to replace the fish that were caught. Communities need to plan how to use their resources.

CHECKING IN

To assess your student's understanding of the lesson, show your student a picture of land where there has been an oil spill. Have your student suppose he or she is a squirrel. Ask your student to write down three reasons why he or she wouldn't want to live there.

Study a Habitat

Look at each picture. See how all living creatures are meeting their needs. Write how each animal uses the environment to meet its needs.

owl _____

_____

squirrel _____

_____

deer _____

_____

duck _____

_____

What's Next? You Decide!

Now it's your turn to choose what to do next in the lesson. Read the activities and decide which one you want to do—you may want to try them both!

Meet an Ecologist

MATERIALS

- ❑ 2–5 blank sheets paper

STEPS

An ecologist is a scientist who studies how animals and people live together in an environment. Use the Internet to learn more about an ecologist. Two famous ecologists are Rachel Carson and Eugene Odum.

- ❑ Find out what you have to do to become an ecologist.
- ❑ Take notes about what you learn.
- ❑ Share what you learn with others.
- ❑ How do ecologists help our understanding of nature's importance?

Stop That Dirt!

MATERIALS

- ❑ 2 shallow trays or boxes
- ❑ plastic food wrap to cover both trays
- ❑ grass to fill bottom of 1 tray or box
- ❑ soil to fill both trays
- ❑ 1 watering can

STEPS

Soil is an important natural resource. Tree and plant roots hold the soil in place. When people cut down too many trees at once, soil can be washed away when it rains.

- ❑ Line two shallow trays with plastic.
- ❑ Cut a square of grass and put it in the bottom of one tray. Put loose soil in the other.
- ❑ Set the trays up at equal angles. You might want to put the end of each up on a block. This acts like a hill.
- ❑ Pour water into a watering can.
- ❑ Slowly, like rain falling, pour half of the water onto the first tray. What happens?
- ❑ Slowly pour the second half of the water onto the second tray. What happens?

Recognizing Our Changing Environment

While some environmental changes are natural and healing, others can cause irreversible harm. We should all work together to take good care of our environment.

OBJECTIVE	BACKGROUND	MATERIALS
To help your student understand changes in the environment and their effects on living things	As responsible citizens, we can teach our students to understand which changes in the environment are beneficial and which are detrimental. In this lesson, your student will learn how natural events and human actions affect the environment and ways we can care for the environment.	■ Student Learning Pages 6.A–6.D ■ 1 picture of a tropical rain forest showing a variety of plants and animals

VOCABULARY

WIND EROSION the process of wind breaking solid rock into smaller particles and carrying them away

NATURAL DISASTER a force of nature that causes a sudden change in Earth's environment, such as a tornado or hurricane

SPECIES a group of plants or animals that reproduce only with each other

EXTINCT no longer existing

ENDANGERED SPECIES a plant or an animal species that is threatened by extinction

GREENHOUSE EFFECT a slow rise in the environment's temperature due to an increase in carbon dioxide and water vapor

CONSERVATION planned use and protection of natural resources

ENVIRONMENTALISTS conservationists who work to protect Earth

NATURAL RESOURCES the living things and materials that are naturally found on Earth that people use

Let's Begin

1   **INTRODUCE** Explain that some changes to our environment occur because of natural causes. Some of these changes occur very slowly, such as with **wind erosion.** Some changes occur rapidly, such as with a flood. Ask your student to guess the meaning of the term **natural disaster.** Then share the definition with him or her. Together brainstorm a list of natural disasters, such as earthquakes, floods, volcanoes, tornadoes, and fires. Save the list as a reference for later on in the lesson.

2 **EXPLAIN** Have your student consider a forest fire, often sparked by lightning. The immediate effects may be seen as a tragedy. Animals that can't outrun the fire or fly away will die. Many trees and plants will burn. But the fire alters the environment in a positive way as well. The ash, which contains needed nutrients, mixes with the soil. More sunlight reaches the forest floor. The plants that burned have deep roots that stay alive. These plants grow new stems and leaves. They mature and make seeds. Nature begins to restore itself and the forest grows again. Ask, *How does nature restore itself after a forest fire?* [ash fertilizes the soil, sunlight reaches the forest floor, roots grow into new plants and make seeds]

DID YOU KNOW?

One type of pinecone only releases its seed under intense heat, such as that from a forest fire.

3 **DISTRIBUTE** Distribute Student Learning Page 6.A. Read the directions with your student. Together complete the first entry for Forest Fire. The "What Happens" section should describe the natural disaster. The "How Nature Restores Itself" should describe how the habitat returns to normal over time without human intervention. Then help your student complete the chart for three other natural disasters from your list in Step 1. Help him or her use research sources as needed. You can visit Web sites such as http://www.thehomeschool.com and search for natural disasters.

4 **EXPLORE** Explain that natural disasters and other changes in the environment can be threats to the survival of plant and animal **species.** Some plants and animals adapt to the changes. Others grow so few in number that they cannot reproduce and the species becomes **extinct.** Point out that Earth has gone through many natural waves of extinction and repopulation. Like a natural disaster, extinction on Earth also rebalances itself over time. Explain that the actions of people also can cause species to become extinct. Ask, *Can you think of a human action that can cause a species to become extinct?* [hunting, polluting the environment, destroying natural habitats]

5 **DISTRIBUTE** Distribute Student Learning Page 6.B. Help your student find information sources about extinct plants and animals. Ask him or her to choose one plant and one animal to learn more about. Have your student follow the directions: draw a picture of each one and identify how and when it became extinct.

DID YOU KNOW?

The Endangered Species Act was passed in 1973. It outlaws hunting, collecting, or harming any endangered plant or animal.

6 **DISCUSS** Point out that today many species of plants and animals are in danger of becoming extinct. We call these **endangered species.** These animals and plants are having trouble adapting to environmental changes. Many of these species are losing their natural habitat because humans are developing more cities and farmland. Endangered species in North America include the grizzly bear, Florida panther, Canada lynx, spotted owl, and the gray wolf. Ask, *Do you think the number of endangered and extinct species is increasing or decreasing? Why?*

7   **DESCRIBE** Show your student a picture of a rain forest. One very large and well-known rain forest is the Amazon rain forest in Brazil. Point out the lush vegetation and animals in the picture. Explain that hundreds of thousands of species of plants and animals live in the rain forest. There are many that scientists still don't know about yet. Unfortunately, many of them are currently endangered. Explain that people are cutting down trees in the rain forest for lumber or to clear the land to plant crops or graze animals. Help your student choose a specific rain forest area in the world to learn more about. Together, find out about the animals and plants that live there and how people are affecting their environment.

8   **EXPLAIN** Explain that the **greenhouse effect** is the name scientists use to describe another change that is happening in Earth's environment. Ask your student if he or she has ever been in a greenhouse, zoo with a jungle habitat, or botanical garden and how it felt. The hot, humid feeling of a greenhouse is like the greenhouse effect. Explain that gases from cars and factories trap heat in the atmosphere causing Earth's temperature to rise slowly. Have your student research the greenhouse effect and how it changes the environment. Discuss.

9   **RELATE** Many people are working to find ways to keep Earth's environment healthy for living things. Some people are focusing on reducing air and water pollution. Others try to protect the natural resources of Earth like trees and water. These people are called **environmentalists** and what they do is called **conservation.** Look up one or two conservation groups with your student. Together, find out what aspect of the environment the group focuses on, what the primary problems are that they try to solve, and what they do to help the environment. Some conservation groups will send brochures out or put you on their mailing lists to get regular updates about important issues and events.

10   **ACT** Explain that one of the things the environmentalists are concerned about is **natural resources.** These are the things that Earth provides for us to use, like trees, water, fresh air, and fertile soil. Sometimes people take natural resources for granted, and they begin to use them unwisely or too fast. Explain that there are small things your student can do every day to help conserve natural resources. Some examples include not letting the water run for too long when brushing his or her teeth, turning the lights off when they aren't being used, and walking somewhere close instead of driving in a car. Tell your student that by doing these things he or she can become an environmentalist, too. Ask your student to look up some periodicals that feature environmental topics at the library. Together, review articles that talk about the positive work that is being done to help the environment.

11   **DISTRIBUTE** Remind your student that water is one of our most important natural resources. All plants and animals need clean

     Recognizing Our Changing Environment

water to live. However, water pollution is becoming a problem. Water pollution happens when anything harmful is added to rivers, lakes, oceans, and groundwater. Have your student read more about water pollution, its sources, and how it affects the environment.

12 **DISTRIBUTE** Distribute Student Learning Page 6.C. Have your student look at the drawing and identify two sources of water pollution and how it can harm the river ecosystem. Then visit a water habitat, such as a lake or river. Ask your student to look for evidence of water pollution there and to speculate on the effect it might be having on the things that live there. Then help your student look up the Federal Clean Water Act at the library or on the Internet at http://www.epa.gov and write a few sentences about its benefits.

13 **EXPAND** Point out that **recycling** is another way that your student can help the environment. Recycling is when material is reused or changed into something else that can be used again. Explain that recycling cuts down on the amount of garbage we have to put in landfills. It also reduces the amount of natural resources we use. For example, recycling paper keeps us from having to cut down more trees. Do some research with your student to find out about how recycling is being done in your community.

Branching Out

TEACHING TIP

When discussing the importance of being an environmentalist, discuss the trash in your house: what is thrown away and what happens to it once it leaves your home. Together with your student, make an agreement to pay more attention to reuse and recycle the things that you previously thought of as garbage.

FOR FURTHER READING

Endangered Species, by Mike Unwin (Millbrook Press, 2000).

Natural Disasters, by Patrick L. Abbot (McGraw-Hill Science/Engineering/ Math, 2002).

A River Ran Wild: An Environmental History, by Lynne Cherry (Harcourt, Inc., 2002).

CHECKING IN

Ask review questions relating to changes in the environment and taking care of Earth: *How does nature cause sudden changes to the environment and how does nature repair itself afterward? Why are some animals and plants becoming endangered or extinct? Why is it important to protect Earth? What can we do to protect Earth?* Listen for answers that explain important points from the lesson.

Explore Natural Disasters

Use what you learned during the lesson about forest fires to complete the first row of the chart. Then complete the chart for three other types of natural disasters.

Natural Disaster	What Happens	How Nature Restores Itself
forest fire		

Learn About Extinct Plants and Animals

In the first column, draw a picture of an extinct plant. Then write how and when it became extinct. In the second column, draw a picture of an extinct animal. Then write how and when it became extinct.

Extinct Plant

Extinct Animal

Find Sources of Water Pollution

Look for two sources of water pollution in this picture. Write each source. Then write how it can harm the river ecosystem.

1. Source _____

_____

_____

_____

_____

_____

2. Source _____

_____

_____

_____

_____

_____

Ask an adult to help you research the Clean Water Act. On a separate sheet of paper, write a few sentences about how it has helped keep water clean.

What's Next? You Decide!

Now it's your turn to choose what to do next in the lesson. Read the activities and decide which one you want to do — you may want to try them both!

Create a New Planet

MATERIALS

❏ construction paper
❏ crayons or markers

STEPS

A planet similar to Earth has been found. Scientists have asked you to create a plan for how we could live on the planet and protect the planet's environment.

❏ Come up with a plan that includes ways to build homes, schools, and other buildings while still caring for the environment.
❏ Draw pictures that show what the planet would look like.
❏ Share your plan with an adult.

Make Recycled Crayons

MATERIALS

❏ 3 or 4 old crayon nubs of different colors
❏ 1 foil cupcake liner
❏ 1 cookie sheet

STEPS

Instead of throwing crayons away, you can recycle them and use them again!

❏ Ask an adult to help you preheat the oven to 250 degrees.
❏ Collect three or four old, used crayons and take off the paper.
❏ Put the crayons in a foil cupcake liner.
❏ Put the cupcake liner on a cookie sheet. Ask an adult to help you put the crayons in the oven and heat them for 5–10 minutes.
❏ When the crayons have melted together, have an adult help you take them out of the oven and let them cool. Be sure to turn off the oven.
❏ Peel the cupcake foil off and draw yourself a picture with your recycled, multicolored crayon!

Recycling Is Fun!

Understanding Muscles and Bones

Your bones and muscles work together to create a wonderful you.

OBJECTIVE	BACKGROUND	MATERIALS
To help your student understand how muscles and bones support his or her body	Muscles and bones work together to keep the body moving. In this lesson, your student will learn about the composition of muscles and bones and how they work together to support the body.	■ Student Learning Pages 7.A–7.B ■ colored pencils ■ 1 calendar

VOCABULARY

SKELETAL SYSTEM the framework of bones

MUSCULAR SYSTEM the muscles all over the body

VOLUNTARY MUSCLES muscles you can control

INVOLUNTARY MUSCLES muscles that work on their own

LIGAMENTS tissues that connect bones

TENDONS tissues that help muscles move bones

CONTRACTION the pulling of a muscle

Let's Begin

1 **EXPLAIN** Tell your student that all human bodies have a **skeletal system** and a **muscular system** that hold the body's shape and keep it upright. Tell him or her that the bones and muscles work together to allow the body to move. Give your student the definitions above. Have him or her write them in his or her science notebook. Tell him or her that this lesson will focus on where the different kinds of muscles in the body are and how they work. Point out that later in the lesson he or she will learn how muscles work together with bones.

2 **PREVIEW** Ask your student to tell what he or she already knows about muscles. Prompt your student to mention ways that he or she uses his or her muscles. Talk about sports or other activities in which your student or other family members are involved. Emphasize that none of these activities would be possible without healthy, working muscles. Have your student share activities that he or she does every day that require the use of muscles.

3 **EXPLAIN** Explain to your student that different kinds of muscles make up the muscular system. Explain that the **voluntary muscles** are those we use through conscious effort as when playing a sport such as basketball. Point out that **involuntary muscles** are those that work on their own with no direction from us. They allow our bodies to digest food, breathe, and keep our hearts beating. Help your student understand that this system is totally necessary for life and that it is important to understand how it works in order to keep muscles healthy. Have him or her record as many ways as possible that he or she uses his or her muscles.

4 **DESCRIBE** Explain to your student that the muscles in the body must be used in order for them to stay healthy and strong. Remind your student that voluntary muscles are those you must think about to use. Tell your student that skeletal muscles, or those that help move bones, move according to messages and directions from their owner. Ask your student to speculate about how these skeletal muscles help move bones. Discuss your student's ideas with him or her.

DID YOU KNOW?

Tell your student that the body has more than 600 muscles in total and they make up almost half a body's total weight.

5 **EXPLORE** Have your student move his or her hand and observe the muscles moving under the skin. Ask, *When you make a fist, how do you think the muscles in your hand help the bones move?* [accept reasonable answers] Ask him or her to consider what happens when swallowing a drink of water. Talk about the muscles used to swallow and what would happen without them. Ask, *What do you think would happen if these muscles moved without directions from their owner?* Discuss your student's answers with him or her. Tell your student that these muscles allow all movement. Direct him or her to conduct research at the library or on the Internet to find out about how the muscles of the arms, legs, feet, and hands help to lift bones and allow them to move. Encourage him or her to share his or her findings in a report.

6 **EXPLAIN** Tell your student that other muscles in the body work on their own. Explain that he or she does not need to think about what he or she is doing for these muscles to work. Point out that these muscles are called involuntary muscles. Ask, *What are some things your body does without you thinking about it?* [breathes, heart beats] Emphasize that the heart uses a cardiac muscle to pump blood and the muscles around the lungs allow breathing without the need to think about either. Have your student feel the pulse of his or her heart's muscle working on its own.

7 **SHOW** Show your student this diagram of the heart. Ask your student what he or she knows about the heart. Discuss.

8 **RESEARCH AND ILLUSTRATE** Invite your student to use the Internet to learn more about the three different types of muscles that comprise the muscular system. Have him or her create a book to explain cardiac, skeletal, and smooth muscles.

9 **DISTRIBUTE** Distribute Student Learning Page 7.A. Have your student use his or her research and the Internet to find information on voluntary and involuntary muscles in different parts of the body.

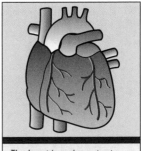

The heart is an important involuntary muscle.

10 **EXPLAIN** Explain to your student that four kinds of bones make up the skeletal system. Talk with your student about how bones move and also how they protect vital organs; for example, the skull protects the brain and the ribs protect the lungs. Tell him or her that the types of bones include long bones found in the legs, short bones found in the hands and feet, flat bones found in the skull and ribs, and irregular bones found in the face, ear, and backbone. Tell him or her that just as muscles need to be used in order to keep growing and stay healthy, it is important to get enough rest, exercise, and eat healthily to keep bones healthy. Ask, *What do you think bones are made of?* [minerals, calcium, blood vessels]

11 **EXPLORE AND RESEARCH** Have your student use the library to find books or search the Internet to learn more about the different types of bones. Ask him or her to find out how bones grow and how they repair themselves throughout life. When he or she completes his or her research, have him or her write a summary of what was learned and create a model of a long, a short, a flat, or an irregular bone of the body. Encourage him or her to draw a diagram of the inside of the bone to display with the model.

12 **EXPLAIN** Explain to your student that tissues called **ligaments** connect bones and that other tissues called **tendons** help muscles move bones. Point out that these tissues allow the bones and muscles to work together to let us move. Ask your student to hypothesize about how muscles actually move bones.

Have him or her flex a foot or lift an arm. Ask him or her to observe the muscle as he or she moves. Explain that when it moves it is pulling a bone. Point out that the muscle pops out because it is pulling together. Explain that this pulling is called **contraction.** Encourage your student to draw a picture that shows how the arm or leg muscles move short or long bones.

 PRACTICE Distribute Student Learning Page 7.B. Have your student choose an activity to complete for additional practice.

Branching Out

TEACHING TIP

Find children's anatomy books at the library. Have your student refer to them to review parts of the lesson.

CHECKING IN

You can assess your student's understanding of muscles and bones by having him or her create a short health bulletin accurately describing the three types of muscles and four types of bones in the body and their importance.

FOR FURTHER READING

Human Anatomy Made Amazingly Easy, by Christopher Hart (Watson-Guptill Publications, Inc., 2000).

Muscles and Bones, by Andreu Llamas and Luis Rizo, ill. (Gareth Stevens Audio, 1998).

Watch Me Grow: Fun Ways to Learn About My Cells, Bones, Muscles, and Joints, by Michelle O'Brien-Palmer and Fran Lee, ill. (Chicago Review Press, Inc., 1999).

Identify Muscles

The body has three different kinds of muscles. Some are voluntary and others are involuntary. Use what you learned in the lesson or from your research to complete the chart.

Body Part	Muscle Type	Voluntary/Involuntary
1. Stomach		
2. Heart		
3. Arm		
4. Leg		
5. Throat		
6. Foot		
7. Hand		

Student Learning Page 7.A: Identify Muscles **191**

What's Next? You Decide!

Now it's your turn to choose what to do next in the lesson. Read the activities and decide which one you want to do—you may want to try them both!

Discover How Muscles and Bones Work Together

MATERIALS

❑ 2–3 cotton swabs

❑ modeling clay

STEPS

❑ Use library books or search the Internet to study more about how muscles and bones work together.

❑ Choose a part of the body, such as the arm, leg, hand, or foot, to learn more about.

❑ Learn what bones, muscles, tendons, and ligaments are inside the part. Find out how the bones, muscles, tendons, and ligaments fit together.

❑ Using cotton swabs as bones and modeling clay as muscles, make a model of the joint.

❑ Explain your joint model, including the different parts and how it moves, to an adult.

Keep a Health Diary

MATERIALS

❑ 1 posterboard

Day	March 16	March 17
Foods I Ate	cornflakes, milk, peanut butter, bread, juice, cookie, apple, chicken, rice, peas, carrots	
Hours of Sleep	10	
Exercise I Did	played kick-ball	
How I Felt	energetic, happy	

STEPS

❑ Make a 14-day chart like the one here on posterboard.

❑ Write down the foods you eat, the number of hours you sleep, any sports or exercise you do, and describe how you feel each day for 14 days.

❑ Then look to see what activities, rest, and foods made you feel good.

Relating Health and Nutrition

In this day of convenience and fast food, it is critical to teach young people the importance of good nutrition.

OBJECTIVE	BACKGROUND	MATERIALS
To teach your student about food groups and nutrition	In 1992, the U.S. Department of Agriculture (USDA) created the food guide pyramid for Americans to use as a guide to a balanced diet. Learning about balanced nutrition will help your student make healthy food choices. This lesson introduces your student to the different types of nutrients, the food groups, and their importance.	■ Student Learning Pages 8.A–8.B

VOCABULARY
NUTRIENTS substances in food that provide the body with energy to build and repair tissues and to control body activities
FOOD GUIDE PYRAMID a guide to healthy food choices created by the U.S. Department of Agriculture

Let's Begin

1 **EXPLAIN** Tell your student that food provides **nutrients** that your body needs. Point out that some foods have more nutrients than others. Ask your student to think about what he or she has eaten in the last 24 hours. Have him or her write down each item. Then ask your student to make a prediction about which of these foods have the most nutritional value and contribute to a balanced diet. Have your student write down the predictions.

2 **INTRODUCE** Distribute Student Learning Page 8.A. Present the concept of a pyramid. Ask, *When building a pyramid, why should the base be longer than the other parts?* Relate this idea to the **food guide pyramid.** Explain that the pyramid can help your student remember how to eat a balanced diet in order to get the nutrients his or her body needs each day. Distribute Student Learning Page 8.A to your student. Explain that he or she is going to learn where different types of food go on the pyramid.

3 **GUIDE AND EXPLAIN** Ask your student to count the number of sections in the pyramid. Each section represents a different food

group. Explain that we need more foods from the bottom of the pyramid than the top. Discuss each group and have your student write the name of the group beside the appropriate section, draw pictures of food corresponding to each group, and write the number of servings you need from the group each day.

- **Bread, cereal, rice, and pasta group:** The foods in this group give us energy to move, play, and do work. The recommendation is six to eleven servings of food from this group each day.

- **Fruit group:** Fruits come from plants. They give us energy and help our bodies use energy and fight illness. Two to three servings of fruit are recommended each day.

- **Vegetable group:** Vegetables also come from plants. They have many nutrients and are important for staying healthy. Three to five servings from the vegetable group are recommended each day.

- **Meat, poultry, fish, dry beans, eggs, and nuts group:** The foods in this group provide our bodies with building materials to help your body grow and work properly. The recommendation is two to three servings from this group each day.

- **Milk, yogurt, and cheese group:** These foods also help our bodies grow and function. Three to four servings of foods from this group are recommended each day.

- **Fats, oils, and sweets:** These foods, such as cake, sodas, and candy, do not have many nutrients. It is recommended to eat only a small amount of these foods.

4 **REVIEW** Once your student has completed the food guide pyramid, have him or her review the list of foods from Step 1. Then have your student compare his or her food list against the recommendations in the food guide pyramid. Were his or her predictions correct? Discuss.

ENRICH THE EXPERIENCE

Water is the most important nutrient. It keeps our bodies hydrated and has many minerals, such as sodium, calcium, magnesium, and potassium.

FOR FURTHER READING

Healthy Foods Unit Study: A Guide for Nutrition and Wellness, by Leanne Ely (Champion Press Ltd., 2001).

Nutrition for Dummies, by Carol Ann Rinzler (John Wiley and Sons, 1999).

Branching Out

TEACHING TIP

Have your student identify the foods in each food group that he or she likes best. Discuss what your student ate for breakfast. How can it be more balanced?

CHECKING IN

Have your student create a three-day meal plan for himself or herself that follows the food guide pyramid recommendations. Ask, *What do you think is more nutritious, a serving of baked potato or a serving of potato chips? Why?* [baked potato; it has less fat and isn't processed]

Complete the
Food Guide Pyramid

Look at the pyramid. Write the name of the food group next to the matching part of the pyramid. Then draw pictures showing the foods that belong in that food group. Write the number of servings you need from that food group each day.

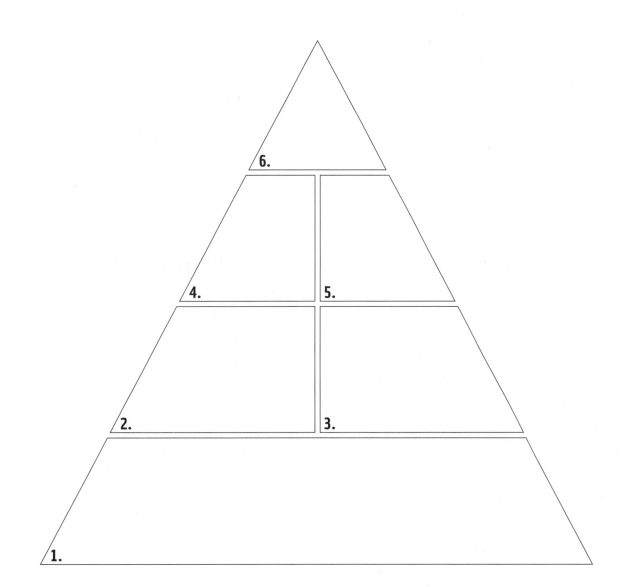

Student Learning Page 8.A: Complete the Food Guide Pyramid **195**

What's Next? You Decide!

Now it's your turn to choose what to do next in the lesson. Read the activities and decide which one you want to do—you may want to try them both!

Open Your Own Restaurant

 MATERIALS

- ❑ old food magazines or grocery store flyers
- ❑ 1 pair scissors
- ❑ 1 paper plate
- ❑ glue
- ❑ 1 posterboard
- ❑ markers or crayons

■ **STEPS**

Suppose that you've opened a new restaurant in your town. It serves healthy food that tastes great.

- ❑ Think of a name for your restaurant.
- ❑ Use what you learned about a balanced diet and the food guide pyramid to plan a menu for the restaurant. Include at least three main dishes, three side dishes, and two desserts on your menu.

- ❑ Then choose one main dish and one side dish from your menu and find pictures of the foods in food magazines or grocery store flyers.
- ❑ Cut out the pictures and glue them on a paper plate the way they would be served in your restaurant.
- ❑ Glue the sample plate to the posterboard and create a poster to advertise your restaurant.

Write a Poem

■ **STEPS**

What is your favorite food? What food group does it belong to?

- ❑ Write a poem about your favorite food, telling how it tastes, how it makes you feel, what it looks and smells like.
- ❑ Find out one or two nutritional facts about your favorite food. Include this information in your poem.
- ❑ Read your poem aloud to an adult.

Learning About Safety

There is a saying "An ounce of prevention is worth a pound of cure." We need to learn how to prevent injuries in order to avoid needing "the cure."

OBJECTIVE	BACKGROUND	MATERIALS
To teach your student about preventing and treating injuries	Preventing and treating injuries are the topics of this lesson. Your student should understand how to prevent an injury by wearing appropriate safety equipment when playing sports or working. He or she should also know how to treat minor injuries and when to seek professional help.	■ Student Learning Pages 9.A–9.B ■ photos from magazines or sporting goods catalogs showing athletes and workers wearing protective gear ■ 1 first-aid kit

VOCABULARY

SPRAIN when a body part, such as the ankle or wrist, is hurt from twisting or placing too much pressure on it
NASAL SEPTUM the membrane between the nostrils

Let's Begin

1 **INTRODUCE** Describe a familiar scenario, such as the following, to your student in order to help him or her begin to think about avoiding injuries. *Joshua has a baseball game. He gets his baseball gear and gets on his bicycle. "Be safe," Joshua's mom calls out. "I will," he replies.* Ask your student to explain what Joshua's mother means when she tells him to be safe.

2 **GUIDE AND EXPLAIN** Present the photos to your student. Lead him or her in a discussion of what the people in the photos are doing and what safety equipment each person is wearing or using. Point out and discuss the following safety equipment.

- **Helmet:** A helmet should be worn on your head when bicycling, skating, or playing sports, such as football. A helmet can prevent head injuries. Construction workers wear plastic or metal helmets called hard hats.
- **Pads:** Depending on your activity, different parts of the body need to be protected by pads. Football players should wear shoulder, hip, spine, and thigh pads. Skaters should wear elbow pads and knee pads.

FOR FURTHER READING

First Aid Manual: A Comprehensive Guide to Treating Emergency Victims of All Ages in Any Situation, by the American College of Emergency Physicians, Peter Beale and Jon R. Krohmer (DK Publishing, Inc., 2001).

Healthy Me: Fun Ways to Develop Good Health and Safety Habits: Activities for Children 5–8, by Michelle O'Brian-Palmer (Chicago Review Press, 1999).

The Kids' Guide to First Aid: All About Bruises, Burns, Stings, Sprains and Other Ouches, by Karen Buhler Gale (Williamson Publishing, 2002).

- **Guards:** Different sports require different guards to protect different parts of the body. Skaters should wear wrist guards to protect the wrist during a fall. Soccer players should wear shin guards.
- **Goggles:** Swimmers should wear goggles to keep chemicals out of their eyes. People who mow lawns should also wear goggles to keep flying objects from hitting their eyes.

3 **DISCUSS** Point out additional safety rules that should be followed. For example, talk about seat belt safety: *It is very important that each person riding in a car wear a seat belt. Children under the age of 12 should ride in the backseat. Children weighing less than 80 pounds should sit in a booster seat. Babies and small children should always ride in car seats.*

4 **APPLY** Distribute Student Learning Page 9.A. Ask your student to examine the people and identify what safety equipment each one should have on. Have your student draw in the missing equipment on each person and write the name of the equipment.

5 **MODEL** Discuss basic first aid with your student. Explain that some injuries can be treated at home. Examine the contents of a first-aid kit. Model the following procedures:

- **Cuts:** Wash the cut with clean water and soap. Allow the cut to dry. Put on first-aid cream. Cover the cut with a bandage. For deep or long cuts, press down on the cut with a clean cloth to slow the bleeding. Elevate the cut above the heart.
- **Sprains:** Elevate the injured area. Apply ice to the sprain for the first two or three days. This keeps the swelling down. Then apply heat to help the sprain heal.
- **Nosebleeds:** Sit Down. Lean forward and pinch the sides of your nose for at least ten minutes. Putting pressure on the **nasal septum** will stop the blood flow.

6 **EXPLAIN** Tell your student that some injuries are emergencies and require professional care. Discuss how and when to dial 911.

Branching Out

TEACHING TIP

Tell your student that if he or she sees someone receive a serious injury, remember the following rules: Stay calm. Tell an adult you need help. Have the hurt person lie still. Keep the injured person warm.

CHECKING IN

Review the photos with your student. Have him or her identify the various safety equipment and its purposes. Set up injury scenarios based on a photo and have your student describe the necessary response.

Search for Missing Safety Gear

Look at the picture. Draw the right safety gear on each person. Then write the names of the missing safety gear.

Missing Gear

On man: _____

_____

On girl: _____

_____

What's Next? You Decide!

Now it's your turn to choose what to do next in the lesson. Read the activities and decide which one you want to do—you may want to try them both!

Preparing for an Accident

MATERIALS

- ❑ 10 index cards
- ❑ 1 first-aid kit

STEPS

In the lesson, you learned what to do if you or someone you're with has a nosebleed, a sprain, or a cut. What would you do if you got a different injury?

- ❑ Use the Internet to find out what to do if you get a burn, a bruise, a black eye, a tooth injury, an insect bite or sting, or a bump on the head. You might use Web sites such as http://www.aap.org.
- ❑ For each injury make an index card. Write the type of injury as the title on each card.
- ❑ List the steps in treating the injury. Don't forget to make cards for the injuries you learned about in the lesson.
- ❑ Put the finished index cards in your first-aid kit to use.

Call for Help

MATERIALS

- ❑ 1 unplugged or toy telephone
- ❑ 1 first-aid kit (with finished index cards from the left, if done)

STEPS

- ❑ With a friend, act out different injuries and actions. For example, your friend might pretend to fall off a bike and sprain his or her ankle.
- ❑ You should say what the injury is and act out helping your friend.
- ❑ If the injury is an emergency, use an unplugged or toy phone to act out dialing 911 for help.

Understanding the Five Senses

Take time to stop and smell the roses.

OBJECTIVE	BACKGROUND	MATERIALS
To help your student understand the five senses: sight, sound, smell, taste, touch	Understanding how the five senses work will not only give your student an understanding of their functions, but it also will give your student an appreciation of how important they can be. In this lesson, your student will learn about sight, sound, smell, taste, and touch.	■ Student Learning Pages 10.A–10.B ■ 1 handheld mirror ■ 1 lemon slice ■ 1 pinch sugar ■ 1 pinch salt ■ 1 teaspoon horseradish ■ crayons

VOCABULARY
TASTE BUDS tiny bumps on the tongue for tasting

Let's Begin

1 **EXPLAIN** Explain to your student that he or she will be studying the five senses in this lesson: sight, sound, smell, taste, and touch. Ask, *What do you know about your senses and how they work?* [possible answers: eyes see, ears hear, nose smells things, mouth (or tongue) tastes things, skin feels things] Discuss his or her answers.

2 **REVEAL: SMELL** Mention to your student that the nose and sense of smell help him or her get information about odors. Point out that when he or she breathes, smells are absorbed by the nose. The nose then sends signals about the odors to the brain. Ask your student to tell you what odors he or she smells right now. Then discuss.

3 **EXPLAIN: TASTE** Explain to your student that your tongue and your sense of taste allow you to taste things. Point out that those bumps on our tongues are called **taste buds.** They allow us to tell if something tastes sweet, salty, sour, or bitter. Invite your student to touch his or her tongue or examine it with a handheld mirror to look at the taste buds.

4   **EXPERIMENT**   Point out that the nose is involved in the sense of taste. Have your student try this experiment. Cut equal-sized cubes of raw apple and raw potato. Have your student pinch his or her nostrils shut and take a bite of each. Ask, *What do you taste?* [most people can't taste the difference between these two with their nose plugged]

5   **TASTE AND DISTRIBUTE**   Offer your student a taste of lemon juice, a pinch of sugar, a pinch of salt, and a taste of horseradish. Ask him or her to describe each taste and try to determine which part of the tongue has more receptors for each type of taste. Walk through the diagram of the tongue on Student Learning Page 10.A with your student. Ask him or her if he or she tasted the different items in these places.

6   **DISCUSS: SOUND**   Tell your student that we use our ears and our sense of sound to hear things. Have your student close his or her eyes as you prompt him or her to listen to various sounds in your home right now, for example, birds, refrigerator hum, music, traffic. Ask, *What sounds do you hear the loudest?* [possible answers: music, traffic] *What kind of background noises do you hear?* [possible answers: furnace or air conditioning, clock] Explain that the ears contain parts that work together to allow people to hear and to balance as they move around. Refer your student to the picture of the ear on Student Learning Page 10.A.

7   **EXPLAIN: TOUCH**   Explain that skin covers our body and that any part of the body can be used to touch and feel things. Gather various household objects and have your student describe how they feel.

8   **DISCUSS: SIGHT**   Show your student the picture of the eye on Student Learning Page 10.A. Together walk through the parts of the eye. Then reveal that the eye allows us to see things at different distances and in different colors. Now have your student complete Student Learning Pages 10.A and 10.B.

Branching Out

TEACHING TIP

There are many documentary films that show how people overcome obstacles caused by not having one or more senses fully functioning.

CHECKING IN

You can assess your student's understanding of the senses by having him or her divide a large posterboard or paper into five parts and draw pictures that represent the five senses.

FOR FURTHER READING

Feeling Your Way: Discover Your Sense of Touch, by Vicki Cobb and Cynthia Copeland Lewis, ill. (Millbrook Press, 2001).

Follow Your Nose: Discover Your Sense of Smell, by Vicki Cobb and Cynthia Copeland Lewis (Millbrook Press, 2000).

Your Tongue Can Tell: Discover Your Sense of Taste, by Vicki Cobb and Cynthia Lewis, ill. (Millbrook Press, 2000).

Understand the Senses

Look at each picture. On a separate sheet of paper, draw and color each picture. On the tongue, write one of your favorite foods that is bitter, sour, salty, or sweet on that part of the tongue. On the eye, color it to match your eyes.

Taste

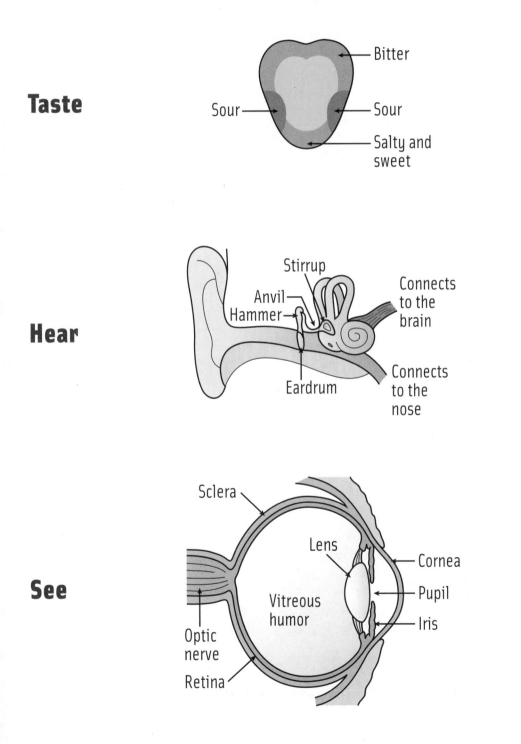

Bitter

Sour —— Sour

Salty and sweet

Hear

Stirrup

Anvil

Hammer

Connects to the brain

Eardrum

Connects to the nose

See

Sclera

Lens

Cornea

Pupil

Iris

Vitreous humor

Optic nerve

Retina

Puzzle the Senses

Read each clue. Then write the answer in the crossword puzzle.

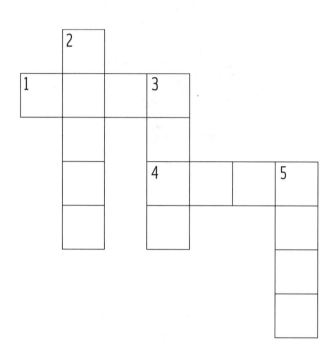

Across

1. what you use to smell with

4. what you use to hear with

Down

2. what you use to eat and taste with

3. what you use to see with

5. this covers most of our body

Now write your own crossword puzzle. Use what you've learned in the lesson.

Exploring Matter, Substances, and Energy

Anything that you can touch or that takes up space is made of matter.

OBJECTIVE	BACKGROUND	MATERIALS
To help your student understand matter, substances, and energy	Matter is all around us! Learning about matter will help your student understand the natural world. In this lesson, your student will study matter, its composition, properties, and states. He or she will learn about elements and compounds and consider energy and how it's used.	■ Student Learning Pages 11.A–11.B ■ 1 measuring cup filled with milk or juice ■ 1 carbonated beverage ■ 1 ice tray ■ 1 tin can ■ 5 pennies ■ $\frac{1}{4}$ cup lemon juice ■ 1 flat-bottomed bowl ■ crayons or markers

VOCABULARY

MATTER   anything that takes up space and has weight

ATOM   the smallest piece of matter; the building blocks of matter

STATES   different forms of matter: solid, liquid, gas

PROPERTIES   different characteristics of matter: size, color, shape

EVAPORATION   the process of a liquid changing to a gas

ELEMENT   matter that is made of only one type of atom

COMPOUNDS   mixtures of two or more elements

SUBSTANCES   the elements and compounds that make up all matter

MIXTURE   a combination of two or more substances

Let's Begin

1 **INTRODUCE** Tell your student that **matter** is anything that takes up space and has weight. Explain that an **atom** is a very small piece of matter. Atoms are so small that even the smallest piece of matter that you can look at with a magnifying glass contains many atoms. To give your student an idea of the relative size of atoms, have him or her picture an orange growing to the size of Earth. The atoms in the peel of the Earth-size orange would be about the size of marbles. Discuss.

2 **EXPLAIN** Continue by explaining that matter can exist in three different **states,** or forms. Matter can be a solid, such as a rock; a liquid, such as water; or a gas, such as oxygen. Have your student label three pages in his or her notebook solid, liquid, and gas. Tell him or her to write the examples rock, water, and oxygen on the correct pages. Encourage your student to list more examples for each state of matter, observations, and other things that he or she learns about each state of matter throughout the lesson.

3 **REVEAL AND DISCUSS** Explain that each state of matter has certain **properties.** Properties are the characteristics we use to describe matter. For example, an apple is red or green or yellow. It's round with a smooth surface. It's soft enough to cut or bite into. These are its properties. Ask your student to describe the properties of a tennis ball. [round, yellow, firm, rubbery on the inside and textured on the outside] Then have him or her describe the properties of several other objects around your home.

4 **EXPAND** Point out that apples and tennis balls are solids. The properties of solid objects include shape, size, color, and texture. The shape and size of a solid stays the same. Liquids can also be described by their color and texture. Grape juice is purple and sticky. Milk is white and thicker than grape juice. However, unlike solids, liquids take on the shape of their container. Have your student experiment with the changing shape of liquids. Pour milk or juice into a measuring cup. Have your student select three containers of different shapes and pour the liquid into each one and observe its shape. Then pour the liquid back into the measuring cup to show that the amount of liquid never changed, just the shape.

DID YOU KNOW?

A simple solution of sugar, citric acid, and baking soda can turn any juice into a carbonated drink.

5 **RELATE** Explain that matter in the form of gas also has specific properties. The properties of gases can be less obvious than those of liquids and solids. Some gases, such as car exhaust, have a smell and a color, but others, such as oxygen, don't smell at all and are clear. Helium is a gas that makes balloons float. Show your student a carbonated drink. Explain that the bubbles are made of a gas called carbon dioxide. Have your student record more examples and ideas about the states of matter in his or her notebook.

One property of helium is that it's lighter than air.

6 DISTRIBUTE Have your student complete Student Learning Page 11.A to practice identifying the states and properties of matter.

7 REVEAL Explain that matter can change from a solid to a liquid to a gas. This is because the atoms in matter are always in motion. Even the atoms in the wall of your house are moving all the time. The atoms in the wall are moving slowly because the wall is solid. Atoms in liquid move faster and are not compressed together as much. Atoms in gases move even faster than liquids. Heat makes atoms move faster. That's why heat changes ice into water. Ice is simply water atoms that have slowed down. Have your student freeze water in an ice tray or a plastic cup. Then together put the ice in the sun or in a pot on the stove over low heat. Observe that eventually the melted water completely disappears. Explain that when a liquid changes to a gas it's called **evaporation.**

8 EXPLAIN Tell your student that when matter is made up of only one kind of atom it's called an **element.** There are more than 100 elements that have been identified by scientists. Some are metals, such as silver, copper, and iron. Other elements, such as helium, are gases. Point out that no matter where an element is found, it always has the same properties as any other sample of that element. Ask, *What other elements can you name?* [gold, aluminum, oxygen, zinc] If you have access to the Internet, encourage your student to explore the periodic table of elements at http://www.chem4kids.com/files/elem_intro.html or review a periodic table from a book.

9 EXPLORE Explain that all matter is made up of elements or mixtures of elements called **compounds.** Compounds form when the atoms from two or more elements combine. Water is an example of a compound made up of hydrogen and oxygen atoms. Point out that another word that scientists use to describe elements and compounds is **substances.** Have your student read more about substances at the library or on the Internet. Ask him or her to identify elements and compounds that are common in your home and list them in a notebook. [table salt, aluminum foil, copper pots]

10 REVEAL Explain to your student that a **mixture** is a combination of two or more substances. Some examples of mixtures are soil (sand, silt, and clay), lemonade (water, sugar, and lemon juice), and breakfast cereal with milk. When two substances come together to make a mixture, they both keep all of their own properties. Point out that when some substances are combined a chemical change happens. This chemical change forms a substance with new properties. Discuss what happens when a tin can is left in water. Tin and water create a chemical change and rust is formed. Have your student put a tin can in water and observe its changes over time. Then have your student research to find other examples of chemical changes. Discuss.

ENRICH THE EXPERIENCE

Your student can find out more about stored energy and how energy is used at http://www.energyquest.ca.gov/story/index.html.

SCIENCE

LESSON 3.11

? DID YOU KNOW?

The volt, a measure of electricity, was named after the Italian Count Alessandro Volta. He invented the first battery, called a Voltaic Pile, around the year 1800. Your student can learn more about him at http://www. energyquest.ca.gov/ scientists/volta.html.

FOR FURTHER READING

Energy, by Alvin Silverstein, Virginia Silverstein, and Laura Silverstein Nunn (Millbrook Press, 1998).

Eyewitness: Matter, by Christopher Cooper (DK Publishing, Inc., 1999).

The Magic School Bus in the Arctic: A Book About Heat, by Joanna Cole, Ann Schreiber, and Art Ruiz (Scholastic, Inc., 1998).

Pocket Pals: Super Science: The Complete Kit, by Sterling Publishing (Sterling Publishing Company, 2001).

11 **EXPLAIN** Explain that energy is what gives us the ability to move and change and make things happen. Heat and light are forms of energy. Explain that energy can be stored up. When an athlete eats pasta the night before an event, his or her body stores some of the energy from the food and uses it later to be able to run fast, jump, or swim. Batteries, matches, and gasoline are other examples of stored energy. Ask, *What happens when you don't eat for a long time?* [your body gets tired] *Why?* [because it runs out of stored energy]

12 **REVEAL** Tell your student that, like matter, energy changes form. One example of energy changing form is a car using gasoline. When the stored energy in gasoline burns and creates heat in the engine, it becomes chemical energy. When the car parts move, the heat becomes mechanical energy, or energy in motion. Moving energy can also be observed in a pen rolling off a table onto the floor or a person riding a bicycle. Similarly, the chemical energy in a match changes to heat and light when it's lit. Ask your student to explain how energy changes form when he or she uses a wind-up toy. [when the toy is wound up, the energy is stored; when you let the toy go, the stored energy becomes motion]

13 **RELATE** Explain that heat given off during energy changes makes life possible. We get light and heat from the sun. We use heat to cook and heat our homes. Heat can also become mechanical energy to run machines and make cars, planes, and trains move. Heat energy also becomes electricity. Electrical energy gives us light, radio, television, computers, and many other things. Point out that when your student moves his or her body, heat is created. Talk with your student about a time when he or she was playing and had to take off a coat or sweater to cool off. Ask, *What was happening in your body?* [stored energy in his or her body was changing into heat and motion]

Branching Out

TEACHING TIP

Matter and energy are things that exist within us and all around us. Guide your student to see that matter and energy can be observed in his or her own body! Point out that your student's body is made up of combinations of compounds and elements. Use examples such as lifting a box, a heartbeat, or talking to show energy being used.

CHECKING IN

To assess your student's understanding of the lesson, show him or her three examples of matter: a bowl of water, a rock, and a balloon filled with air. Have your student explain their states and several of their properties.

Find Forms of Matter

Draw a picture of a solid, a liquid, and a gas found around your home. Then write two properties of each.

Solid:	Liquid:	Gas:

Solid Properties

1. _____

2. _____

Liquid Properties

1. _____

2. _____

Gas Properties

1. _____

2. _____

Create a Chemical Change

Have you ever noticed that a new penny is shiny and bright but an old penny is dull? A penny becomes dull because of a chemical change in the copper on the penny's surface. The chemical reaction creates tarnish. Try this experiment to make a chemical reaction that will remove the tarnish.

MATERIALS

- ❏ 5 pennies
- ❏ $\frac{1}{4}$ cup lemon juice
- ❏ 1 flat-bottomed bowl
- ❏ crayons or markers

STEPS

1. Put some pennies into a small bowl and look at them. How tarnished are they?

2. Find a crayon or marker that is the same color as the pennies. Color a small circle with the crayon or marker in your notebook.

3. Pour lemon juice into the bowl so that the pennies are covered. Wait 10 minutes.

4. After 10 minutes, rinse off the pennies. Then look at their color again. What color are the pennies?

5. Find a crayon or marker that's the same color as the new color of the pennies.

6. Color a small circle in your notebook next to the old color. Look at the difference.

7. In your notebook, write what color the new pennies are and why you think they changed color.

Investigating Light and Sound

Light and sound help us to find out about our world.

OBJECTIVE	BACKGROUND	MATERIALS
To introduce your student to the properties of light and sound	Light and sound are forms of energy that are important in our everyday lives. In this lesson, your student will learn about the properties of light and sound.	■ Student Learning Pages 12.A–12.B ■ 1 flashlight ■ 1 long cardboard tube ■ 1 flat mirror ■ 1 bell ■ 1 cotton ball ■ 1 sheet construction paper ■ 1 sheet clear plastic wrap ■ 1 sheet tissue paper ■ 1 sheet aluminum foil ■ 1 book

VOCABULARY

TRANSPARENT allowing light to clearly pass through

TRANSLUCENT allowing only some light to pass through

OPAQUE not allowing light to pass through

Let's Begin

LIGHT

1 **EXPLAIN** Ask your student to think about why plants, animals, and people need light. Explain that light is energy that travels in waves. Discuss with your student sources of light. Explain that light travels in a straight line, but it can also be bent. Have your student shine a flashlight through a long cardboard tube and observe what happens. Then have your student bend the tube and shine the flashlight again, observing the difference. Discuss what your student observes.

2 **RESEARCH** Explain to your student that he or she can see objects because light bounces off them. Have your student research how his or her eyes allow him or her to see. Use the Internet to find a diagram of the eye. Have your student copy the diagram and discuss the different parts of the eye.

A rainbow shines in the sky.

FOR FURTHER READING

Exploring Light and Color: A Hands-On Approach to Learning, by Heidi Gold-Dworkin (McGraw-Hill Trade, 2000).

Light and Sound, by Chris Oxlade (Heinemann Library, 1999).

Sound and Light, by Sarah Angliss, contribution by Maggie Hewson (Kingfisher, 2001).

3 **INSTRUCT** Have your student look at his or her reflection in a mirror. Tell your student that he or she can see himself or herself because a flat mirror has a shiny, flat surface. Explain that the light rays bounce off the surface of the mirror in a regular way, allowing your student to see his or her reflection.

4 **EXPERIMENT** Tell your student that when light hits different types of materials, different things can happen. Instruct your student to read the definitions of **transparent, translucent,** and **opaque** on Student Learning Page 12.A. Then have your student use a flashlight to classify the materials listed. Discuss.

5 **ASK** Ask, *What would happen if you left an ice cream cone outside on a sunny day?* Explain that when sunlight is absorbed, it changes to heat. Heat from the sun melts the ice cream. Discuss how the sun's heat affects other objects.

6 **EXPLAIN** Explain that a shadow is created when an opaque object, such as a person, blocks a light source. Shine a light onto a wall and let your student experiment with making shadow puppets on the wall.

7 **EXPLORE** Relate to your student that white light is a mix of colors like those seen in a rainbow. Explain that he or she can see these colors if he or she looks at light through a prism.

SOUND

1 **DISCUSS** Tell your student that sound is a kind of energy. Sounds are made when matter vibrates, or moves quickly back and forth. Vibrating matter causes all the sounds that your student hears. Have your student ring a bell. Ask your student how a bell makes a sound. [the clapper hits the inside of the bell, causing it to vibrate]

2 **RESEARCH** Instruct your student to research how people and animals use vocal cords to produce sound.

Branching Out

TEACHING TIP

Help your student create a simple drum with a coffee can and a balloon stretched over the top, secured with a rubber band. Let your student adjust the rubber band and the balloon to change the sound.

CHECKING IN

Assess your student's understanding of the lesson by having him or her summarize the lesson in his or her own words.

Investigate Light with Objects

Read the definitions in the chart.

Kind of Material	Definition	Example
Transparent	Material that allows light to clearly pass through it	Clear drinking glass
Translucent	Material that lets only some light pass through it	Tracing paper
Opaque	Material that doesn't let light pass through it	Cardboard

Read the list of materials. Try to shine a flashlight through each. Use what you notice and the definitions to label each: transparent, translucent, or opaque. Write your answers. Then write a paragraph about what you learned about light in this experiment.

1. Cotton ball: _____

2. Construction paper: _____

3. Clear plastic wrap: _____

4. Tissue paper: _____

5. Aluminum foil: _____

6. Book: _____

_____

_____

_____

What's Next? You Decide!

Now it's your turn to choose what to do next in the lesson. Read the activities and decide which one you want to do— you may want to try them both!

Investigate Black and White Materials

MATERIALS

- ❏ 1 ice cube tray full of ice cubes
- ❏ 1 white square construction paper
- ❏ 1 black square construction paper
- ❏ 1 flashlight

STEPS

Do this activity to find out which color of clothing is a better choice to wear on a hot, sunny day.

- ❏ Place an ice cube tray full of ice cubes on a flat surface.
- ❏ Cover one ice cube with a black square of construction paper. Cover one ice cube with a white square of construction paper.
- ❏ Shine a flashlight on the ice cubes and observe which ice cube melts first.

Observe Changing Shadows

MATERIALS

- ❏ 1 piece chalk (optional)

STEPS

- ❏ Go outside in the morning and stand in a sunny place.
- ❏ Look at your shadow. If you'd like, you can have a family member or friend trace the outline of your shadow with chalk to make it easier to see the shape and size.
- ❏ Then go outside to the same place at noon and notice how your shadow looks compared to how it looked earlier in the day.
- ❏ Look at your shadow again at 5:00 P.M.
- ❏ Look through books to explain what you notice.

Learning About Forces and Simple Machines

We use simple machines all the time to help us do work.

OBJECTIVE	BACKGROUND	MATERIALS
To introduce your student to forces and simple machines	Simple machines are an important part of science that your student encounters in his or her everyday life. This lesson introduces your student to the concepts of force, work, and simple machines.	■ Student Learning Pages 13.A–13.B

VOCABULARY
FORCE an energy that pushes or pulls
WORK when a force moves an object over a distance
FRICTION the force of two things rubbing against one another
SIMPLE MACHINES machines with few or no moving parts that help a person do work
INCLINED PLANE a flat surface that is higher at one end than the other, like a ramp
WHEEL AND AXLE a machine that has a wheel that turns a post or an axle
PULLEY a machine made of a rope placed around a wheel
LEVER a rod that turns around a point called a fulcrum
SCREW a nail-shaped machine with spiral grooves wound around it that holds things together
WEDGE an object that tapers to an edge and is used to push things apart

Let's Begin

1 **INTRODUCE** Ask your student what he or she knows about forces. Explain that a **force** is a push or a pull. Tell your student that when he or she throws a ball, leans against a wall, or writes with a pencil, he or she is using force. Explain that an object can't move unless a force is exerted on it. For example, tell your student that when a person rides a scooter, he or she pushes off the ground with his or her foot. Those pushes cause the wheels of the scooter to turn and move. Ask, *Can you name other ways forces cause objects to move?*

2 **DEFINE** Ask your student to define the word **work.** Tell your student that in everyday language we usually define work as doing a job. Scientists say that work is done when a force makes an object move over a distance. Explain that a person pushing a

grocery cart is doing work because he or she is using force to make an object move. Point out that if a person pushes on a wall, no work is done. Although force is used to push against the wall, if the wall doesn't move, there is no work. Ask, *Can you think of three examples of work that you did today?*

3 **EXPLAIN** Tell your student that force can be measured. Explain that when someone steps on a scale to weigh himself or herself, that person is measuring the force of gravity on his or her body. Talk with your student about some everyday examples of how we use weight to measure force. [to weigh produce at the market]

4 **RELATE AND EXPERIMENT** Explain that **friction** influences force. Point out that friction is present whenever two things touch each other. When a person walks, it's the friction between his or her feet and the ground that allows the person to take a step. Other examples of friction include a diver jumping into water or a ball rolling only a short distance on a shag carpet. Have your student conduct a friction experiment. In a room with a tile or wood floor, ask your student to carefully try walking and sliding across the floor in stocking feet, with shoes, and in bare feet. Ask, *Which has the least friction? Which has the most?* [stocking feet probably have least; shoes or bare feet will probably have more]

5 **REVEAL** Point out that when we think of a machine we often think of complicated things such as washing machines or car engines. Explain that **simple machines** are machines with few moving parts that don't use electricity and help a person do work. Examples of simple machines are pull-tops on beverage cans, pedals on a bicycle, seesaws, scissors, and wrenches. These simple machines are grouped into different categories depending on how they work. Categories are **inclined plane, wheel and axle, pulley, lever, screw,** and **wedge.** Now distribute Student Learning Page 13.A.

Branching Out

FOR FURTHER READING

Forces and Movement (Straightforward Science), by Peter D. Riley (Franklin Watts, 1998).

Simple Machines (Starting with Science), by Deborah Hodge (Kids Can Press, 2000).

TEACHING TIP

Help your student identify some examples of simple machines around your house.

CHECKING IN

To assess how well your student understands simple machines, discuss with him or her several scenarios where work needs to be done, such as moving a large crate onto a truck or prying open a jammed door. Have him or her explain which type of simple machine would be best for accomplishing the job.

Learn About
Simple Machines

Look at each picture. Write the type of simple machine
each is: screw, wedge, lever, wheel and axle, pulley, or
inclined plane.

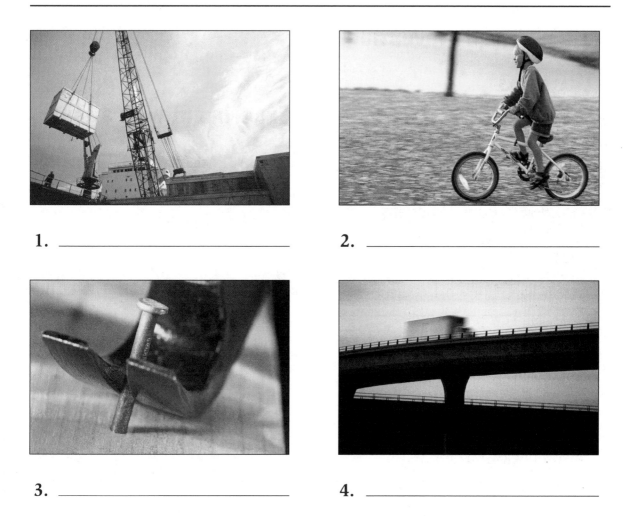

1. _____

2. _____

3. _____

4. _____

**Find three simple machines in your home. Write their names and
what type of simple machines they are.**

Name   Type of Simple Machine

5. _____   _____

6. _____   _____

7. _____   _____

What's Next? You Decide!

Now it's your turn to choose what to do next in the lesson. Read the activities and decide which one you want to do—you may want to try them both!

Design a Not-So-Simple Invention

MATERIALS

❑ 1 book about Rube Goldberg
❑ crayons or markers

STEPS

Rube Goldberg

Rube Goldberg was an artist and a cartoonist. He was known for drawing very complex machines that were meant to do very simple jobs.

❑ Read about Rube Goldberg and his cartoons. You can also check him out at http://www.rubegoldberg.com.
❑ Choose a simple task that you would like to accomplish.
❑ Create an invention that could accomplish this simple task. Be sure to include simple machines in your invention.
❑ Draw a picture of your invention.

❑ Then write a description of how your invention works and share it with an adult.

Experiment with a Lever

MATERIALS

❑ 1 desk or table
❑ 3 or 4 large books
❑ 1 ruler or meterstick

STEPS

❑ Stack three or four large books on a flat surface, such as a desk or table.
❑ Use a ruler or meterstick as a lever. Place the lever underneath the books and try to lift them by pulling up on the lever.
❑ Experiment with moving the lever so that more or less of the lever is sticking out from under the books.
❑ Observe how changing the position of the lever affects how much effort it takes to lift the books.

Understanding Electricity

Electrical energy makes our lives easier.

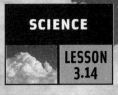

SCIENCE

LESSON
3.14

OBJECTIVE	BACKGROUND	MATERIALS
To introduce your student to the concept of electricity	It would be difficult to go through a day in our modern world without using electricity. Whether riding an elevator, turning on a computer, or blow-drying our hair, we are very accustomed to having electricity. This lesson introduces your student to electrical energy, electromagnets, and static electricity.	<ul><li>Student Learning Pages 14.A–14.B</li><li>2 balloons</li><li>2 pieces 16-inch string</li><li>1 piece wool cloth</li><li>1 bar magnet</li><li>4–5 metal paper clips</li><li>1 copy Web, page 354</li></ul>

VOCABULARY

ELECTRIC CURRENT the flow of electricity along a path
ELECTRICAL ENERGY the electric current that flows through wires
CIRCUIT the pathway that electrical energy follows
MAGNETISM the ability of a magnet to exert a force
ELECTROMAGNETS magnets made up of a core of iron inside a wire coil that carries electric current
STATIC ELECTRICITY electricity that forms when electrical charges build up between two objects

Let's Begin

ELECTRICAL ENERGY

1 **INTRODUCE** Explain that the **electric current** that flows through wires is called **electrical energy.** Electrical energy can be changed into other forms of energy. For example, electrical energy is changed into light in a lightbulb, into heat energy on a stove, and into mechanical energy in a washing machine. Ask your student to list 10 objects in your home that are powered by electricity.

2 **EXPLAIN** Explain that electrical energy is made from other sources of energy, such as coal, nuclear energy, or wind power. Power plants have machines called generators that use these forms of energy to make electrical energy. Tell your student that electrical energy needs a pathway to follow to move from place to place. The pathway that electrical energy follows is called a **circuit.** Electrical energy that flows through a circuit is called electric current. A circuit must be continuous like an unbroken chain. Explain that the electric power lines that connect the

power plant to your home are a circuit. If a power line near your home is damaged, the circuit is broken and the power will go out. Ask, *What are some things you couldn't do if the power was out?* [use computer, turn on lights, keep food cold]

ELECTROMAGNETS

1 **EXPLAIN** Give your student a bar magnet and four or five metal paper clips. Tell your student to hold the magnet over the paper clips and observe what happens. Tell your student that magnets exert a force that attracts them to iron-containing objects. The ability of a magnet to exert a force is called **magnetism.** Then have your student complete Student Learning Page 14.A.

2 **DIRECT** Explain that magnets can also be made with electricity. They are called **electromagnets.** Doorbells, telephones, cars, televisions, and stereo systems all contain electromagnets. Have your student find out how electromagnets are used in one of these household devices. Ask him or her to show how the device works.

STATIC ELECTRICITY

1 **ASK** Ask your student if he or she has ever gotten a shock after walking on a carpet and touching a metal object. Explain that electrical energy is all around us. Everything is made up of forces called electrical charges. When two objects rub together, more electrical charge builds up on one of the objects. Explain that the electricity that forms when electrical charges build up between two objects is called **static electricity.**

2 **EXPERIMENT** Have your student blow up two balloons. Tie a piece of string to each balloon and hold the balloons by the string so they hang down. Bring the balloons close together. Have your student observe how they attract or repel one another. Now rub both balloons with the wool cloth. Bring the balloons close together again. Have your student observe how they attract or repel one another.

FOR FURTHER READING

Electricity (Simply Science), by Darlene R. Stille (Compass Point Books, 2001).

The Magic School Bus and the Electric Field Trip, by Joanna Cole (Scholastic Paperbacks, 1999).

Branching Out

TEACHING TIP

Go to http://ippex.pppl.gov for more on electricity.

CHECKING IN

To assess how well your student understands the concepts in this lesson, have your student fill in a copy of the Web found on page 354. Tell your student to write "electricity" in the center and then summarize all of the important ideas of the lesson in his or her own words on the Web.

Experiment with Magnets and Electricity

Read the steps. Then magnetize a nail so it acts like a temporary magnet.

MATERIALS

- ❏ 1 large nail
- ❏ several paper clips
- ❏ 1 bar magnet

STEPS

1. Place the bar magnet on a table.

2. Pull the nail over one side of the magnet at least 10 times. Be sure to go in the same direction, from right to left or left to right, every time. The nail will become more magnetized with each pull.

3. Lay a few paper clips on the table. Test the nail's magnetism on the paper clips. How does it compare to the magnetic power of the bar magnet?

4. If the nail doesn't attract the paper clips, try the experiment again with a different nail. Be sure to follow the instructions carefully.

5. Once you have tested the nail with the paper clips, wait one or two hours and test it again. Then test it once more one or two hours later. What do you notice?

6. You can also try charging the nail and then dropping it on the floor. Does it lose magnetic energy?

7. Write about what you found in your notebook.

What's Next? You Decide!

Now it's your turn to choose what to do next in the lesson. Read the activities and decide which one you want to do—you may want to try them both!

Observe Changes in Magnetic Force

MATERIALS

- ❑ 1 plastic cup
- ❑ 1 paper clip
- ❑ 1 magnet
- ❑ 1 paper box or metal pan

STEPS

- ❑ Put a paper clip in a plastic cup.
- ❑ Use the magnet from outside the cup to try to move the paper clip up the side of the cup.
- ❑ Then put the paper clip inside a paper box or metal pan.
- ❑ Try to move the paper clip again, using the magnet from the outside. Before you start, make a prediction about whether the magnet will be able to attract the paper clip through the container.
- ❑ Write your predictions and observations in your notebook. What have you learned?

Suppose You Didn't Have Electricity

MATERIALS

- ❑ 1 small notepad

STEPS

- ❑ Think about all the ways you use electricity every day.
- ❑ Put a small notepad in your pocket and for one full day keep a list of every time you use electricity and how you use it—for light, to wash clothes, to watch television, and so on.
- ❑ Then suppose that you're living before electricity was available. Make a second list of how you would do each of the things from the first list without using electricity. How would your day be different? What activities would change?
- ❑ Share your list with an adult.

Exploring Earth, the Moon, and the Sun

It's good to get to know your neighbors.

OBJECTIVE	BACKGROUND	MATERIALS
To have your student learn about Earth, the moon, and the sun	Astronomy is often considered one of the world's oldest sciences and something your student can use on a daily basis. This lesson introduces your student to the relationship between Earth, the sun, and the moon, as well as to other parts of our solar system.	■ Student Learning Pages 15.A–15.B ■ 1 flashlight ■ 1 weather section of local newspaper ■ crayons

VOCABULARY
PLANET a body in space that travels around a star **ORBIT** the path that one body in space, such as a planet, travels around another body, such as a star **AXIS** the straight line that a planet rotates on

Let's Begin

THE SUN

1   **DISCUSS AND EXPERIMENT** Discuss what your student has observed about shadows. Explain that an opaque object is an object that blocks light. Ask your student to name some examples of opaque objects. Point out that the larger an object is, the larger its shadow will be. Also, point out that the closer an object is to a light source, the larger its shadow will be. Give your student a flashlight and let your student experiment with shining the flashlight on different objects and observing the shadows that result. Your student also can shine the flashlight on the objects from different distances to see how the shadows change.

2   **REVEAL** Reveal that the sun's light makes objects on Earth have shadows. Discuss with your student what he or she knows about the sun. Tell your student that the sun is a star. The sun looks so much larger than other stars because it is the closest star to Earth. Explain that the sun is a ball of hot gases that provides the light and heat necessary for life on Earth, and that the sun is at the center of the solar system. Everything that

travels around the sun is part of the solar system. Ask, *How long does it take for Earth to go all the way around the sun?* [1 year or about 365 days]

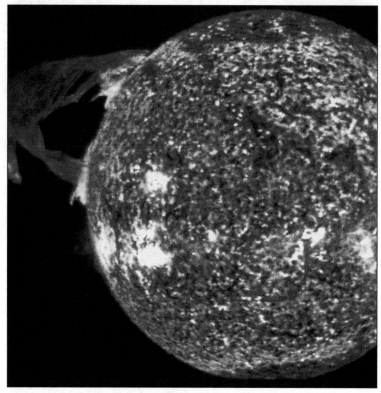

The sun is a star that gives Earth heat and light.

THE MOON

1 **DISCUSS** Now discuss with your student what he or she has observed about the moon. Explain that when there is a full moon, like the sun, it also can make shadows. Mention that although it might seem as if the moon shines, it doesn't make any light of its own. The moonlight we see is actually sunlight reflected off the surface of the moon. The sun is always shining on part of the moon. As the moon travels around Earth, the amount of reflected light we can see depends on where the moon is in its orbit around Earth. Discuss the last time there was a full moon. Does your student recall what it looked like?

2 **EXPLORE** Explain that the different amounts of reflected light that can be seen are known as the phases of the moon. Have your student research the phases of the moon in books or on the Internet, such as at World Almanac for Kids at http://www.worldalmanacforkids.com. You also can show your student the weather section of your local newspaper. Most newspapers include information about the current phase of the moon. Have your student follow the phases of the moon, in the sky or in the newspaper, for several days and give you a summary of what he or she noticed.

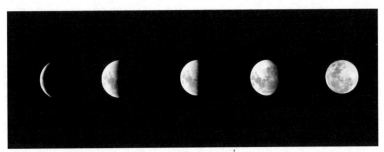

The moon changes phases gradually. It takes about $29\frac{1}{2}$ days for the moon to complete its cycle from new moon to new moon.

3 **ASK AND RESEARCH** Ask your student if he or she knows that people have gone to the moon many times. Go to the library with your student and research information about moon explorations. Have him or her tell you what types of transportation have been used to go to the moon, when the first trip to the moon occurred, and why people would want to go to the moon. Then ask him or her if he or she would want to go to the moon and why.

PLANETS

1 **RELATE** Explain that because Earth is a planet, it revolves, or travels around, the sun in a path called an **orbit**. A **planet** is a body in space that moves around a star. Explain that Earth's revolution around the sun (along with its tilt) gives us seasons during the year. The planets also rotate, or spin around, on an **axis**. An axis is an invisible straight line around which an object rotates. It takes Earth about 24 hours to complete one rotation. Tell your student that Earth's rotation is what causes day and night. Ask, *What is the difference between rotation and revolution?* [rotation happens around an axis inside the planet, revolution is when a moon or planet travels around another object—such as the sun]

DID YOU KNOW?

Recent scientific investigations have led scientists to speculate if Pluto should be considered a planet in our solar system.

The cloudy, blue appearance of Earth from space is because of the large amounts of water on our planet.

ENRICH THE EXPERIENCE

Schedule a field trip to a planetarium or an observatory to offer your student firsthand glimpses of what he or she is studying in this lesson.

Exploring Earth, the Moon, and the Sun   **225**

2 **INVESTIGATE** Point out that not everyone on Earth has sunlight at the same time. Together with your student look at your local newspaper's sun rising and setting times. Have your student check these times daily for a week. Then have him or her tell you about what he or she has discovered.

3 **SHARE** Move on to discuss the other planets in the solar system. Reveal that our solar system consists of the sun and nine planets: Mercury, Venus, Earth, Mars, Jupiter, Saturn, Uranus, Neptune, and Pluto. Ask your student what he or she knows about planets and discuss.

4 **DISTRIBUTE** Distribute Student Learning Page 15.A. Have your student read the directions out loud. Help him or her find research books to answer the questions.

5 **EXPLORE** Explain that one way that scientists get their information about the planets, the sun, and the moon is by observing them through a telescope. Ask your student what he or she knows about telescopes. Explain that telescopes are scientific instruments that scientists use to observe things in space. Mention that one important telescope is the Hubble Space Telescope, a large telescope that has been orbiting Earth since 1990. Go to http://hubble.nasa.gov and check out photographs taken from the Hubble Telescope. You may want to preview them first and select certain images to show your student for discussion.

Branching Out

TEACHING TIP

Your library may have several videos about Earth, the sun, and the moon to enhance the lesson. You may want to view them first to make sure they are age appropriate.

CHECKING IN

To assess how well your student has learned the concepts in the lesson, have him or her "teach" the lesson back to you. Encourage him or her to include drawings or other visuals in the lesson.

FOR FURTHER READING

DK Space Encyclopedia, by Nigel Henbest and Heather Couper (DK Publishing, 1999).

Planets Around the Sun, by Seymour Simon (SeaStar Books, 2002).

What the Moon Is Like, by Franklyn Mansfield Branley and True Kelley, ill. (HarperCollins Children's Books, 2000).

Research a Planet

Choose one planet in the solar system. Research the planet. Read the questions. Then write the answers.

Name of planet: _____

Number of moons: _____

Temperature: _____

What the planet is made of: _____   _____

Now draw a picture of the planet you chose.

What's Next? You Decide!

Now it's your turn to choose what to do next in the lesson. Read the activities and decide which one you want to do— you may want to try them both!

Check Out the Moon

MATERIALS

❑ 1 ruler

STEPS

❑ Use a ruler to draw a grid on a sheet of paper. Your grid should include 30 boxes— 6 boxes going across the page and 5 boxes going down the page. Make the boxes large enough to draw a picture inside each one.

❑ Starting with today's date, write the date in the upper left corner of each box for the next 30 days.

❑ Each night, go outside after sunset and observe the moon. Then draw a picture of how the moon looks.

❑ If the night is too cloudy to see the moon, draw a cloud in the

box. If the night is clear but you can't see the moon, write "can't see moon" in the box.

❑ After you have observed the moon for 30 nights, look back at your drawings.

Create a Planet

MATERIALS

❑ construction paper
❑ 1 unused shoebox
❑ glue
❑ 1 pair scissors
❑ various pieces colored yarn
❑ 1 handful of buttons, craft sticks, or other craft items

STEPS

❑ Suppose you discovered a planet. What would it look like?

❑ Turn the shoebox on its side. Create a scene inside the shoebox of what your planet might look like.

❑ Use the paper and craft items to build a scene from your planet.

Examining Earth

Studying the ground we walk on may seem basic, but there are amazing forces at work shaping, bending, breaking, and changing Earth.

OBJECTIVE	BACKGROUND	MATERIALS
To introduce your student to Earth's composition	Learning about Earth's composition and formation is an important aspect of science that your student can observe in the land right under his or her feet. This lesson introduces your student to Earth's layers, forces that change Earth's surface, and soil.	■ Student Learning Pages 16.A–16.B ■ 1 U.S. map ■ 1 small jar with lid, filled halfway with water ■ handfuls of different kinds of soil from your neighborhood ■ 1 copy Web, page 354 ■ 1 old shirt or smock ■ newspapers (enough to cover workspace) ■ 1 small plastic soda bottle, filled more than halfway with warm water ■ 1 aluminum pie pan ■ 1 package modeling clay ■ 4 drops red food coloring ■ 6 drops liquid dish soap ■ 1 funnel ■ 2 tablespoons baking soda ■ 1 bottle vinegar ■ $\frac{1}{2}$ cup water

VOCABULARY

CRUST the outer layer of Earth

MANTLE the layer of Earth below the crust that's made up of hot, melted rock

CORE the layer of Earth below the mantle that's made up of metal; the center of Earth

LAVA the liquid rock flowing out of a volcano

FAULTS breaks in Earth's crust where earthquakes can happen

SOIL a mixture of rock particles and decayed plants and animals

Let's Begin

EARTH'S SURFACE

1 **DISCUSS** Ask your student if he or she has ever thought about what is found deep inside Earth. Tell your student that Earth has many layers. Earth's outermost layer is called the **crust.** Explain

that the layer underneath the crust is called the **mantle.** The mantle is solid and made mostly of rock. The lower part of the mantle is soft, and the upper part of the mantle is hard. Tell your student that the center layer of Earth is called the **core.** The core is divided into two layers. The outer core is made of metals that are so hot they are liquid. The inner core is also made of very hot metal, but because the pressure of Earth's center is so strong, the inner core is solid. Have your student draw and label a model of Earth's layers. Discuss the completed model with your student.

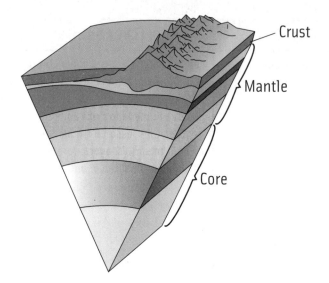

DID YOU KNOW?

Earth's crust is so thin compared to Earth's other layers that if Earth were the size of an apple, Earth's crust would be as thin as the apple's peel.

2 **MODEL** Show your student a hard boiled egg in the shell. Explain that the egg can be a model for the layers of Earth. With the shell still on, cut the egg in half. Point out that the egg shell is like Earth's crust, the white is the mantle and the yellow is the core.

3 **RESEARCH** Tell your student that Earth's surface is always changing. Movements inside Earth, gravity, water, and wind are all forces that work to change Earth's surface. Explain that some changes happen very quickly while other changes take place over millions of years. Explain that formations such as mountains, plains, valleys, and islands are all created by these forces. Together with your student, research how each of these forms. Then have your student summarize each in his or her notebook.

4 **EXPLAIN** Tell your student that some changes in Earth's surface take place very slowly. A glacier is an example of a force that causes slow changes on Earth's surface. Explain that a glacier is a mass of ice that flows slowly over land. When a glacier moves, rocks are carried along with it. The pressure from the movement of the glacier and the scraping of the rocks against the land creates new landforms. Point out that thousands of years ago the Great Lakes were formed by glaciers. Have your student locate the Great Lakes on a United States map.

When large amounts of snow compress into ice, glaciers form. Gravity moves glaciers downhill.

5 **RELATE** Tell your student that some changes on Earth's surface happen very quickly. Forces that change Earth's surface quickly include earthquakes and volcanoes. Explain that a volcano is a land formation created by the eruption of liquid rock from under Earth's crust. Explain that when there is a weak spot in the crust, molten rock from the mantle forces its way to the surface and erupts as **lava.** Have your student research volcanoes and find out about the different kinds of volcanoes and where many of the world's volcanoes are found. Also have your student choose one volcano that erupted recently and find out what changes occurred. Ask, *What happened to the plants, animals, and people who lived close to the volcano?*

6 **DISTRIBUTE** Distribute Student Learning Page 16.A. Assist your student in preparing and conducting the experiment.

7 **EXPLAIN** Tell your student that an earthquake is a sudden movement of Earth's crust. Explain that earthquakes happen because forces inside Earth push and pull on rocks. Sometimes these forces are strong enough to cause rocks to suddenly slip along cracks in Earth's crust called **faults.** Together with your student, find out about a major earthquake, how scientists measure earthquakes, and how people prepare for them.

SOIL

1 **EXPLAIN AND MODEL** Explain that **soil** is found in Earth's crust. Give your student a small jar that is filled halfway with water. Tell your student to put a handful of soil in the jar and screw the lid on the jar. Then tell your student to shake the jar and set it aside. After about ten minutes, have your student observe the jar and describe what he or she sees. The soil should settle into layers. You may want to extend this activity by trying different kinds of soil, such as clay soil or very sandy soil.

2 **ASK** Ask your student where he or she thinks soil comes from. Tell your student that over time soil is formed as rocks break apart from wind, rain, ice, and water. Over thousands of years the rocks slowly crumble and become soil. Soil also contains humus, or the decayed remains of dead plants and animals. Humus adds nutrients to the soil that help plants and animals live. Explain that soil is very important to life on Earth. Plants need certain types of soil to be able to grow. Animals need healthy plants to eat. Ask, *Why do you think certain areas are better for growing certain foods, such as pineapples in Hawaii?* [because of the type of soil and the weather]

3 **REVEAL** Explain that soil is not the same in different parts of the world. There are three main types of soil: clay, sand, and silt. Together, research clay soil, sandy soil, and silt. Find out about their color, ability to hold water, how much humus they have, and what plants like them best. Then ask, *What kind of soil is best for growing a garden?* [plants will grow best in soil that has an equal mixture of the three because a balanced amount of water can then be held in the soil]

4 **DISTRIBUTE** Distribute Student Learning Page 16.B for an experiment on soil.

FOR FURTHER READING

Atlas of Geology and Landforms: An A–Z Guide, by Cally Oldershaw (Scholastic Library Publishing, 2001).

Earthsteps: A Rock's Journey Through Time, by Diane Nelson Spickert (Fulcrum Publishing, 2000).

How the Earth Works: 60 Fun Activities for Exploring Volcanoes, Fossils, Earthquakes, and More, by Michelle O'Brien-Palmer (Chicago Review Press, 2002).

The Science of Soil (Living Science), by Jonathan Bockneck (Gareth Stevens, 1999).

Branching Out

TEACHING TIP

Videos on Earth's layers, volcanoes, earthquakes, glaciers, and soil may enhance the content of this lesson. You may want to preview the videos first.

CHECKING IN

To assess how well your student understands the concepts of the lesson, have your student fill in a copy of the Web found on page 354. Instruct your student to include all of the major concepts from the lesson. Discuss the completed Web with your student.

Model a Volcano

Read the materials. Then read the steps. Conduct this experiment to make a model volcano.

SCIENCE

16.A

MATERIALS

- ❏ 1 old shirt or smock
- ❏ newspapers (enough to cover workspace)
- ❏ 1 small plastic soda bottle, empty
- ❏ 1 aluminum pie pan
- ❏ 1 package modeling clay

- ❏ warm water
- ❏ 4 drops red food coloring
- ❏ 6 drops liquid dish soap
- ❏ 1 funnel
- ❏ 2 tablespoons baking soda
- ❏ 1 bottle vinegar

STEPS

1. Ask for an adult's help before beginning.

2. Wear a smock and cover your work area with newspapers.

3. Place the soda bottle in the pie pan.

4. Put modeling clay all over the soda bottle to make a mountain shape around the bottle. Don't cover the opening of the bottle or put clay inside the bottle.

5. Fill the bottle more than halfway with warm water, but don't fill it to the top.

6. Add four drops of red food coloring and six drops of soap to the bottle.

7. Use the funnel to add two tablespoons of baking soda to the bottle. Use the funnel to slowly pour the vinegar into the bottle until your volcano "erupts" and "lava" flows down the sides of your volcano.

8. Think about how this model is like a real volcano.

Lava coming out of a volcano

Test the Soil

Read the materials and the steps. Conduct this experiment to find the amount of sand, silt, and clay in soil.

MATERIALS

❑ soil from your neighborhood

❑ $\frac{1}{2}$ cup water

STEPS

1. Collect a bit of soil from around your house about the size of a large marble.

2. Wet it with a few drops of water.

3. Try to flatten it between your hands like a thin pancake.

4. If it's crumbly and won't make a pancake, there's a lot of sand in it. If it makes a pancake but then falls apart, there's a lot of silt in it. If it makes a pancake and sticks together well, there's a lot of clay in it.

5. Write two or three sentences in your notebook about what happened to the soil. Then write about how much silt, sand, or clay you think it has.

6. Share your ideas with an adult.

Soil is all around us.

In Your Community

To reinforce the skills and concepts taught in this section,
try one or more of these activities!

Different Kinds of Telescopes

Is your student interested in astronomy? Find
out if there's an exhibit that shows the evolution of the telescope at a museum of science
and industry or planetarium in your town. Take
a visit to see the telescopes firsthand. If you
aren't near a planetarium or museum, you may
be able to find an astronomy group that meets
in your area. Many astronomy groups have
Web sites. Arrange for a time when you and
your student could attend a gathering and look
at the stars and planets through telescopes.

Soil in Your Neighborhood

There are thousands of different kinds of soil
on Earth. Have your student examine the soil
around your home. He or she will need a magnifying lens, a small spatula, and a surface to
work on that has good lighting. Ask your student to collect a handful of soil from several
inches under the surface of the ground. Show
him or her how to use the spatula and magnifying glass to examine the color and texture of
the soil. Remind your student what you covered in lesson 3.16 about sand, silt, and clay.
Have your student determine which is more
present in the soil around your home. Ask him
or her to consider how this might affect the
way the soil is used in your community.

Endangered Animals Close to Home

There are hundreds of animals in the United
States that are on the endangered species list.
Together with your student, use the Internet or
contact a local ecology center to find out about
the animals that live in or close to your community that are endangered. Have your student
choose one animal to learn more about. Ask
him or her to find out how the people in your
community can help protect this animal. Then
have your student make a poster that teaches
other people about the animal and how they
can help. After getting permission, have your
student display the poster at your local library
or other public place.

Community Recycling

Does your community have a recycling program? Together with your student, find out
how your recycling program works. What gets
recycled? Where do they recycle it? How long
does it take? What gets made from the recycled
material? If you can, visit the recycling center
in your area. See if you can arrange a guided
tour or an interview with a manager there for
your student. If there isn't a recycling program
in your community, have your student find out
why not. See if you can create a plan to start a
recycling program together and propose it to
your city hall.

We Have Learned

Use this checklist to summarize what you and your student
have accomplished in the Science section.

❏ **Plants and Animals**
❏ classifying plants and animals
❏ predators, prey, food chains, life cycles

❏ **Habitats**
❏ organisms, their needs, their
environment
❏ ecosystems

❏ **Humans in the Ecosystem**
❏ how people affect the environment
❏ natural resources

❏ **Changes in the Environment**
❏ natural disasters, restoration
❏ extinct and endangered plants and
animals

❏ **Taking Care of Earth**
❏ conservation, environmentalists
❏ your role in taking care of the
environment

❏ **Muscles and Bones**
❏ voluntary muscles, involuntary
muscles
❏ how muscles and bones work
together

❏ **Five Senses**
❏ senses of touch, sight, sound
❏ senses of smell, taste

❏ **Health and Nutrients**
❏ basic food groups
❏ benefits of good nutrition

❏ **Personal and Community Safety**
❏ avoiding injuries, using protective
equipment
❏ basic first aid, emergency action

❏ **Matter, Substances, and Energy**
❏ properties and states of matter
❏ elements, compounds, chemical
changes

❏ **Light and Sound**
❏ sources and travel of light and sound
❏ reflections, mirrors, shadows

❏ **Simple Machines**
❏ force, work
❏ inclined planes, pulleys, levers,
wheel and axle

❏ **Electricity**
❏ electric current, magnetism
❏ effects of static electricity

❏ **Earth and Space**
❏ Earth, sun, moon, solar system
❏ telescopes, constellations

❏ **Earth's Crust, Mantle, and Core**
❏ glaciers, volcanoes, earthquakes
❏ rocks, minerals, soil

We have also learned:

_____

_____

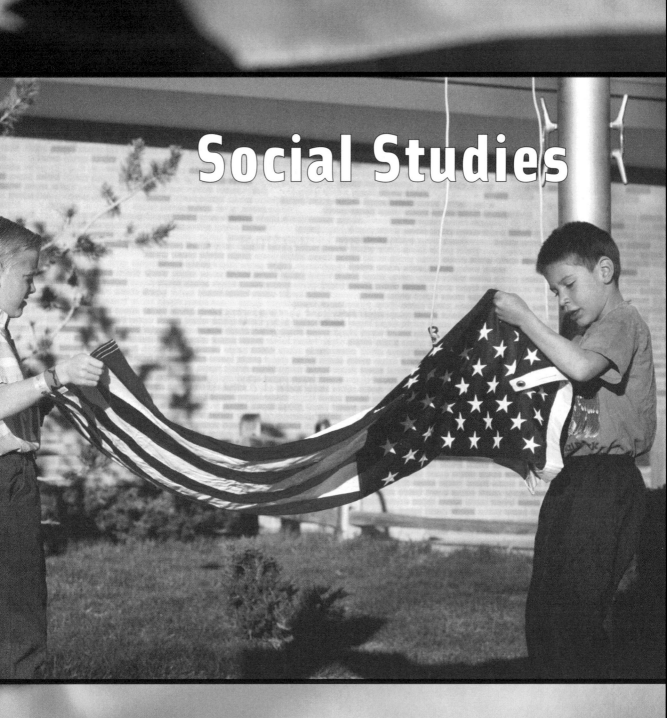

Social Studies

Social Studies

Key Topics

Communities and Neighborhoods
Pages 239–242

Maps and Directions
Pages 243–246

Comparisons of Communities
Pages 247–256

Community Features and Resources
Pages 257–266

Communities of the Past
Pages 267–278

Beginnings of the United States
Pages 279–282

Immigration
Pages 283–288

Citizenship
Pages 289–294

National and Local Community Symbols
Pages 295–300

Discovering Community

People naturally come together to live.

OBJECTIVE	BACKGROUND	MATERIALS
To help your student understand the components of a community	Every community is unique, but all communities share some basic components. As your student learns the meaning of community, he or she will be able to decide what makes his or her community special. Throughout this lesson, your student will learn about the different components of a community and why each component is important.	■ Student Learning Pages 1.A–1.B ■ 1 copy Web, page 354

VOCABULARY

COMMUNITY an area where a group of people live, work, interact, and have fun; usually includes several neighborhoods

NEIGHBORHOODS sections of a community where people live near one another

GRID MAP a type of map that uses letters and numbers to show where different places are located

SYMBOLS something that stands for something else

Let's Begin

1 **INTRODUCE** Encourage interest in the topic of **community** by asking your student to share some of the ideas he or she already has about community. Ask, *What do you think a community is?* Consider your student's answer and relate it to how you present the next step.

2 **EXPLAIN** Explain that a community is a group of **neighborhoods** where many different people live. Tell the student that you will be learning why neighborhoods, people, and services are important parts of a community. Invite the student to create a checklist titled "Community." Under the title, he or she can write "neighborhood," "people," and "services." The student can check off each of these components as he or she learns more about them.

3 **DEFINE** Explain that a community is made up of more than one neighborhood. A neighborhood is a section of a community where people live near one another. Ask, *What makes a neighborhood and a community different?* [a neighborhood is a smaller part of the larger community; a community is made up of a group of neighborhoods]

4 **REVEAL** Tell your student that a community has many different people: children, adults, men, and women. The people in a community do different things. They are teachers, firefighters, nurses, students, secretaries, and so on. Reveal how different people make one community by comparing a community to a puzzle. Explain that puzzle pieces come in different shapes, but each different piece is needed to make the whole picture. Have your student brainstorm some different types of people that are part of a community and then think about why they are important. Discuss.

Police Officer   Nurse   Teacher

5 **EXPLAIN** Explain that in a community there are various places where people can get different services they need. Tell your student that a community has services such as libraries, parks, schools, hospitals, and businesses. The different services in a community give people places to work, play, learn, get medicine, and shop. Ask, *What services can you name in our community?*

6 **DISTRIBUTE AND PRACTICE** Distribute Student Learning Page 1.A. Explain that the page shows a **grid map,** a type of map that uses letters and numbers to show where different places are located. Tell the student that this type of map is very useful when you want to find a certain location or service. Show the student that the **symbols** at the bottom of the map represent certain places. Have your student complete the questions.

Branching Out

TEACHING TIP

While you are out in the community with your student, identify the different types of people you encounter and discuss why they are important in your community.

CHECKING IN

Review what your student has learned about community by having him or her fill in a copy of the Web found on page 354. Have your student title the Web "A Community" and describe the different important parts that make a community in the outer ovals.

A BRIGHT IDEA

Take an old puzzle with 6 to 12 pieces and label them with names of different jobs people have in your community. Show the student that if one of those jobs is missing, then the puzzle is incomplete. Every person and every person's job in the community is important and valuable.

FOR FURTHER READING

Communities (Social Studies), by Lisa Trumbauer and Gail Saunders-Smith (Pebble Books, 2000).

What Is a Community from A to Z, by Bobbie Kalman (Crabtree Publishing, 2000).

Discover Community

Look at the map. Then answer the questions.

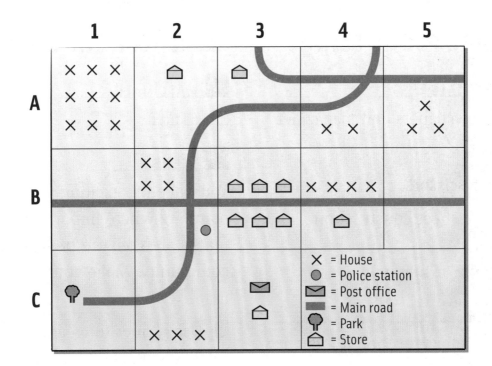

1. What service is located in square B2? _____

2. Which square has the most stores? _____

3. What services are located in square C3? _____

4. Which square is the park located in? _____

5. Which square has the most houses? _____

What's Next? You Decide!

Now it's your turn to choose what to do next in the lesson. Read the activities and decide which one you want to do—you may want to try them both!

Create a People Collage

MATERIALS

❏ old newspapers and magazines

❏ glue

❏ 1 pair scissors

❏ 1 large sheet construction paper

❏ crayons or markers

STEPS

Create a collage of the different types of people in a community.

❏ Use your crayons or markers to title the collage "People in a Community."

❏ Look through newspapers and magazines for pictures of people who have various jobs in a community. You can also draw people doing different jobs that help a community.

❏ Cut out the pictures and glue them onto a sheet of construction paper.

❏ Write the name of each job under the picture. Try to fill the entire page with pictures.

Make Your Own Grid Map

MATERIALS

❏ 1 ruler

STEPS

You have the exciting job of planning where important places are going to be in a new community. Make your own grid map.

❏ Use a ruler to create grid boxes. Label them with letters and numbers. Look on Student Learning Page 1.A for an example.

❏ Think of the different services that are important to a community.

❏ Create a symbol for each important place and decide where to put the places on the map.

❏ Don't forget to think of a name for your new community!

SOCIAL STUDIES

LESSON 4.2

Discovering North, South, East, West

Learning north, south, east, and west will be useful to your student as he or she gets older and more independent.

OBJECTIVE	BACKGROUND	MATERIALS
To have your student learn how to identify and use the directions *north, south, east,* and *west* on a map	Learning how to use the directions *north, south, east,* and *west* is an important skill in determining the specific and relative location of objects or places. In this lesson, your student will use a simple map of a park in order to practice using these directions.	■ Student Learning Pages 2.A–2.B ■ crayons or colored pencils

VOCABULARY

LEGEND the part of a map that identifies what the symbols on a map mean
COMPASS ROSE a symbol that tells where *north, south, east,* and *west* are located on a map

Let's Begin

1 **DISTRIBUTE** Distribute Student Learning Page 2.A. Explain that this map is an overhead view of a park. Make sure that your student is looking at the map with *north* pointing up. Point out *north* on the map and mention that on most maps, *north* usually points toward the top of the page.

2 **RELATE** Point out that the **legend,** or key, explains the symbols or marks used in a particular map. Identify the **compass rose** in the legend. Explain that a compass rose often is found in the legend in most maps, and it points out the directions *north, south, east,* and *west.* Review the rest of the legend's symbols.

3 **EXPLAIN** Explain that *north, south, east,* and *west* are directions, just like *forward* and *backward, up* and *down,* and *right* and *left* are directions. Direct your student to the star in the center and show how it points to *north, south, east,* and *west.*

4 **CLARIFY AND MODEL** Use the following activity to distinguish between *north, south, east,* and *west* and other directions, such as right or left.

ENRICH THE EXPERIENCE

Encourage your student to write a song or poem based on what he or she learns in this lesson. The song or poem may include terminology from the lesson, such as *north, south, east, west, compass, legend,* or *map.*

SOCIAL STUDIES

LESSON 4.2

Stand next to your student. Have him or her tell you to walk a few steps to the right or left. Offer that *left* and *right* mean the same direction to both of you right now. Then stand facing your student. Have him or her tell you to walk a few steps to the right or left. Now offer that this type of direction doesn't mean the same thing to both of you, which is why *right* and *left* aren't always useful in maps.

5 **MODEL AND ASK** Now have your student look at the map again. Show your student that to walk from the star in the middle to the basketball court, he or she would walk east. To walk back, he or she would walk west. Explain how every object in the map is *north, south, east,* or *west* of another object. Have your student color the swings, basketball court, flower garden, and barn. Then ask, *What is north of the swings?* [basketball court] Then ask, *What is south of the flower garden?* [barn]

6 **DEVELOP MORE SKILLS** Introduce the combined directions: *northwest, northeast, southwest,* and *southeast.* Explain that not every object on a map is directly *north, south, east,* or *west* of another object. Point out that the flower garden is not directly *north* or *west* of the center star but *northwest.* Have your student color the picnic tent. Then ask, *What direction would you be facing if you were standing in the center star looking at the picnic tent?* [southwest] Have your student color the pond. Then have him or her ask you a question about where another part of the park is in relation to the pond. For example, *What is south of the pond?* [basketball court]

7 **DISTRIBUTE AND PRACTICE** Distribute Student Learning Page 2.B to provide your student with additional practice using directions. Have your student complete this page using Student Learning Page 2.A. When your student has finished, review his or her work.

GET ORGANIZED

Allow enough time to teach, explore, and enjoy a subject or concept—even if you only have time to teach one area. Reorganize plans for the next few days to catch up.

FOR FURTHER READING

Map Mania: Discovering Where You Are and Getting to Where You Aren't, by Michael A. Dispezio and Dave Garbot, ill. (Sterling Publishing Company, Inc., 2002).

There's a Map in My Lap!, Tish Rabe and Aristides Ruiz, ill. (Random House, Inc., 2002).

Branching Out

TEACHING TIP

Your student may at times become disoriented or confused when using a map to locate an object or a landmark. In such cases have your student begin the exercise again using *north* as a starting point.

CHECKING IN

To assess your student's understanding of directions have him or her draw a simple overhead map of his or her bedroom. The map should contain all of the relevant objects, such as bed, dresser, and so on. On the back of the map have your student write five statements that show his or her ability to express the location of objects using directions. For example, *The bed is north of the closet.*

Explore a Map

Investigate North, South, East, West

Look at the map. Read each question. Then write the answer.

1. What direction would you go if you were at the barn and walked to the picnic tent? _____

2. What direction would you go if you were at the flower garden and walked to the swings? _____

3. If you were at the center star looking at the pond, what direction would you be facing? _____

4. If you were at the center star looking at the basketball court, what direction would you be facing? _____

Read each sentence. Then write the answer to complete the sentence.

5. The barn borders the picnic tent on the barn's _____ side.

6. The pond borders the flower garden on the pond's _____ side.

7. The _____ tells where north, south, east, and west are located on a map.

8. A _____ gives clues about the items, or symbols, in a map.

Comparing Communities

We can celebrate the diversity of the world's communities.

OBJECTIVE	BACKGROUND	MATERIALS
To help your student recognize the similarities and differences of communities across the United States and around the world	Every community is unique, and it is important for your student to be able to appreciate diverse types of communities. In this lesson, your student will learn to describe the similarities and differences among many different communities.	■ Student Learning Pages 3.A–3.B ■ 1 map of your state ■ 1 U.S. map ■ 1 globe ■ 1 world map ■ tape ■ 1 sheet construction paper ■ 1 pair scissors

VOCABULARY

URBAN relating to the area made up of a city and the regions close to the city

RURAL relating to the area away from the city where people live in smaller towns and on farms

SUBURBS areas that are near the city but not part of the city

GLOBE a round model of Earth

CONTINENTS the different landmasses on Earth

NORTH POLE the farthest northern point on Earth

SOUTH POLE the farthest southern point on Earth

EQUATOR an imagined circle around Earth that is an equal distance from the North Pole and the South Pole

Let's Begin

1 **EXPLAIN** Explain that there are communities all across the United States and around the world. Communities have many things in common. All communities are places where different types of people work, live, play, and learn together. But communities are also different from each other. The differences make every community special and unique. Have your student identify a few things that make his or her community special.

2 **DISCUSS** Point out that how we describe a community depends on what we are comparing it to. Have your student suppose that he or she is from Bally, a town in Pennsylvania with about 1,000 people. Point out that if he or she went on a vacation to Salt Lake City, Utah, which has more than 170,000 people, Salt Lake City would seem like a large community. But to someone from

Los Angeles, California, where more than 3 million people live, Salt Lake City would seem small. Have your student research the number of people who live in your community. Ask, *Do you think your community is large or small? Why?*

3 **USE A MAP** Explain that maps can help tell us the size of a community. Often a city's name is printed in small letters if it has a small population and in big letters if it has a big population. Help your student find his or her community on a map. Show the student that the map shows us where different communities are located as well as about how many people live in that community. Have the student create a list of or point out communities that are bigger and smaller than his or her community.

4 **DEFINE** Explain that many communities can be described as either **urban** or **rural.** Urban communities are made up of a city and the neighborhoods around the city. Urban communities have a lot of people and the buildings are close together. In rural communities, the towns and buildings are spread out and less people live in a larger area of land. Most rural communities in the United States are close to farmland. Show your student these three photos.

Minneapolis, Minnesota, is an urban community.

These rolling hills are part of a rural community in Tennessee.

Many people enjoy living in the suburbs.

Explain that some communities are described as being **suburbs.** A suburb is an area that is near a city but not part of the city. It's not as far from a city as rural areas. Ask your student if he or she would consider your community urban, rural, or suburban.

5 **DESCRIBE** Explain further the differences between urban and rural communities. Explain that Chicago, Illinois, is an urban community. More than 3 million people live in the city of Chicago. There are more than 600 schools there. Many people work in tall office buildings. In comparison, Cissna Park is a rural town in central Illinois where 800 people live. Many people there work on farms. Ask, *Which community has more people, an urban community or a rural community?* [urban]

6 **SHOW AND DISCUSS** Show your student that the location of a community is part of what makes the community special. A community's location influences the types of jobs people have and what they do for fun. Have your student find Boulder, Colorado, on the map. Point out that the foothills of the Rocky Mountains are close to Boulder. Many people who live there have fun hiking in the mountains. Then have your student locate New York City. Explain that there are many restaurants and theaters in New York City, so a lot of people there have fun going to see plays and dining out. Next have your student find Clearwater Beach, Florida, on the map. Ask, *What do you think people do for fun in Clearwater Beach?* [swim, go to the beach] *What about in your community?*

7 **EXPLORING DIFFERENCES** Explain to your student that different kinds of communities need different types of transportation. In an urban community people drive cars, but people also use trains, buses, subways, and taxis to get around the city. Because places are close together, people in urban areas can easily walk to stores and restaurants. In a rural community places are spread farther apart. People need to use cars to travel around their community. It may be more difficult for someone in a rural community to walk to a store or restaurant because his or her house may be far away from the places he or she wants to go. Ask your student to make a list of or discuss the kinds of transportation people use in his or her community.

8 **DISCUSS** Discuss with your student the fact that every community has some difficulties and problems. In an urban community there are a lot of people living close together. When all these people are traveling to and from work in their cars, the highways and streets get very crowded, causing traffic jams. The exhaust from so many cars also causes air pollution. In rural communities there are different problems. For example, if the plants and crops don't grow in a rural farming community, then the farming families won't have anything to sell to make money. Have your student investigate some things that people in cities can do to prevent air pollution. Discuss. [carpooling, using public transportation, walking, riding bikes]

9 **SHOW AND TELL** Show your student a **globe.** Explain that a globe is a round model of Earth. Then show your student a map of the world. Together locate the seven **continents** and the oceans on both the globe and the map. A globe shows us the sizes and shapes of the land and water on Earth in visually accurate scale. Ask, *What is the same about the globe and the map?* [both show all the continents and the oceans] *What is different about the globe and the map?* [the map is flat and shows distorted shapes and sizes; the sizes and shapes of the land and water are more accurate on the globe] Then point out the **North Pole** and the **South Pole** on the globe. Explain that the North Pole is the northernmost point on Earth and the South Pole is the southernmost point on Earth.

(?)

DID YOU KNOW?

Cars are a major source of air pollution. People can help reduce air pollution by buying a vehicle that gets good gas mileage, keeping tires inflated, not overfilling your gas tank, and keeping your air-conditioning system free of leaks.

10 **CONNECT** Twirl the globe and point to a place on it. Discuss with your student the environment, weather, culture, customs, and people of the place you pointed to. Get books or tourist information about that area. In your discussion, make connections to the similarities of this area to your community.

11 **IDENTIFY** Point out the **equator** to your student. Tell your student that the equator circles all the way around Earth at an equal distance between the North Pole and the South Pole. If we looked at a photograph of Earth, we would not see the equator. The equator divides the globe into two halves: the northern half and the southern half. Have your student use the globe to identify three countries in the northern half of Earth [possible answers include the United States, Mexico, and Spain] and three countries in the southern half of Earth [possible answers include Australia, Peru, and Zimbabwe].

12 **DISCUSS** Reveal that Earth's climate changes the farther away from the equator one gets. Share that it's very hot at or near the equator. Countries such as Brazil and Kenya are on the equator. Explain that countries that are far away from the equator, such as Russia and Canada, can be very cold. Identify these places on the globe. Together discuss what your student knows about these places.

Branching Out

TEACHING TIP

When your student researches information using the Internet, remember that there are sites that may be inappropriate for children. Be sure to pay close attention to what information your student is getting. You may also want to review it to make sure that it's age appropriate.

CHECKING IN

You can assess your student's ability to compare and contrast communities by having him or her describe what kind of community he or she would most like to live in and why.

FOR FURTHER READING

America's Top 10 Cities, by Jenny E. Tesar (Blackbirch Marketing, 1998).

I Live on a Farm, by Stasia Ward Kehoe (PowerKids Press, 1999).

Compare Communities

Use this newspaper page to write a short story about Sandra and Justin and their communities. Sandra is nine years old and lives in the city. Justin is eight and lives on a farm.

In the City	On the Farm
Sandra	Justin

What's Next? You Decide!

Now it's your turn to choose what to do next in the lesson. Read the activities and decide which one you want to do—you may want to try them both!

Illustrate What You've Learned

MATERIALS

❑ 1 sheet construction paper
❑ crayons or markers

STEPS

Create a picture of all the things you've learned about urban and rural communities.

❑ Take a sheet of construction paper and fold it in half.
❑ Title one side "urban" and the other side "rural."
❑ Use your markers and crayons to draw what an urban community looks like.
❑ Then use your markers and crayons to draw what a rural community looks like.
❑ What are the differences? What are the similarities?

Play Globe Hunt

MATERIALS

❑ 1 globe
❑ at least 10 paper strips
❑ 1 hat or bowl

STEPS

❑ Cut five strips of paper for each player.
❑ Have the players think of five different countries, continents, or oceans and write each on a separate strip of paper. Make sure they fold the strips of paper so no one can see what they wrote.
❑ Put all the papers in a hat.
❑ Players take turns picking a strip of paper and trying to find the place on the globe.
❑ After a player finds the place, he or she should point out if the place is on the northern or the southern half of the globe.

Exploring U.S. Geography

The regions of land of the United States are just as varied as its inhabitants.

OBJECTIVE	BACKGROUND	MATERIALS
To help your student become familiar with the geography of the United States	The geography of the United States is very interesting. It includes a variety of landforms, bodies of water, and climates. In this lesson, your student will learn about the various landforms and regions of the United States.	■ Student Learning Pages 4.A–4.B ■ 1 U.S. map ■ 1 North America map ■ crayons or colored pencils

VOCABULARY
COUNTRY the land and the people of a particular area
OCEAN a large body of salt water
LAKE a large body of freshwater
RIVER a stream of moving water
MOUNTAIN raised land that's higher than a hill
HILL a usually rounded height of land smaller than a mountain
PLAIN an area of flat land without trees
PLATEAU a flat area of land that is higher than the land around it
DESERT dry land with few plants and little rainfall
CLIMATE the average weather conditions of an area over a long period of time
LANDFORM MAP a map that shows the natural features of the land's surface

Let's Begin

1 **DISCUSS AND LABEL** Explain to your student that each state may differ in its appearance. For example, some states have mountains while others do not. Then explain that the United States is made up of 50 states. Show your student a map of the United States. Help your student locate his or her state on the map. Distribute Student Learning Page 4.A and have your student turn the page 90 degrees so that the map is easy to read. Then have him or her color his or her state red. Then have him or her color the rest of the states green.

Show your student a map of North America. Point out Canada and Mexico. Explain that Canada is a **country** that is close to the United States and that Mexico is another. Ask, *Which country is north of the United States?* [Canada] *Which country is south of the United States?* [Mexico]

2 **DEFINE AND COLOR** Tell your student that an **ocean** is a large body of salt water, a **lake** is a large body of freshwater, and a **river** is a stream of moving water. Help your student locate the Atlantic and Pacific Oceans, the Great Lakes, and the Mississippi River on the U.S. map. Have your student color in blue the Atlantic and Pacific Oceans, the Great Lakes, and the Mississippi River on Student Learning Page 4.A.

3 **LOCATE LANDFORMS** Inform your student that a **mountain** is raised land that is higher than a hill. A **hill** is a rounded height of land that is smaller than a mountain. A **plain** is a flat area of land without trees. A **plateau** is an area of flat land higher than the land around it. A **desert** is an area of dry land with few plants and little rain. Help your student locate the Rocky Mountains and the Sonora Desert on the U.S. map. Have him or her color them brown on Student Learning Page 4.A.

The Rocky Mountains are in Colorado.

The Great Plains are located in the central part of the United States.

4 **DESCRIBE** Tell your student that **climate** is the average weather conditions of an area. Climates can be hot, cold, warm, dry, or rainy. The climate and geography of an area affect the clothes people wear and the things they do for fun. Ask, *What is your climate like? What do people wear? What do they do for fun?*

FOR FURTHER READING

Bill Nye the Science Guy's Big Blue Ocean, by Bill Nye, Ian Saunders, and John S. Dykes (Disney Press, 1999).

Destination: Rocky Mountains, by Jonathan Grupper (National Geographic Society, 2001).

Geography Inside Out, by Richard Symanski (Syracuse University Press, 2002).

Branching Out

TEACHING TIP

Read the weather section of the newspaper with your student. Note the different climates of the United States as you learn about the daily weather.

CHECKING IN

Have your student suppose that he or she was going on a trip across the United States. Ask your student to make a list of the different types of land and water he or she might see.

Explore U.S. Geography

Look at the map. Color your state red. Color the rest of the states green. Then color the oceans blue.

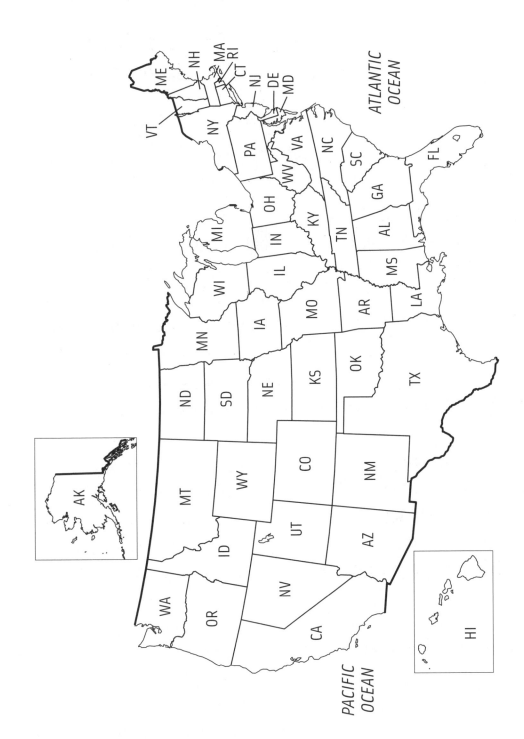

What's Next? You Decide!

Now it's your turn to choose what to do next in the lesson. Read the activities and decide which one you want to do—you may want to try them both!

Write a Letter

MATERIALS

❏ 1 stamp
❏ 1 envelope

STEPS

Get more information and practice writing a letter! You can learn a lot about a state by writing a letter to the state's Visitor Information Center.

❏ Choose a state that interests you.
❏ Write a letter to the visitor information center of that state asking for information on that state.
❏ You'll have fun seeing pictures and reading interesting facts about the state that you chose.
❏ You may have to ask an adult to help you mail your letter.

Speak a Different Language

MATERIALS

❏ construction paper
❏ markers or crayons
❏ 1 pair scissors

STEPS

In our neighboring countries, the people speak different languages. Many people in Canada speak French and people in Mexico speak Spanish.

❏ Imagine you are traveling to Mexico or to a part of Canada that speaks French.
❏ Go to the library or look on the Internet to find out how to say *hello, goodbye, please,* and *thank you* in Spanish and French.
❏ Cut out note cards from the construction paper.
❏ Write your words on note cards.
❏ Decorate each note card.

Recognizing the Natural Resources of the United States

People's lives are shaped by the natural resources available to them.

OBJECTIVE	BACKGROUND	MATERIALS
To help your student identify natural resources and why they are important	Where people live and what they do depend on the natural resources available to them. The United States has many kinds of natural resources. In this lesson, your student will learn what natural resources are available in the United States and why natural resources are important.	■ Student Learning Pages 5.A–5.B ■ newspaper articles about natural resources ■ colored pencils

VOCABULARY

NATURAL RESOURCES things in the environment that people can use

NATURAL GAS a kind of gas found deep underground that is used for heating fuel

MINERALS nonliving substances found in the earth such as iron, salt, or diamonds

FUEL something that can be burned to supply heat or power

RECYCLE to use something over again

Let's Begin

1 **EXPLAIN** Explain to your student that **natural resources** are things from nature that people need or use. Air, water, forests, oil, coal, **natural gas,** and **minerals** are all natural resources. Some natural resources are important for survival, such as air, water, and soil. Other natural resources are important because of their usefulness. For example, trees are used for several things. Trees are used as wood for building, as **fuel** for heating, and for making paper. Ask, *What are some ways that water is useful?* [for drinking, growing plants, transporting, cooking, and washing]

2 **DISCUSS** Discuss with your student natural resources. If you'd like, have him or her make a list of natural resources. Encourage him or her to think about how people use each of the resources you discuss. Then review the newspaper articles on natural

Trucks carry logs to their destination.

resources with your student. Talk with him or her about what resources contributed to what he or she is wearing or ate for breakfast.

3 **RELATE** Explain that the United States has more natural resources than most other countries in the world. However, the resources are not distributed equally throughout the country. For example, some areas have large forests, while others have good soil for farming. Some areas have minerals, such as iron or coal, while others have rivers or seas for shipping and fishing. Have your student think about the natural resources available in his or her area. Then draw a map together.

4 **DISTRIBUTE AND IDENTIFY** Distribute Student Learning Page 5.A. Ask, *What does this map show?* [some resources that the United States has and where they are located] Direct your student to point to the map key. Ask, *What is the purpose of a map key?* [It tells what the symbols on the map represent] Ask, *What do the squares represent?* [iron] *What do the triangles represent?* [forests] *What do the circles represent?* [oil] Have your student color the triangles green, the circles red, and the squares blue. Remind him or her to color the symbols on the key as well. Ask, *Which of these resources does Alaska have?* [forests and oil] *South Dakota?* [iron] Then have your student point to his or her state and tell which of these resources, if any, his or her state has.

5 **EXPLAIN AND DISCUSS** Explain to your student that protecting natural resources is important. One way people help to protect natural resources is by replacing them. Planting a tree is an example of replacing a natural resource. Another way to protect natural resources is by recycling. To **recycle** is to use something over again. Discuss with your student what his or her community does to protect its natural resources.

📖
FOR FURTHER READING

Earth Day: Keeping Our Planet Clean, by Elaine Landau (Enslow Publishers, Inc., 2002).

A River Ran Wild: An Environmental History, (Read Rainbow Book) by Lynne Cherry (Voyager Books, reprinted 2002).

Sharing Nature with Children, by Joseph Cornell (Dawn Publications, 1998).

Branching Out

TEACHING TIP

Help your student make the connection between the abundance of natural resources in the United States and the country's quality of living. Point out that the United States is able to grow more food than any other country because of its good soil. Also, because the United States has an abundance of rivers and lakes, people have enough water to drink.

CHECKING IN

Assess your student's understanding of natural resources and their importance by having him or her draw a picture that illustrates how people use at least three natural resources.

Use a Map Key and Symbols

Read this map to find out which states have forests, oil, and iron. Use the map key and symbols to help you.

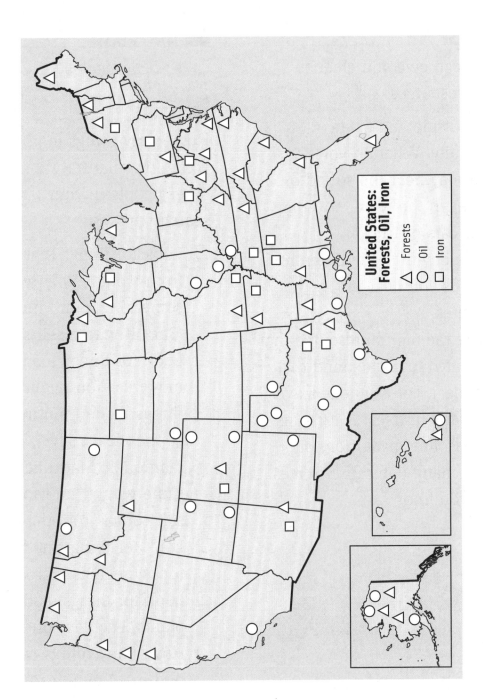

United States:
Forests, Oil, Iron

◁ Forests
○ Oil
□ Iron

What's Next? You Decide!

Now it's your turn to choose what to do next in the lesson. Read the activities and decide which one you want to do—you may want to try them both!

Listen for Clues

STEPS

Sounds can give you clues to natural resources.

❏ Go outside and listen carefully. What do you hear? You may hear the sound of leaves in the wind. You may hear cars or trucks.

❏ Write down all the different sounds you hear in five minutes.

❏ Write the natural resource that is related to each sound that you hear. For example, leaves are parts of trees. A car runs on gasoline made from oil.

❏ How many natural resources did you find?

Lead a Resource Hunt

MATERIALS

❏ self-stick notes

STEPS

How many things in your home come from natural resources? Ask other people in your family to search with you.

❏ Look for things that are made from wood. When you find something, don't move it. Mark it with a self-stick note.

❏ Look for things made from minerals. You might find things made from iron, copper, lead, silver, gold, or diamonds. Mark them in the same way. (Don't forget that salt comes from the earth!)

❏ Look for things made from rocks, such as marble.

❏ Look for things made from plants, such as cotton.

❏ How many things can you find in 10 minutes? Share what you find with others.

Recognizing the Features of a Community

A community's success depends on the contributions of the people who live in it.

OBJECTIVE	BACKGROUND	MATERIALS
To help your student identify the features of past and present communities	Two hundred years ago, travel and long-distance communication were limited and communities were isolated from each other. Today, new ways of travel and communication have brought communities together. In this lesson, your student will learn about the features of a community and how these features have changed over time into the communities we know today.	▪ Student Learning Pages 6.A–6.B ▪ 1 present-day U.S. road map ▪ 1 copy major newspaper ▪ 1 copy Web, page 354 ▪ 1 copy Sequence Chain, page 354

VOCABULARY

TRANSPORTATION a way of moving people or goods from one place to another

TECHNOLOGY the use of new tools and ideas to solve problems

COMMUNICATE to exchange information by talking, signaling, or writing

TELEGRAPH a machine that sends coded words long distances over electrical wires

CONSUMERS people who buy goods or services

EMPLOYER the person in a business who hires people to do work

MANUFACTURE to make raw material into useful products using machines or human labor

ASSEMBLY LINE a sequence of workers and machines a product passes through from start to finish

TRADE the buying and selling of goods between communities or countries

Let's Begin

1 **EXPLAIN** Explain that before the early 1800s, traveling from one community to another in the United States was difficult and time-consuming. There were no paved roads like the ones we have today, only rough paths and trails. Most of the time people walked from one place to another. To travel long distances, people rode horses or mules, or used animal-drawn wagons. If they could, they traveled by water in boats and canoes. If you'd like, tell a story about what a child in the 1800s saw as changes in his or her life. Ask, *How would your life be different if you had to travel the way people did before 1800?* [would have to

walk to school or ride a horse; couldn't visit friends and relatives, vacation in distant places, or travel to buy things]

2 **RELATE** Explain that in the 1800s **transportation** improved. In the early 1800s, people began to build roads. The busiest road was the National Road, completed in 1839. It was about 575 miles long and ran from Baltimore, Maryland, to near St. Louis, Missouri. **Technology** also improved travel. Robert Fulton introduced his steamboat, the *Clermont,* in 1807. For the first time, boats could move up rivers easily. By the 1820s, steam engines were used to power railroad trains as well. Railroads began to crisscross the country. Ask, *Why would a community in the 1800s want a railroad nearby?* [railroads made it easier for people to travel and get supplies from other places]

3 **EXPAND** Tell your student that in the early 1900s two inventions changed the way people traveled. Henry Ford invented an affordable car in 1908 called the Model T. Many people bought cars and were able to travel wherever they wanted—and get there relatively quickly. At about the same time, Orville and Wilbur Wright made the world's first successful airplane flight. Throughout the 1900s, technology changed and improved these two inventions. Point out that today people can even travel in space! We drive cars every day on a huge network of wide, smooth roads and interstate highways. Together with your student, brainstorm about how people might travel from place to place in the future.

4 **DISTRIBUTE AND IDENTIFY** Distribute Student Learning Page 6.A and a current U.S. road map to your student. Together, look at the road map. Ask, *What type of map is this?* [transportation map] *What does it show?* [routes people use to travel from place to place] Review the map with your student. Then direct him or her to use it to answer the questions.

5 **EXPLAIN AND DISCUSS** Point out that people need to be able to **communicate** as well as travel between places. Before the 1800s, people communicated through newspapers or listened to town criers shout the news from the town square. In the 1800s, communities that were far apart began to communicate by mail. In 1860, a service called the Pony Express began. It used horseback riders in the western United States who were like a relay team delivering mail. Each rider would hand the mail off to the next rider all along the route. Research with your student the Pony Express and how it worked. Discuss how the Pony Express compares with the way mail is transported and delivered today.

6 **REVEAL** Explain that in 1844 communication improved when a machine called the **telegraph** was invented. Samuel Morse used a special code—Morse code—to send words over electrical wires. Communities that were far apart could now get messages from each other in minutes. People still use Morse code today. Show your student the example of Morse code on the right. Then have him or her read more about Morse code and compare how it was used in 1844 to how it's used today.

7   **EXPAND** Point out that in 1876 Alexander Graham Bell further changed the way people communicated when he invented the first telephone. People were able to talk to each other over long distances directly through wires. In 1895, an Italian inventor named Guglielmo Marconi invented the wireless telegraph. Later, this technology was used to invent the radio. Have your student read more about the invention of the wireless telegraph and the radio and how they affected the speed and distance at which people were able to communicate. Then have your student look in the newspaper for a news story about a distant country. Ask, *If we did not have radios, telephones, or telegraphs, how would we find out about this news? How long would it take?* [we might never find out about it or it could take months for a traveler to relay the news to us]

```
• • • •  = H
•        = E
• — • •  = L
• — • •  = L
— — —    = O
```

8   **RELATE** Mention that technology has given us many new ways to communicate. Most people today have televisions and radios in their homes. People also use computers and the Internet to send and receive mail and search for information. We also use cellular phones, pagers, and fax machines. Ask, *How have these new ways of communicating helped our communities?* [it's easier to contact other communities and learn about different cultures and ideas; businesses can work faster and solve problems more easily]

9   **INTRODUCE AND WRITE** Remind your student that travel in the past was difficult, so most people stayed in their own communities. Explain that since travel was difficult people had to make or grow everything they needed to survive. Today, most people work at jobs to earn money that they use to buy food and goods. They pay for a place to live and the services they need, such as those from doctors or plumbers. When people live this way, they are called **consumers.** Have your student make a list of survival needs and other things that he or she would like to buy. Then have him or her prioritize the list in order of importance, noting the difference between needs and wants.

10   **EXPLAIN AND RESEARCH** Explain that most people work for an **employer,** or someone who owns a business. Some people like to work for employers who need them to make things, such as cars or furniture. Others like jobs that provide a service, such as taking care of people at a hospital. Still others enjoy selling goods such as groceries or clothes. Some people work at home making their own products or using computers. All these workers spend the money that they make from their job to buy things from businesses and stores in their community. The money they spend helps their community grow. Have your student research several jobs that he or she finds interesting.

Help your student choose two or three jobs that he or she would enjoy the most and write a few sentences describing each one.

11   **REVIEW** Remind your student that natural resources are material that we get from Earth. Some people's jobs have to do with turning natural resources into products that we can use. Ask your student to write a list of natural resources in his or her notebook. Your student can review Lesson 4.5 for ideas.

12   **RESEARCH AND DISTRIBUTE** Explain to your student that some businesses in a community **manufacture** products in factories. Many factories have an **assembly line** where each worker or machine completes a part of the product and passes it along until the product is finished. Assembly lines employ a lot of people. Other jobs in manufacturing include product design, engineering, shipping, and sales. Have your student research an example of a product that is made on an assembly line and try to find an illustration of how the product is made. Then have your student use a copy of the Sequence Chain found on page 354 to show the steps of the assembly-line process. You also can have your student make an art project or sandwiches for a crowd using a hands-on assembly line.

13   **RELATE** Explain to your student that communities depend on each other for **trade.** They buy and sell each other's goods and services. A community in California might sell oranges to a community in Wisconsin. A community in Nevada might buy lumber from a company in Oregon. Communities in the United States also trade with other communities all over the world. Ask, *What products or foods does your family buy that are from another state or country?* [oranges from Florida, bananas from Brazil, electronics from Asia, spices from India, and so on] Also, clothes tags indicate where they are manufactured.

DID YOU KNOW?

The name piggy bank has nothing to do with pigs! People in Scotland used to store their money in jars made from a kind of clay called pygg. People called the jars pyggy banks. They weren't shaped like pigs until much later.

Branching Out

TEACHING TIP

As you talk about the different methods of transportation and communication, ask your student to express his or her ideas and feelings about what life was like in communities of the past compared to communities today.

CHECKING IN

You can assess your student's understanding of the features of a community and how they have changed by having him or her create a time line. Using the information in the lesson and your student's own research, have him or her include important events and changes in transportation, communication, the way people work, and what they do.

FOR FURTHER READING

Model T: How Henry Ford Built a Legend, by David Weitzman (Crown Publishing, 2002).

Odd Jobs, by Ellen Weiss and Damon Ross, photographer (Alladin Paperbacks, 2000).

Radio Rescue, by Lynne Barasch (Frances Foster Books, 2000).

Read a Road Map

Look at a present-day U.S. road map. Read each question.
Then write the answer.

1. Your family is driving from Cleveland, Ohio, to
   Columbia, South Carolina. What one interstate
   highway could you take? _____

2. Your family is driving from Albuquerque, New
   Mexico, to Tulsa, Oklahoma. What states will you
   drive through if you take Interstate Highway 40?

   _____

3. Your family is driving from Seattle, Washington, to
   Denver, Colorado. What interstate highways could
   you take? _____

4. Your family is driving from Maine to New York. What
   states will you drive through? _____

5. Which interstate highway is the shortest route from
   Kansas City, Missouri, to St. Louis, Missouri?

   _____

What's Next? You Decide!

Now it's your turn to choose what to do next in the lesson. Read the activities and decide which one you want to do—you may want to try them both!

Make Your Own Map

MATERIALS

❏ 1 posterboard
❏ 1 map of your town
❏ 1 ruler
❏ colored pencils or markers

STEPS

How do you get from one place to another every day? Make yourself a map!

❏ Find a map of where you live. You can use a road atlas or a map from the telephone book as a guide.
❏ Decide what places and streets you want to show on your map. You can show the way from your home to the library or the way from the park to your friend's house. It's up to you.
❏ Be sure to label all the places and roads on your map and give your map a title.
❏ Share your map with an adult.

Plan Your Own Business

STEPS

Do you have an idea for a business? Maybe you make money now by doing chores, mowing grass, shoveling snow, or selling crafts at a fair. Create a plan to turn your idea into a real business.

❏ Write your ideas in your notebook. Write the tools and materials you need to get started and how much they will cost.
❏ Write who will work with you and when you will do your work.
❏ Be sure to think about who will buy your products or services and how they will find out about your business.
❏ Give your business a name.
❏ Read your business plan to an adult and answer any questions he or she has about your business.

Investigating the Anasazi People

Studying past cultures helps us learn about our own cultures.

OBJECTIVE	BACKGROUND	MATERIALS
To help your student understand the ancient Anasazi communities	Studying the culture and traditions of the Anasazi people teaches us the importance of working together as a community and using Earth's resources respectfully. In this lesson, your student will learn to recognize the importance of Native Americans to the history of the United States.	<ul><li>Student Learning Pages 7.A–7.B</li><li>1 map Colorado</li><li>books about Anasazi or Pueblo pottery</li><li>air-dry clay</li><li>paint</li></ul>

VOCABULARY

MESAS   tablelike landforms with steep sides and flat tops

KIVAS   round, underground rooms used for religious gatherings

SIPAPU   a small hole dug in the ground and believed to be a passageway to the spirit world

DROUGHT   a long time with little or no rain when the land becomes very dry

Let's Begin

1   **EXPLAIN** Explain that before Europeans arrived in America there were already groups of people living in communities across what is now the United States. These people are called Native Americans. One of these groups was the Anasazi. They lived in the southwestern part of what we now call Colorado between the years 1100 to 1300 A.D. The place they lived is called Mesa Verde, which means "green table" in Spanish. Have your student locate Mesa Verde, Colorado, on a map.

2   **REVEAL** Point out that Mesa Verde has a hot and dry desert climate with many cliffs and **mesas.** The Anasazi are often called cliff dwellers because they built their homes into the sides of the steep cliffs. Their homes had many small rooms and were built very close together. They used ladders and steps that they had carved into the rocks to climb to the tops of the mesas. The cliffs gave the Anasazi protection from harsh weather and enemies. Ask, *What kinds of landforms are there in southwestern United States?* [cliffs and mesas]

Anasazi cliff dwellings at Mesa Verde

3 **EXPAND** Explain that the Anasazi planted crops on the mesas. There was very little water in the desert, so the Anasazi collected and conserved water. They grew beans, squash, and corn and raised turkeys. They relied on other resources from the desert such as the yucca plant to make clothes, sandals, bedding, and baskets. The Anasazi also made pottery. Everyone in the Anasazi community worked together. Because they lived in harmony with Earth and each other, the Anasazi were able to survive in the challenging desert environment. Make a meal with your student using the foods that the Anasazi used. Discuss what it would have been like to live as the Anasazi did.

4 **RELATE** Explain that in the Anasazi community everyone contributed through work. The families also shared their food with each other. Ask, *What are some of the ways your family and community work together?*

5 **DISCUSS** Point out that religion was important in Anasazi culture. The Anasazi built **kivas,** which were round, underground rooms with wall paintings where people gathered and heard stories. There were many kivas in each community. The men used the kivas the most, but the women used them, too. The Anasazi believed that they came to Earth through special holes in the ground. Every kiva had one of these holes, called a **sipapu.** They also held religious ceremonies and dances outside to celebrate and give thanks for good crops. Discuss with your student some of the things your family or community does to honor your beliefs and to celebrate.

6 **EXPLAIN AND DISTRIBUTE** Mention that the Anasazi left Mesa Verde between 1300 and 1450, but we aren't sure why. Scientists hypothesize that they may have left due to **drought** or were forced to leave by another Native American group. The Pueblo people who live in the southwest today are their descendents. Distribute Student Learning Page 7.A.

Branching Out

FOR FURTHER READING

Anasazi (Ancient Civilizations), by Timothy Larson and Christy Steele (Raintree/Steck Vaughn, 2001).

The Anasazi, by David Petersen (Scholastic Library Publishing, 1998).

TEACHING TIP

You can see photos of the cliff dwellings and find out about Anasazi history in Mesa Verde at http://www.mesa.verde.national-park.com.

CHECKING IN

You can assess your student's understanding of the Anasazi by having him or her give you an oral overview of Anasazi culture and daily life. Ask leading questions such as *What was important to the Anasazi?* [community, religion, safety]

Read and Write About the Anasazi

Become a reporter. Travel back in time to spend a day with the Anasazi. Write a short news story about what you saw and learned on your trip.

_____

_____

_____

_____

_____

_____

_____

_____

_____

_____

Look at a book of Anasazi or Pueblo pottery. Notice the designs on the pottery. Draw a pottery design of your own on a separate sheet of paper. If you like, use air-dry clay to make a small pinch pot. Let it dry. Then color your design on it with paint or markers.

Like the Anasazi, the Pueblo people are excellent potters.

What's Next? You Decide!

Now it's your turn to choose what to do next in the lesson. Read the activities and decide which one you want to do—you may want to try them both!

Make a Book

MATERIALS

- ❏ 1 sheet construction paper
- ❏ 1 stapler
- ❏ 1 sheet blank white paper
- ❏ markers, crayons, or colored pencils

STEPS

- ❏ Fold a sheet of construction paper and a sheet of blank white paper in half.
- ❏ Staple the white paper to the construction paper at the crease so that the construction paper is like a cover for the white paper. This will give your book four white pages.
- ❏ On the bottom of the first page write, "The Anasazi lived in the southwestern United States in Mesa Verde, Colorado."
- ❏ On page 2 write, "They built houses into the sides of cliffs."
- ❏ On page 3 write, "They farmed beans, squash, and corn and raised turkeys in the desert."
- ❏ On page 4 write, "Everyone worked together."
- ❏ Draw pictures on your book's pages.
- ❏ Then write a title for your book on the cover and decorate it.
- ❏ Share your book with your friends and family!

Find Out About Other Native Americans

STEPS

Besides the Anasazi there are other groups of Native Americans who lived in the United States.

- ❏ Look for books at the library or Internet sites about another Native American community, such as the Navajo, Hopi, Lakota, or Cheyenne.
- ❏ Read about them. Then write a paragraph telling how they are similar to and different from the Anasazi.
- ❏ Also write about what Native American communities teach us about life.

Understanding Jamestown

The land and the people together make a community.

OBJECTIVE	BACKGROUND	MATERIALS
To help your student learn about the settlement and people of Jamestown, Virginia	In England, stories about finding gold and riches in America from the Spanish encouraged the English to come to America. As the first English settlement in North America, Jamestown offered protection from enemies and natural resources that provided shelter and food. In this lesson, your student will learn about the English colony at Jamestown, Virginia.	■ Student Learning Pages 8.A–8.B ■ 1 map United States ■ 1 copy Web, page 354

Let's Begin

1 **EXPLAIN** Explain that prior to English colonists' arrival, Native Americans lived in the area known as Virginia. The first English settlers arrived in 1607. They named the area Jamestown after King James. Use a map of the United States to locate Jamestown, Virginia, and the Chesapeake Bay. Ask, *Why do you think English colonists settled in this area?* [it's surrounded by water, easy to see enemies coming, good location for food] Point out that this area has flat lands along the coast and forests.

2 **RELATE** Mention that the Powhatan were Native Americans who had lived in the Chesapeake area for more than 300 years. They learned to use the available natural resources for food, shelter, and transportation. Some were farmers who grew corn, beans, and squash, while others hunted deer and other animals or fished. They learned to preserve their food by drying meat and fish and storing nuts. They made their homes, canoes, bows, and arrows from pine trees. They learned to live with the colonists but often battled over land rights. Ask, *How do you think the Powhatan felt having to battle over land? Why do you think this?*

3 **DISCUSS** Point out that most of the English men who came to Jamestown were not farmers or hunters. Explain that many died from starvation or disease during the first few years. Discuss with your student how the English men might have prepared for the new land. [learned about its weather and food]

ENRICH THE EXPERIENCE

Suggest that your student make a time line of important facts and people of Jamestown. During the lesson, have your student add to his or her time line as he or she discovers additional facts.

4 **RELATE** Mention that the leader of the group, John Smith, organized the colonists to build houses and plant crops. He also made two important decisions. The first decision was to establish a rule that if the colonists worked, then they would eat. The second was to befriend Powhatan, the leader of the Powhatan people. The Powhatan helped the colonists learn how to plant corn, hunt animals, and fish. Ask, *Why were John Smith's decisions good ones? How would you react to the "no work, no food" rule? What would you do?*

5 **EXPLAIN** Mention that despite the many hardships the colonists faced, some good things happened, too. For example, in 1608 they made enough soap, glass, and tar to send some back to England. Also, John Rolfe, a farmer, developed and grew a special tobacco and in 1612 was able to send it back to England for money. Rolfe also helped keep peace with the Powhatan by marrying Powhatan's daughter, Pocahontas, in 1614. Ask, *Why else do you think the marriage between John Rolfe and Pocahontas was important?* [it showed the two groups could learn to get along and like each other]

John Rolfe helped keep peace with the Powhatan by marrying Pocahontas.

6 **DISCUSS AND SUMMARIZE** Mention that the English brought Africans to the new land to work as slaves. As a result of their hard work, Jamestown grew. More settlers from England arrived and set up colonies along the Atlantic coast. They came for a number of reasons: riches, religious freedom, and for the challenge of starting new lives in new land. In all, 13 colonies were established. These colonies formed the beginnings of the United States. Have your student verbally summarize the events of Jamestown from 1607 through 1614. Then distribute Student Learning Page 8.A and have your student apply what he or she has learned about Jamestown.

7 **PRACTICE** Distribute Student Learning Page 8.B. Have your student choose activities to complete to expand his or her knowledge about Jamestown.

FOR FURTHER READING

The Double Life of Pocahontas, by Jean Fritz and Ed Young, ill. (Penguin Putnam Publishing, 2002).

Elizabeth's Jamestown Colony Diaries: Book One, by Patricia Hermes (Scholastic, Inc., 2002).

Jamestown: New World Adventure, by James E. Knight and David T. Wenzel, ill. (Troll Communications L.L.C., 1998).

Branching Out

TEACHING TIP

Periodically, use a map of the United States and your student's time line to help your student get a sense of the location of the first settlement and the events that happened during the early years.

CHECKING IN

Assess your student's understanding of Jamestown by having him or her complete a copy of the Web found on page 354 about Jamestown.

Draw Jamestown

Use the Internet or books to find pictures or a written description of the Jamestown settlement. Then draw a picture of the Jamestown settlement. What types of buildings made up the settlement? What did the colonists look like? Then in your notebook, write a paragraph describing your drawing.

What's Next? You Decide!

Now it's your turn to choose what to do next in the lesson. Read the activities and decide which one you want to do—you may want to try them both!

Discover Important People of Jamestown

MATERIALS

- ❑ drawing paper
- ❑ crayons or markers
- ❑ fasteners or ribbons

STEPS

- ❑ Use books or the Internet to learn more about John Smith, Pocahontas, Powhatan, and John Rolfe.

- ❑ Write a report that tells about one of these people and explains his or her importance in the Jamestown settlement. You may wish to draw a picture of the person.

- ❑ Put together your report into a booklet with fasteners or ribbons.

- ❑ Give your booklet a title and design a cover.

Write a Letter

STEPS

Suppose you're a member of one of the families that settled in Jamestown, Virginia, in 1612, five years after the first settlers had arrived.

- ❑ Write a letter to a friend back in England telling about your new life in Jamestown.

- ❑ Use these topics to help you get started:
  - Description of home
  - Description of daily life: work, play, school
  - Description of people in and around Jamestown settlement

- ❑ Share your letter with another person.

Exploring a Spanish Mission

The influence of one culture can cause another culture to disappear.

OBJECTIVE	BACKGROUND	MATERIALS
To show your student how events in a community's past can shape the present	Today, San Antonio is a metropolitan area with a population of more than a million people. In the past, the area was home to groups of Native Americans who lived along the San Antonio River. The lives of these people—and the area's cultural heritage—changed when Spanish missionaries arrived in the 1700s. In this lesson, your student will learn about early Spanish missions in San Antonio and their effect on the community.	<ul><li>Student Learning Pages 9.A–9.B</li><li>1 map Texas</li><li>1 copy Venn Diagram, page 353</li></ul>

VOCABULARY

MISSIONS communities or settlements built by missionaries

MISSIONARIES people who teach others about their religion

INDEPENDENCE freedom

ARCHAEOLOGISTS scientists who study what humans have left behind, such as goods and materials

HERITAGE something handed down from the past

FIESTA a celebration in San Antonio; the Spanish word for festival or party is *fiesta*

Let's Begin

1 **INTRODUCE AND IDENTIFY** Explain that today San Antonio is a large city in southcentral Texas. It is built along the San Antonio River. Give your student a map of Texas. Have him or her identify San Antonio on the map. Ask, *What foreign country borders Texas?* [Mexico]

2 **EXPLAIN** Explain that for centuries groups of Native Americans called Coahuiltecan (kwah-weel-TEH-kan) lived along the San Antonio River. Survival was not easy for the Coahuiltecan because food was scarce. In the 1700s, life changed for the Coahuiltecan when Spanish-speaking Roman Catholic priests came from Mexico to set up **missions** (places where the priests could teach others about their religion). These priests were called **missionaries.** In the 1700s, missionaries established five

ENRICH THE EXPERIENCE

Spanish explorers first saw the San Antonio River on June 13, the Catholic holy day of Saint Anthony of Padua. To honor him, they gave the river his Spanish name—San Antonio.

The Alamo is shown here.

I Remember the Alamo,
by D. Anne Love
(Random House
Children's Books,
2001).

*Kid's Guide to Exploring
San Antonio Missions,*
by Mary Maruca
(Western National
Parks Association,
2000).

*The Spanish Missions of
San Antonio,* by Lewis
F. Fisher (Maverick
Publishing Company,
1998).

missions in what is now San Antonio. Ask, *Why do you think the priests wanted to teach others about their religion?* [they wanted them to become Roman Catholics]

3 **RELATE AND RESEARCH** Explain that San Antonio's missions continued to operate for more than one hundred years. During that time, many Native Americans became Catholic and spoke only Spanish. Their own culture began to disappear. In 1836, Texas and Mexico went to war over Texas's **independence.** An important battle took place at a mission known as the Alamo. A Mexican army defeated a small group of Texan fighters, who included Davy Crockett, a celebrated hero of the battle. Yet these Texan fighters helped Texas win independence from Mexico, which happened nine years later. Texas joined the United States in 1845. Have your student research and write about Juan Seguin's and James Bowie's roles in the battle at the Alamo.

4 **EXPLAIN AND DISTRIBUTE** Explain that missions offered Native Americans food and a place to live in exchange for learning the Catholic religion and doing work. Women did spinning and weaving, made pottery and baskets, fished, and cared for children. The men made furniture and tools and did farmwork. The missionaries taught children to read and write Spanish, led prayer meetings, and taught religion. Reveal that a lot of what we know about past peoples comes from looking at things these people may have used at that time, such as clothing and pottery. **Archaeologists** (ar-kee-OLL-o-jists) are scientists who study what humans have left behind, such as goods and materials. Now distribute Student Learning Page 9.A.

5 **EXPLAIN** Relate that presently San Antonio's culture reflects its Spanish **heritage.** Many people who live in the city are Mexican-American. People speak both Spanish and English. All five of the missions still exist. Some are still used as churches. The Alamo has become a museum. Each year the people of San Antonio have **Fiesta,** a weeklong celebration in the Spanish tradition. Make a copy of the Venn Diagram found on page 353. Have your student use it to show the similarities and differences between San Antonio in the 1700s and today.

Branching Out

TEACHING TIP

Find more information about San Antonio missions at http://www.nps.gov/saan.

CHECKING IN

Have your student create a time line using the information in this lesson. Have him or her include important people and events.

Study the Past

You're an archaeologist. You're finding things from the Alamo. Read each question. Then draw the answer.

1. Draw pictures of what the Native Americans might have eaten.

2. Draw pictures of what the Native Americans might have done during the day.

You're an archaeologist in the future. You've just found a piece of clothing from your home. You're from the future so you don't know what it is! Read each question. Then write the answer.

3. Describe the piece of clothing. _____
   _____

4. How do you think people used it? _____
   _____

5. Where did you find the piece of clothing? _____
   _____

6. What clues from where you found it tell you about how it's used?
   _____
   _____

What's Next? You Decide!

Now it's your turn to choose what to do next in the lesson. Read the activities and decide which one you want to do—you may want to try them both!

List Celebrations in Your Community

STEPS

San Antonio has Fiesta. What festivals does your community have? What events do you look forward to?

❑ Make a list of as many events as you can.

❑ Write what each event celebrates.

❑ Ask others in your family to make lists, too.

❑ Then compare lists. Who came up with the longest list?

❑ Then choose the event you like best and circle it.

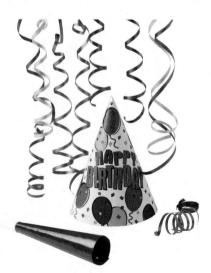

Be a Time Traveler

STEPS

You are a time traveler to the past!

❑ Imagine you have gone to San Antonio in the 1700s.

❑ It's summer and very hot. You are inside the walls of one of the missions. You can look around, but no one can see you! What do you see? What are people doing? How are people keeping cool?

❑ Go inside the church. What does it look like? What does it feel like?

❑ Now it's time to come back to the present. Think about what you saw. Then write a story about your trip. In your story, tell why you would or wouldn't have wanted to live in a mission.

Understanding the Beginnings of the United States

Today is the first day of a new beginning.

OBJECTIVE	BACKGROUND	MATERIALS
To help your student learn how the United States of America came to exist	In the 1700s, 13 English colonies settled along the coast of the Atlantic Ocean and laid the foundation that started the United States. In this lesson, your student will learn how the United States developed.	■ Student Learning Pages 10.A–10.B ■ 1 U.S. map ■ 1 copy Writing Lines, page 355

Let's Begin

1 **DISCUSS** Explain to your student that the United States of America was not a country in the early 1700s. Instead, 13 English colonies made a settlement along the Atlantic coast. Point out to your student the original colonies on a map of the United States. Ask, *How might the location near the ocean have helped the colonies?* [the coast provided ports for trade, more people came to the colonies]

2 **EXPLAIN AND RESEARCH** Explain to your student that once the colonies grew in population and had become successful in farming and trade, they wanted freedom from England. Tell your student that at the time Philadelphia, Pennsylvania, was the largest and the busiest city among the colonies. It was a city that William Penn founded in 1682 for people of all races and religions.

Have your student use the Internet or resource books to learn about Philadelphia in the 1700s. Ask, *Why is Philadelphia an important city of our past?*

3 **DESCRIBE AND RESEARCH** Point out to your student that Ben Franklin moved to Philadelphia when he was 17 years old. He was self-educated, creative, and was an expert printer. He is best known for his *Poor Richard's Almanac,* his inventions, and his role as a statesman. Some of his ideas and inventions include: developing the first lending library, organizing the first volunteer fire department, bifocal reading glasses, and the lightning rod.

DID YOU KNOW?

The 13 English colonies included Massachusetts, New Hampshire, Rhode Island, Connecticut, New York, New Jersey, Delaware, Pennsylvania, Maryland, Virginia, North Carolina, South Carolina, and Georgia. At the time, Maine was part of Massachusetts, and New York and New Hampshire claimed Vermont.

GET ORGANIZED

Suggest that your student begin a time line of important events of the 1700s.

4 **RESEARCH AND WRITE** Distribute Student Learning Page 10.A. Have your student use the Internet or resource books to learn more about Franklin's inventions and his role as a statesman. Ask, *Why were his inventions useful? What was his contribution to uniting the colonies?* Have your student draw a picture of one of his inventions.

5 **RELATE AND CHART** Explain that in the 1770s, when Ben Franklin was in his 60s, he saw his world change. The colonists united to free themselves from England. They wanted to make their own laws and stop paying taxes to England. Fighting among the colonists and the English began in 1775, the beginning of the American Revolution. Have your student use the Internet or resource books to learn more about the American Revolution.

ENRICH THE EXPERIENCE

Have your student add events to his or her time line of the 1700s.

6 **EXPLAIN** Tell your student that to help end the war, the colonists met in Philadelphia. It was in Philadelphia that Thomas Jefferson, a Virginian, wrote the Declaration of Independence. It stated why the colonists should be free. Ben Franklin and 55 other leaders signed and adopted the declaration on July 4, 1776. The war lasted until 1781 when the colonists won their independence and became the United States of America. Ask, *Why was the Declaration of Independence needed?* [colonists needed to let England know why they should be free]

7 **DISCUSS AND SUMMARIZE** Mention that even though the war was over, the United States was not truly united. Again the leaders met in Philadelphia in 1787. They included Franklin, Thomas Jefferson, and James Madison. George Washington, one of the great army leaders during the American Revolution, was elected leader of the group. Together they wrote the Constitution, the framework of our laws and government. In 1789, two years after the Constitution was adopted, Washington became the first president of the United States. In 1791, they added the Bill of Rights to the Constitution, rights protecting our speech and religion. Have your student write a summary of the events from 1787 through 1791.

Branching Out

FOR FURTHER READING

Meet George Washington, by Joan Heilbroner (Random House Books for Young Readers, 2001).

The Thirteen Colonies, by Brendan January (Scholastic Library Publishing, 2000).

Who Was Ben Franklin?, by Dennis Brindell Fradin (Penguin Putnam Books for Young Readers, 2002).

TEACHING TIP

Suggest that your student use a journal to keep track of the information presented in the lesson.

CHECKING IN

Assess your student's understanding of the lesson by having your student choose a person from his or her time line and write a short paragraph about the contribution of the person.

Remember
Benjamin Franklin

Benjamin Franklin gave our country new ideas and inventions. Choose one of his inventions. Draw a picture of the invention. Then, on your copy of the Writing Lines (page 355), write a paragraph about how the invention works.

Benjamin Franklin uses a kite to experiment with electricity.

What's Next? You Decide!

Now it's your turn to choose what to do next in the lesson. Read the activities and decide which one you want to do— you may want to try them both!

Map the 13 Colonies

MATERIALS

❑ 1 map present-day United States

❑ drawing paper

❑ crayons or markers

STEPS

❑ Use a map of the United States as a reference to draw a map of the 13 English colonies.

❑ Label each colony, major city or region, major river or rivers, and the ocean.

❑ Make a map key using color, shading, or design to name each colony.

❑ Then use your map key to color or shade each colony.

Match Nicknames

MATERIALS

❑ resource books

STEPS

In this lesson, you learned about famous people and places.

❑ Match the name of the person or place to the nickname.

> a. Father of the Constitution
> b. City of Brotherly Love
> c. Father of Our Country
> d. Father of the Declaration of Independence

_____ 1. Philadelphia

_____ 2. Thomas Jefferson

_____ 3. James Madison

_____ 4. George Washington

❑ Choose one of the people or places and write a short paragraph that tells why the nickname is a good one.

Understanding Immigration

Move out and move on to expand your knowledge of the world.

OBJECTIVE	BACKGROUND	MATERIALS
To have your student explore immigration to and expansion within the United States	Immigration to and expansion within the United States gave renewed hope to people who were looking for new opportunities. In this lesson, your student will learn about U.S. immigration and expansion.	■ Student Learning Pages 11.A–11.B ■ 1 globe or world map

VOCABULARY

PIONEERS the first people to settle undeveloped land

OREGON TRAIL the path that pioneers took from Missouri westward to Oregon

MINING the act of taking minerals out of the earth

IMMIGRANTS people who leave their country to live in another country

GREAT MIGRATION a time beginning in the early 1900s when large groups of African-Americans moved from the southern parts of the United States to settle in northern cities

OATH a promise to do something

Let's Begin

1 **DISTRIBUTE AND DISCUSS** Distribute Student Learning Page 11.A. Use this map to show your student that the area west of the Mississippi River in the 1840s was not developed or part of the United States. Ask, *Why do you think the land was not settled?* Point to Missouri and then Independence, Missouri, on the map. Mention that Missouri was a settled area at that time. Groups of settlers known as **pioneers** left in wagon trains with as many as 1,000 people to travel the **Oregon Trail.** They traveled by foot, horse, or wagon 2,000 miles over a five-month period to reach Oregon. Their goal was to build a better life for themselves and their families. Discuss why settlers might have wanted to move from the East. [land was expensive; cities were crowded; wanted more money and opportunities]

ENRICH THE EXPERIENCE

With your student, read *Little House on the Prairie* by Laura Ingalls Wilder to give your student a glimpse of prairie life.

2 **RESEARCH AND EXPLORE** Have your student look at the map and locate the Oregon Trail and the California Trail. Ask, *Which current states did the pioneers travel through to reach Oregon? California?* [Kansas, Nebraska, Wyoming, Idaho; Kansas, Colorado, New Mexico, Utah, Nevada] *What kinds of challenges did the pioneers face?* [mountains, rivers, cold weather, storms, sickness]

3 **EXPLAIN AND RESEARCH** Explain to your student that life was difficult for pioneers in Oregon and California. Many of them had few personal belongings and little money. Some of them farmed the land, some opened general stores, and some searched for gold. Point out that with so many wagon trains arriving, communities and **mining** towns grew quickly. By 1869, railroads replaced wagon trains, reducing the time it took to reach the West.

Have your student use the Internet or resource books to research the California Gold Rush of 1849. Using a landform map, indicate the site of the gold rush on the map. Discuss with your student how the land was important in the gold rush.

Direct your student to use the information he or she learned about the Oregon Trail to complete Student Learning Page 11.A. Challenge your student to use adjectives and verbs in his or her writing to bring the trail to life.

4 **EXPLORE** Explain to your student that while the West was continuing to grow, people from Europe were arriving at Ellis Island, New York, in the late 1890s and the early 1900s in large numbers. These people, called **immigrants,** came to the United States to find work and to live in a free world. Most of these immigrants came from Europe. The Statue of Liberty was their first glimpse of America. Other immigrants arrived at Boston, Massachusetts, and San Francisco, California. Those arriving in San Francisco came from Asia (China and Japan). Ask, *What did immigrants contribute or bring to the United States?* [new languages and customs]

ENRICH THE EXPERIENCE

Suggest that your student ask a relative or family friend about someone who came to the United States in the early 1900s. Together have them discuss how the person came, why, and where he or she lived upon arrival.

5 **LOCATE AND DISCUSS** Use a globe or a world map to locate the countries of southern and eastern Europe, such as Italy, Poland, Greece, Russia, Romania, Hungary, and Turkey. Point out to your student that people from these countries left their countries because they wanted cultural freedom. Then point to Ireland, Germany, Sweden, and Denmark on the map or globe. Explain to your student that many of the Irish came to the United States in the 1850s because of the potato famine of 1845. Some continued to leave because of the stories about the better life in the United States. Immigrants from Germany, Sweden, and Denmark came to buy farmland in the Midwest.

6 **DISCUSS AND LOCATE** Explain to your student that while immigrants arrived in the United States, others within the country moved north. It was called the **Great Migration.** Mention that after the Civil War, thousands of African-Americans from the South moved to northern cities such as New York, Philadelphia, Chicago, and Detroit. Use a map of the United States to locate these cities. Ask, *In which states are these cities?* [New York, Pennsylvania, Illinois, and Michigan]

7 **EXPLAIN** Point out that while African-Americans had better jobs and living opportunities in northern cities, they experienced great challenges. For the same job, they were paid less than Caucasian workers. In many places, they had separate lunchrooms, rest rooms, and lodgings. Mention that Martin Luther King Jr. and a group of other Americans worked hard in the 1950s and 1960s to end this treatment and to bring fair treatment to all.

Discuss with your student what he or she knows about Martin Luther King Jr. Ask, *Why does the United States honor Martin Luther King Jr. with a national holiday?* [to honor his memory and accomplishments]

8   **EXPLORE**   Point out that people from around the world still believe that the United States offers a better life than their own country. Immigrants continue to come to the United States. Tell your student that if he or she were to walk around the neighborhood or one of the larger cities in his or her area, he or she would probably hear people speaking many languages. Ask, *Why is it important for immigrants to continue to speak their first languages in their homes?* [it helps them to feel connected to their native countries] *How does learning English help immigrants?* [they may adjust easier to the community]

Suggest that your student write five questions he or she would like to ask a recent immigrant. If possible, have your student use those questions to interview a friend, relative, or neighbor and learn something new about that person's culture.

9   **DISCUSS**   Mention that when immigrants arrive in the United States most plan on becoming citizens. They want to live, work, and vote in the United States. Discuss with your student what he or she thinks it means to be a citizen.

Explain that becoming a citizen of the United States takes time. To apply for citizenship, one requirement is that the person must be 18 years old. Children become citizens once parents become citizens. Mention that immigrants need to first learn enough English to fill out necessary forms, take a test, and say the oath of loyalty. Point out that an **oath** is a promise to do something.

10 **PRESENT** Point out that the Oath of Loyalty has five promises a new citizen must keep. With your student, read the Oath of Loyalty that follows.

Oath of Loyalty

- I declare that I give up my loyalty to any other country.
- I will support, defend, and be faithful to the Constitution of the United States.
- I will join the armed forces or fight in the army when the law requires it.
- I will also do other work for my country when it is required by law.
- I swear that I am freely choosing to promise these things.

Discuss each promise and its meaning with your student.

11 **ILLUSTRATE** Share the following steps to becoming a citizen of the United States with your student.

Steps to an Adult Becoming a U.S. Citizen

1. Enter the United States legally.
2. Live in the United States five years.
3. Fill out an application form.
4. Take and pass a test in American history.
5. Speak with a judge about the application and the test.
6. Say the Oath of Loyalty.
7. Receive a citizenship certificate.

---

12 **PRACTICE** Distribute Student Learning Page 11.B and have your student choose activities to complete for additional practice.

Branching Out

FOR FURTHER READING

Becoming a Citizen, by Sarah De Capua (Scholastic Library Publishing, 2002).

Ellis Island Days, by Ellen Weiss and Betina Ogden, ill. (Aladdin Paperbacks, 2002).

Oregon Trail, by Elizabeth Dana D. Jaffe (Capstone Press, 2002).

TEACHING TIP

Suggest that your student copy the chart on becoming a citizen and the Oath of Loyalty in his or her notebook.

CHECKING IN

Assess your student's understanding of the lesson by having him or her "teach" the lesson to you by retelling the important points he or she learned. Encourage him or her to use visuals or anything else to make the lesson interesting.

Live Life on a Wagon Train

Look at the map. You're traveling from Independence, Missouri, to Oregon with your family. In your notebook, write a journal entry about your trip. Draw pictures to go with what you wrote. Read the questions to help you get started.

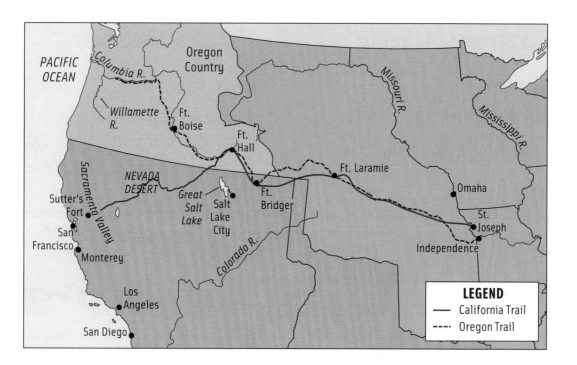

❏ What did you bring? Why?

❏ What things did you leave behind? Why?

❏ How do you spend the day?

❏ What parts of the land did you see?

❏ Where do you sleep?

❏ What do you eat?

❏ What is the best part of the trip?

❏ What is the worst part of the trip?

What's Next? You Decide!

Now it's your turn to choose what to do next in the lesson. Read the activities and decide which one you want to do— you may want to try them all!

Build a Model of the Statue of Liberty

MATERIALS

❑ Internet or resource books

❑ 1 large lump modeling clay

STEPS

❑ Research the Statue of Liberty using the Internet or resource books. Find answers to these questions:

- How tall is it?
- What is it made of?
- Who made it?
- Why is it located on Ellis Island?

❑ What does it stand for?

❑ Write a short report using your research. Then use your research information to make a clay model of the Statue of Liberty.

Make and Draw a Time Line

STEPS

❑ Add five major events in this lesson to the time line. Draw pictures of each major event.

```
←——|——|——|——|——|——→
  1800  1850  1900  1950  2000
```

Cook a Pioneer Meal

MATERIALS

❑ resource books

❑ 1–2 recipe books

STEPS

❑ Research meals the early pioneers prepared.

❑ Choose a meal and use recipe books to prepare the meal for you and your family.

❑ Ask your family members what they like best about the meal. Which part of the meal would they change?

Examining the U.S. Capital and Citizenship

To know your nation's heritage is to know its strength.

OBJECTIVE	BACKGROUND	MATERIALS
To help your student learn about the U.S. capital and citizenship	The location of the capital of the United States was a compromise between members of Congress of northern and southern states. Both regions agreed that the nation's capital belonged to the people and wanted the location to be separate from any state. In this lesson, your student will learn about the U.S. capital and what it means to be a U.S. citizen.	■ Student Learning Pages 12.A–12.B ■ 1 U.S. map ■ 1 map Washington, D.C. ■ 1 world map or atlas ■ 1 copy Venn Diagram, page 353

VOCABULARY

CAPITOL a building in Washington, D.C., where Congress meets

CAPITAL the city where the state or national government is located

CONGRESS a group of people who represent the United States and who help to pass laws

SENATE the upper house of Congress that is made up of two people from every state

HOUSE OF REPRESENTATIVES the lower house of Congress that is made up of people from every state; the number of representatives is based on each state's population

AMBASSADORS people who go to another country to represent their countries' governments

Let's Begin

1 **EXPLORE AND LOCATE** Tell your student that when George Washington served as president (1789–1797), the **capitol** was located in Philadelphia, Pennsylvania. He worked with Pierre L'Enfant, a French designer and builder, to design the new capitol. Later Benjamin Banneker, who had worked with L'Enfant, took over the designing and acted on the plans. Thomas Jefferson, too, offered his ideas for the building's design.

Use a map of the United States to have your student locate Philadelphia and Washington, D.C. Ask, *Why do you think that Washington, D.C., was an ideal location?* [it was in the middle of the states at that time, near a river for transportation and trade]

2 **DISCUSS AND CHART** Point out that the building of the entire U.S. **capital** took a long time. The White House, the first

? DID YOU KNOW?

Two states, Maryland and Virginia, gave the land to the federal government to build the capital city along the Potomac River. Washington, D.C., was named after George Washington. The initials D.C. stand for the District of Columbia.

White House, Washington, D.C.

building to be built, began in 1792. John Adams, the second
U.S. president (1797–1801), was the first president to live in the
White House. His wife, Abigail Adams, thought the White House
was beautiful but couldn't believe that forests surrounded it. She
thought the area would be a bustling city with lots of people
and shops. The Capitol, which houses **Congress**—the **Senate**
and the **House of Representatives**—was completed in 1800.

DID YOU KNOW?

Here's a hint about when
Congress is in session.
When the Senate is
working, a flag is flown
above the north wing of
the Capitol. When the
House of Representatives
is working, a flag is flown
above the south wing of
the Capitol.

3 **COMPARE** Mention that Abigail Adams would be happy living in
Washington, D.C., today. It's a busy city that has lots of people
living and working there. It has many cultural activities and is an
area where many foreign **ambassadors** live. In the capital city,
some of the early buildings have not been replaced. The White
House, though remodeled and updated, remains, and the Capitol
continues to house the Senate and the House of Representatives.
Today the Capitol also has a museum of U.S. history.

Together, look at a map of Washington, D.C. Ask, *In which
ways has Washington, D.C., changed? What new areas and
building do you see listed on the map? What do you notice on
Massachusetts Avenue?* [no paths, horses, or carriages, more
buildings; monuments, memorials, Lafayette Park, Smithsonian
Institute, National Zoo, restaurants, hotels; Massachusetts
Avenue is often referred to as Embassy Row because that's
where many ambassadors live]

4 **RELATE AND RESEARCH** Point out that, since John Adams,
many presidents have lived in the White House. Suggest that
your student use resource books or the Internet to find the
names of the presidents of the United States. Ask, *How many
presidents has our country had? Who is our president today?
Where did he live before the White House? Who was our previous
president?* [43 presidents; George W. Bush; in Texas; William J.
Clinton] Have your student use the Internet or resource books to
learn more about the present president of the United States.

5   **INTRODUCE AND LOCATE** Explain that in 1956 the United States created a program called Sister Cities with cities of the world to learn and share thoughts and work together to solve problems. More than 900 cities in the United States have sister cities in other parts of the world. Point out that Bangkok, Thailand, is a sister city to Washington, D.C. It is also the capital city of Thailand. Work with your student to use a world map or atlas to locate Thailand and Bangkok. Ask, *Which countries border Thailand?* [Laos, Cambodia, Myanmar, Malaysia] *Which body of water is it near?* [Bay of Bengal] Together with your student, find out about Sister Cities programs in your town or other cities in your state.

6   **COMPARE** Explain that Washington, D.C., and Bangkok, Thailand, have many things in common. Both have a special home for their country's leaders, the White House and the Grand Palace. Both establish laws through a constitution, with their supreme courts being the highest court of law. In addition, both cities have similar types of housing, have large immigrant populations, and are located near busy ports for trade, travel, and recreation. Point out that most of the residents of Washington, D.C., and Bangkok differ in the languages they speak, the food they eat, and work environments.

Suggest that your student use the Internet or resource books to find information on the language, food, and work environment of Thailand. Then have your student use a copy of the Venn Diagram found on page 353 to compare the two cities.

An aerial view of Washington, D.C., is shown here at dusk.

Bangkok, the capital of Thailand, bustles with people.

7   **CONNECT AND CHART** Explain that a large part of U.S. heritage is its people. Explain that the United States is founded on the principle of its citizens showing responsibility. One responsibility is being a good citizen. Discuss with your student what being a good citizen means to him or her. Explain that for adults, voting and being active in government at the town, city, state, or national level are two ways of being a good citizen.

Discuss with your student ways he or she can be a good citizen. [being loyal to our country, working to help other people, getting involved in the community by volunteering, helping neighbors with yard work and cleaning out garages, cleaning up litter, collecting bottles and cans] Suggest that your student make a chart listing ways to be a good citizen.

8 **RELATE AND EXPLAIN** Point out that citizens of the United States have certain rights. One of them is voting. Discuss with your student why being able to vote is a special right. [In many countries, people aren't allowed to vote and cannot change government rules and policies. People need to speak their opinions on matters that will affect them and change their society.]

9 **DISCUSS AND SUMMARIZE** Have your student skim a local newspaper to find articles that talk about changes in his or her community. Examples may include cutting back school budgets, increasing rates of trash collections or water usage, or building a new store or road. Together, discuss why speaking out and voting can make a difference in the community.

10 **DISTRIBUTE AND DISCUSS** Distribute Student Learning Page 12.A. Discuss the three rights of U.S. citizenship listed on the page with your student. Then have your student complete the exercise.

Branching Out

TEACHING TIP

You may wish to suggest that your student copy into his or her notebook the text of the Pledge of Allegiance. Discuss with him or her what the pledge means and how it relates to being a good citizen.

CHECKING IN

Assess your student's understanding of the lesson by having your student say or read the Pledge of Allegiance and then write a paragraph on what it means to him or her to be a good citizen. Ask, *What are you promising when you say the Pledge of Allegiance?*

Speak About Your Rights

Read the two American citizens' rights. Talk with an adult to find out what they mean. Then suppose you're president of the United States. Give a speech about why these are important. Use this page to write notes.

❑ the right to vote
❑ the right of free speech

_____

_____

_____

_____

_____

_____

_____

_____

_____

_____

_____

_____

_____

_____

_____

_____

_____

_____

_____

What's Next? You Decide!

Now it's your turn to choose what to do next in the lesson. Read the activities and decide which one you want to do—you may want to try them both!

Discover Interesting Facts About the White House

STEPS

Did you know that the White House has an indoor pool, a bowling alley, and 28 fireplaces?

❑ Use the Internet or resource books to find five interesting facts about the White House.

❑ Write your facts in your notebook. Do any of the facts surprise you?

❑ Share them with another person. Did he or she know the facts? Did any of the information surprise him or her?

Draw a Memorial

MATERIALS

❑ 1 map Washington, D.C., showing locations of memorials and monuments

❑ drawing paper

❑ crayons or markers

STEPS

❑ Look at the map and any books of the memorials and monuments in Washington, D.C.

❑ Choose one. Find out who designed it and when, and note special features of it.

❑ Draw a picture of it.

❑ Then write a description of it. Why would you choose this place to visit? What makes it special?

Abraham Lincoln Memorial, Washington, D.C.

Recognizing Our National Symbols and Holidays

Past and present actions tell a lot about who you are and what you represent.

OBJECTIVE	BACKGROUND	MATERIALS
To help your student learn about the United States through its symbols, landmarks, and holidays	From early on Americans have honored and celebrated their unity, history, and strength in many ways. In this lesson, your student will learn about the identity of the United States through examples of its national symbols, landmarks, and holidays.	■ Student Learning Pages 13.A–13.B ■ 1 U.S. map ■ 1 photo or illustration Statue of Liberty

VOCABULARY
EMBLEM a sign or symbol that represents something **COAT OF ARMS** a shield with symbols that represent what a group stands for

Let's Begin

1 **RECALL AND EXPLAIN** Point out that the capital of the United States is a place for all Americans. Recall with your student why the Washington, D.C., area was developed and what early buildings, monuments, and memorials were built. [as a central place for our president to live and for our senators and representatives to govern our country and make laws; White House, Capitol, Washington Monument, Lincoln Memorial, Jefferson Memorial]

Review with your student the reason for building the Capitol. [to house the members of the Senate and the House of Representatives, who make plans and laws for our country] Have your student use the Internet or resource books to explore the design and architecture of the Capitol. Ask, *What does the statue of the woman on top of the dome stand for?* [freedom]

2 **DISCUSS AND RELATE** Explain that each country in the world creates its own identity through culture, beliefs, dress, and government. Ask, *What parts of your identity make you different from others?* [personality traits, looks, actions] Mention that the United States of America has its own identity. Explain that certain symbols, landmarks, and holidays reveal its identity.

3 **EXPLORE AND CONNECT** Have your student think about some of the things that identify the United States. [the flag, the Pledge of Allegiance, the bald eagle, the Great Seal of the United States, the Capitol, the Statue of Liberty, holidays] Call attention to the U.S. flag. It is a national symbol that stands for the freedom of the people of the country. The first flag had 13 stars and 13 stripes to stand for the original 13 colonies. More stars were added as more territories became states. Ask, *What does our flag look like today? What does each part of the flag represent?* [50 stars and 13 stripes; 50 stars to stand for the 50 states and 13 stripes to represent the original 13 colonies]

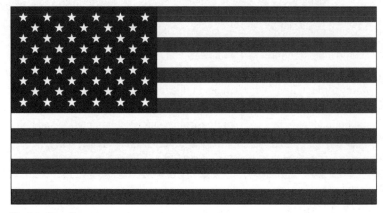

The American flag

Mention that at different times since the 1870s individual states have declared June 14 to be Flag Day. This day recognizes the anniversary of the decision of Congress to have a national flag. It was not until 1949 that President Harry Truman gave the date of June 14 as the official holiday honoring the U.S. flag.

4 **RELATE AND EXPLAIN** Point out that the bald eagle is another national symbol. Show your student a one-dollar bill and the bald eagle on it. Have your student describe other items on the bill. [picture of George Washington, signature, numbers, "In God We Trust," the Great Seal of the United States] Explain that the bald eagle was chosen as a symbol of the United States because the first settlers of America found thousands of bald eagles. They studied the strength and gracefulness of the eagle. They were impressed with how the eagle got its prey and how it survived. In 1782, the bald eagle officially became the national bird of the United States, representing strength, freedom, and courage. Mention that in addition to the one-dollar bill, the bald eagle is found on the president's flag, federal agency seals, and the Great Seal of the United States.

5 **DISCUSS AND RESEARCH** Call attention to the bald eagle that is on the Great Seal of the United States. Explain that the bald eagle is an **emblem,** and the Great Seal is a **coat of arms** for our nation. It took three people—Benjamin Franklin, John Adams, and Thomas Jefferson—six years, from 1776 to 1782, to design and finalize the emblem.

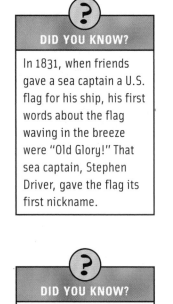

? DID YOU KNOW?

In 1831, when friends gave a sea captain a U.S. flag for his ship, his first words about the flag waving in the breeze were "Old Glory!" That sea captain, Stephen Driver, gave the flag its first nickname.

? DID YOU KNOW?

Bald eagles are not really bald. They have white feathers on their heads and around their necks.

Have your student use the Internet or resource books to find out more about the Great Seal of the United States. Suggest that your student draw a picture of it. Ask, *What does the seal look like? What do the objects on the seal stand for? What is on the backside of the seal? What is it used for?*

6 **PRESENT AND RESEARCH** Tell your student that the Liberty Bell is another symbol of the United States. Explain that the Liberty Bell was made of copper and tin in London, England, in 1752 for the Pennsylvania State House (now known as Independence Hall). The bell cracked and was remade three times in its long history. When the Declaration of Independence was signed in 1776, the bell was rung to symbolize freedom. Every year on July 4, the bell was rung to celebrate U.S. freedom. It rang for the last time in 1846 to honor George Washington's birthday. Today, the bell is located at the Liberty Bell Pavilion in Philadelphia, Pennsylvania.

Have your student use the Internet or resource books to find articles and pictures of the Liberty Bell. Direct him or her to the words inside the bell. Ask, *What do you think the words inside the bell mean?* [freedom for all] *Why do you think it was first located at Independence Hall in Philadelphia?* [the Declaration of Independence and the Constitution were written there]

7 **RECALL AND CONNECT** With your student, use a map of the United States to locate New York Harbor. Point out that the Statue of Liberty is located there and is an important symbol of the United States. Explain to your student that the Statue of Liberty was originally named Liberty Enlightening the World. More than a hundred years ago, the people of France gave the statue to the United States as a symbol of its liberty.

Use a picture of the Statue of Liberty to continue to discuss the symbol with your student. Explain that the burning torch stands for liberty, the flowing robes and the spikes on the crown stand for the continents and seas, and the notebook in her left hand has the date July 4, 1776, in Roman numerals. Ask, *What do you think the date in Roman numerals symbolizes?* [U.S. independence from England]

ENRICH THE EXPERIENCE

Suggest that your student make a chart of the U.S. symbols discussed so far and their importance. Have him or her add symbols to the list throughout the lesson.

8 **EXPLORE** Mention that in addition to symbols, countries have holidays and songs that reveal their identity. The United States celebrates many kinds of holidays. Some are national celebrations, some are religious or ethnic holidays, and some are just fun days. Discuss with your student holidays that he or she knows. Ask, *Which holidays do you celebrate throughout the year?*

9 **DISCUSS AND CHART** Explain that many U.S. holidays identify what America means to its people. Discuss with your student the meaning of some U.S. holidays, such as Martin Luther King Jr. Day, President's Day, Memorial Day, Independence Day, Veteran's Day, and Thanksgiving.

SOCIAL STUDIES

LESSON 4.13

10 **SUMMARIZE** Discuss with your student why learning about some of the symbols, landmarks, and holidays of the United States is important. [to learn about the identity and history of the United States] Explain that the United States also has songs that symbolize the country. Ask, *Why are there songs about the United States of America?* [to show pride in the United States]

Have your student use the Internet or resource books to make a list of songs that symbolize the United States. ["America," also known as "My Country 'Tis of Thee," "America the Beautiful," "The Star-Spangled Banner," "Yankee Doodle"] Obtain a recording of one of the songs and listen to it with your student.

11 **PRACTICE** Direct your student to Student Learning Page 13.A. Have him or her use the Internet and resource books to find and interpret symbols for his or her state. One Internet site to try is http://www.50states.com where the official flags, birds, and songs are listed for each state. Then direct your student to Student Learning Page 13.B for more activities.

Branching Out

TEACHING TIP

Together with your student listen to a recording of one or more songs about the United States of America. If possible, find the written words of one or more songs and discuss the meaning of some of the phrases.

FOR FURTHER READING

America: A Patriotic Primer, by Lynne Cheney and Robin Preiss Glasser, Ill. (Simon and Schuster Children's, 2002).

Fifty States (Fandex Family Field Guides), by Tom J. Craughwell (Workman Publishing Company, Inc., 1998).

The Spirit of America: A Collection of Favorite American Quotes, Poems, Songs, and Recipes, by Barbara Milo Ohrbach (Crown Publishing Group, 2002).

CHECKING IN

Assess your student's understanding of the lesson by having him or her fill in a word web about the United States. Use the example below to help direct your student.

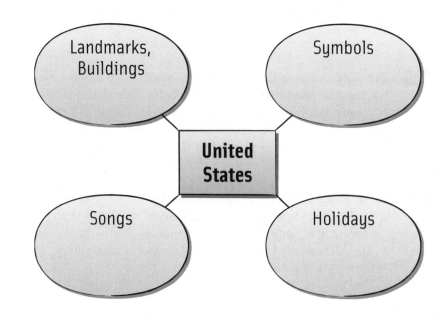

© 2003 by Barron's Educational Series, Inc. All Rights Reserved.

Make a State Symbol Chart

Each state in the United States has its own symbols. Use the Internet or resource books to find your state's symbols. Write each symbol in the chart.

My State: _____

Symbol	My State
1. Flag	
2. Song	
3. State seal	
4. Animal	
5. Bird	
6. Flower	
7. Tree	
8. Dog	
9. Fruit	
10. Insect	

Now choose three symbols from the chart and write one fact about each. Write your facts in your notebook.

What's Next? You Decide!

Now it's your turn to choose what to do next in the lesson. Read the activities and decide which one you want to do—you may want to try them both!

Make a U.S. Booklet

MATERIALS

- ❏ drawing paper
- ❏ crayons or markers
- ❏ fasteners or ribbons

STEPS

What does the United States mean to you? Which symbols, landmarks, and holidays would you include in your booklet?

- ❏ Decide what the United States means to you.
- ❏ Research ideas and objects that symbolize the identity of the United States.
- ❏ Prepare a booklet about the United States. Draw pictures that show symbols, landmarks, and holidays you feel best represent the United States.
- ❏ Under each drawing, write a paragraph that tells about it and about why you feel it best shows the meaning of the United States.

Learn About Another Country's Symbols

MATERIALS

- ❏ drawing paper
- ❏ crayons or markers

STEPS

You've learned about the identity of the United States. Other countries have their own identities.

- ❏ Choose one of the following countries and research some of its symbols, landmarks, and holidays: Kenya, Ireland, Egypt, Peru, or India.
- ❏ Draw and write about two symbols, two landmarks, and two holidays of the country. How does each symbol, landmark, and holiday identify the country?
- ❏ You may also choose another country that may interest you more than the ones suggested.

The Eiffel Tower in Paris, France, has become a symbol of France.

In Your Community

To reinforce the skills and concepts taught in this section,
try one or more of these activities!

People and Jobs

One of the best ways for your student to find out about jobs is to talk to people who have them. Have your student choose two or three jobs that he or she finds interesting. Ask other people in your family to use their network to find people who have those jobs. Arrange interviews for your student and go with him or her on the interviews. Have your student prepare a list of three to five questions for each person and write a paragraph about what he or she learned about each job. Suggest that your student write thank-you notes to the people he or she interviewed.

Multicultural Awareness

The United States is a multicultural country. Chances are your community or a neighboring one is multicultural, too. Have your student find out about the different cultures that are represented in your community. Ask your student to choose one of the cultures to learn more about. You could even visit a restaurant or musical performance from that culture with your student.

Natural Resources in Your Area

The natural resources in your area will vary depending on where you live. Your community may rely on mining, farming, harvesting oil, forestry, coastal fishing, or great spots for tourism. Have your student find out what the one or two primary natural resources are in your area. Make arrangements to visit with your student an area where these resources are being accessed or harvested. Guide your student to make the connection between the resource that Earth provides and the prosperity of the people in your community.

A Map of the Park

Have your student create an imaginary map of a park or another community place that you like to visit together. Visit the park with pencil and paper. Ask your student to draw the perimeter of the park and include a map key and a compass rose to show north, south, east, and west. Have your student include all the places or objects in the park, including swings or monkey bars, trees, benches, water fountains, and so on. After the map is complete, challenge your student to write a list of directions for another person to follow. For example, *Start at the swings. Walk north until you reach the fountain, then walk east. What will you run into?*

The Beginnings of Your Community

Understanding how your community began can help your student find a sense of pride and connection. Have your student contact the local historical society or civic center and find out what year your town or city was founded. Find out if there are any books in the community library about the history of your town and when the first European settlers arrived. What was the land like? What did the people have to do to survive? Your student may also be interested in finding out about the Native American people who lived on the land before your town was there.

We Have Learned

Use this checklist to summarize what you and your student
have accomplished in the Social Studies section.

❑ **Community**
❑ neighborhoods, people, services
❑ community maps
❑ understanding north, south, east, west
❑ comparison of communities
❑ using globes

❑ **Geography of the United States**
❑ U.S. map
❑ U.S. states
❑ neighboring countries
❑ U.S. climate, geography
❑ natural resources of land, water

❑ **Features of a Community**
❑ transportation
❑ communication
❑ work, jobs, money
❑ producing goods

❑ **Communities of the Past**
❑ Anasazi Native Americans
❑ English colony at Jamestown
❑ Spanish mission at San Antonio

❑ **Beginnings of the United States**
❑ Philadelphia and the first president
❑ traditions and culture
❑ immigration
❑ moving west and growth of cities
❑ how and why people immigrate today
❑ who first lived in your community
  and why

❑ **Community Government and Citizenship**
❑ U.S. capital
❑ the meaning of good citizenship
❑ symbols of a community
❑ comparing international communities

We have also learned:

_____

_____

_____

_____

_____

_____

_____

_____

_____

_____

_____

_____

_____

_____

1. Which is a complete sentence?

   A Tacoma, Washington, for vacation.

   B Rodney went to Tacoma, Washington, for vacation.

   C For vacation, Tacoma, Washington.

   D Rodney to Tacoma, Washington, for vacation.

2. What type of sentence is this?

   | I can't wait to go to the fair! |

   A declarative

   B interrogative

   C exclamatory

   D imperative

3. What type of sentence is this?

   | How are you feeling today? |

   A declarative

   B interrogative

   C exclamatory

   D imperative

4. What is one way to keep listeners interested when telling a story?

   A One way is to make eye contact with your listeners.

   B One way is to use the same tone of voice throughout your story.

   C One way is to speak really quickly to make the story shorter.

   D One way is to look down when you speak to your listeners.

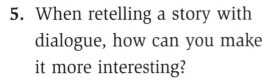
5. When retelling a story with dialogue, how can you make it more interesting?

   A The storyteller can speak very softly.

   B The storyteller can look happy when speaking.

   C The storyteller can read the dialogue more quickly than the other words.

   D The storyteller can change the tone of voice to show emotions of the characters.

6. Which sentence is correct?

   A The boy "said I don't want to go to the park."

   B "The boy said I don't want to go to the park."

   C The boy, said I don't want to "go to the park."

   D The boy said, "I don't want to go to the park."

7. Which sentence is correct?

   A "Please help me with the dishes," said Mom.

   B "Please help me with the dishes said Mom."

   C Please help me with the dishes, "said Mom."

   D "Please help me" with the dishes said Mom.

8. When writing a research report, what should you do first?

   A choose a topic

   B make an outline

   C find source materials

   D edit your materials

9. Checking for capitalization, punctuation, and spelling errors in a research report is called—

   A outlining.

   B editing.

   C notetaking.

   D publishing.

10. Which date is written correctly?

   A April 23 1954

   B 1954 April 23

   C 1954, April 23

   D April 23, 1954

Read each passage. Decide which type of writing it is. Circle the letter of the correct answer.

---

11. Drive north on Pine Street until you get to the third stoplight. Turn left at the stoplight onto Main Street. Drive two blocks and turn right onto Davis Court.

   A biography

   B rhyming poetry

   C science fiction

   D instructional

12. Mr. Norton's experiments with time travel have been very successful. So far, he has traveled back to the past three times and into the future twice.

   A biography

   B rhyming poetry

   C science fiction

   D instructional

13. James was born on July 13, 1926, in Houston, Texas. His family was very large. He had eight brothers and sisters.

   A biography

   B rhyming poetry

   C science fiction

   D instructional

Read the sentence in the box. Choose the synonym of the underlined word. Circle the letter of the correct answer.

Read each selection. Read the questions and answer choices that go with each selection. Circle the letter of the correct answer.

14.

The play was <u>excellent.</u>

A acceptable

B horrible

C poor

D outstanding

15.

My <u>trip</u> went well.

A travel

B vacation

C stumble

D party

16.

<u>Fall</u> is my favorite season.

A stumble

B autumn

C crumble

D winter

Use for 17–23.

A Canoe Trip with Buddy

It was in August that we took our first canoe trip. My older brother Matt rowed in the front. I rowed in the back. Our dog Buddy sat in the middle. The river was calm and peaceful. It was a beautiful day.

Then Buddy spotted a squirrel. The peacefulness turned into <u>chaos.</u> Buddy jumped out of the boat and tried to climb up the <u>bank.</u>

"I'll get him, Elizabeth," said Matt.

"Be careful!" I yelled as he jumped into the water.

It took Matt a few minutes to swim to where Buddy was. Then he realized he wouldn't be able to get Buddy to swim back to the boat.

"Bring the boat over here!" Matt yelled.

I rowed over to where they were and Matt lifted Buddy back into the boat. Matt was tired from wrestling with Buddy in the water, so I rowed for the rest of the trip.

Matt and I went on many more canoe trips after that, but we usually left Buddy at home.

Characters	
Setting	
Plot	The characters go on a canoe trip.

17. What should be written next to "Characters" in the chart?

    A Elizabeth, Buddy

    B Elizabeth, Matt, Buddy

    C Matt, Buddy

    D Elizabeth

18. What should be written next to "Setting" in the chart?

    A ocean and summertime

    B river and winter

    C ocean and winter

    D river and summertime

19. What is the meaning of the underlined word in the sentence below?

    The peacefulness turned into <u>chaos.</u>

    A softness

    B disorder

    C order

    D separation

20. What is the meaning of the underlined word in the sentence below?

    Buddy jumped out of the boat and tried to climb up the <u>bank.</u>

    A side of a river

    B a place to keep money

    C rely on

    D row a canoe

Use for 21–24.

Behind our house, there is a stream that seems to come from nowhere and then end suddenly. One day I asked Mother, "Why is it there?"

Mother said, "I will tell you the story of that stream. A very long time ago, a young girl lived with her family on this land. She was a very happy girl. Her favorite thing to do was ride her horse, Mabel. She always took very good care of Mabel. She combed her <u>mane</u> and braided her tail every morning. Then she spent every afternoon riding Mabel."

Mother continued, "One day, Mabel became lost. The girl didn't know where to find her. She looked everywhere to find Mabel, but the girl could not find her. Finally, a farmer found Mabel wandering near a dirt road. The girl cried so many tears of joy when Mabel returned that her tears formed this stream."

21. Why is the narrator curious about the stream?

   A It seems to come from nowhere.

   B The horse likes to drink from the stream.

   C The water is bright blue.

   D Many people like to drink the water from the stream.

22. This story is an example of—

   A a biography.

   B a legend.

   C nonfiction.

   D poetry.

23. Who tells the story of the girl and the horse?

   A the narrator

   B Mother

   C Mabel

   D the girl

24. What is the meaning of the underlined word in the sentence?

> She combed her <u>mane</u> and braided her tail every morning.

A hooves

B back

C hair

D neck

Read each sentence. Rewrite each sentence with correct punctuation.

25. How old are you

_____

_____

26. Sally had a bowl of cereal an apple and a glass of orange juice for breakfast

_____

_____

_____

Read each sentence. Rewrite each sentence with correct capitalization.

27. my best friend lives in st. louis, missouri.

_____

_____

_____

_____

_____

_____

28. my favorite day of the week is saturday.

_____

_____

_____

_____

_____

_____

Read the selection. Rewrite the selection in past tense.

29. My family is going on a trip to Washington, D.C. It will take us eight hours to get there. We are going to visit the White House, the Capitol, and the Washington Monument. We will visit many other sites, too. We are staying in Washington, D.C., for five days.

_____

_____

_____

_____

_____

_____

_____

_____

_____

Read the note card. Use the note card to help answer the questions.

Blue Whale
1. Mammal
2. Largest animal ever, up to 100 feet long
3. Found in all oceans
4. Almost extinct, only 5,000 left in the world

30. What is the main heading?

_____

_____

31. What are the details?

_____

_____

_____

_____

_____

_____

_____

_____

_____

_____

| Read each set of words. Write the contraction for the words. |

32. you are _____

was not _____

33. she will _____

it is _____

| Read the selection. Rewrite the selection with quotation marks to show dialogue. Correct any mistakes in grammar, spelling, capitalization, and punctuation. |

34. I just made a new friend named marsha. when we were playing at the park yesterday we started talking about birthdays. When is your birthday I asked marsha. she said my birthday is March 19th. when is yours? i said my birthday is on March 21st, only two days after yours

_____

_____

_____

_____

_____

_____

_____

_____

_____

_____

_____

_____

_____

_____

_____

_____

_____

_____

_____

_____

_____

_____

_____

Read the selection and the questions that follow. Answer the questions in complete sentences.

The easiest way to build a snowman is to have several friends help you. The first thing you do is roll three balls of snow. One ball should be really big. This is the base of the snowman. Another ball should be medium-sized. The third ball should be smaller. This is the head of the snowman.

Second, stack the balls of snow on top of each other. The largest ball goes on the bottom. The medium-sized ball goes in the middle. The smallest ball goes on top. Now the hardest part is done.

Third, give the snowman arms and a face. You can use tree branches for the snowman's arms. The eyes and mouth can be made from rocks or other small objects. Use a carrot to make the nose. If you want, you can even give the snowman a hat, scarf, and gloves. Now your snowman is complete.

35. What is the purpose of the passage?

_____

_____

_____

_____

36. Why do you think it's a good idea to have others help you?

_____

_____

_____

_____

37. List in order the three main steps for building a snowman.

_____

_____

_____

> Read each question. Write the answers in complete sentences.

38. Write a paragraph that describes a person, a place, an event, or an object. Write a topic sentence and supporting details.

_____

_____

_____

_____

_____

_____

_____

_____

_____

_____

_____

_____

_____

39. Miguel's Aunt Kay sent him his favorite board game as a gift. Write a thank-you note to Aunt Kay from Miguel.

_____

_____

_____

_____

_____

_____

_____

_____

_____

_____

_____

_____

40. Choose something you are good at doing. Write a paragraph that gives instructions for doing it. Include steps that should be followed in order.

_____

_____

_____

_____

_____

_____

_____

_____

_____

_____

_____

_____

_____

_____

_____

1. Which is 823 rounded to the nearest ten?

   A   800

   B   820

   C   830

   D   900

2. What is the place value of the 5 in 15,427?

   A   ones

   B   tens

   C   hundreds

   D   thousands

3. How much money is shown?

   A $1.31

   B $1.37

   C $2.35

   D $2.36

4. Which set of coins makes 80 cents?

   A   one quarter, two dimes, and two nickels

   B   one quarter, three dimes, and three nickels

   C   two quarters, two dimes, and two nickels

   D   three quarters, three dimes, and one nickel

5. Janet had $3.00. Her friend Ben gave her a quarter and three nickels. How much money does Janet have now?

   A $3.35

   B $3.40

   C $3.45

   D $3.50

6.   52
   <u>+ 63</u>

   A   105

   B   106

   C   115

   D   116

7.
$$
\begin{array}{r}
223 \\
+\ 308 \\
\hline
\end{array}
$$

   A 530

   B 531

   C 608

   D 681

8.
$$
\begin{array}{r}
19 \\
37 \\
+\ 48 \\
\hline
\end{array}
$$

   A 56

   B 67

   C 85

   D 104

9.
$$
\begin{array}{r}
224 \\
-\ \ 79 \\
\hline
\end{array}
$$

   A 145

   B 146

   C 155

   D 156

10.
$$
\begin{array}{r}
489 \\
-\ 231 \\
\hline
\end{array}
$$

   A 258

   B 268

   C 278

   D 288

11.
$$
\begin{array}{r}
2,896 \\
-1,324 \\
\hline
\end{array}
$$

   A 1,470

   B 1,472

   C 1,570

   D 1,572

12. Lena and Malcolm each own 9 books. They each bought 3 new books at the book sale. How many books do they have in total?

   A 22

   B 23

   C 24

   D 25

13. There are 196 students in Michael's school. Next year 27 students are leaving. How many students will return next year?

   A 169

   B 176

   C 223

   D 233

14. How many pints equal 8 cups?

   A 1

   B 2

   C 3

   D 4

15. Which is the best unit to use for measuring the weight of a pear?

   A foot

   B ounce

   C meter

   D pound

16. Which is the best unit to use for measuring the amount of water in a bathtub?

   A milliliter

   B gram

   C liter

   D kilogram

17. Choose the best estimate for the weight of the bicycle shown below.

   A 150 g

   B 150 ft

   C 150 m

   D 150 kg

18. What is the temperature?

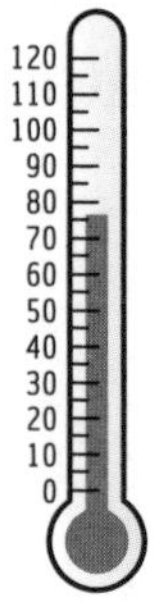

A 72°F

B 74°F

C 76°F

D 78°F

19. 11 × 4 =

A 34

B 44

C 54

D 64

20. 12 × 10 =

A 110

B 120

C 210

D 220

21. 214 × 13 =

A 2,173

B 2,177

C 2,782

D 2,783

22. 2 × 3 × 5 =

A 20

B 25

C 30

D 35

23. 65 ÷ 5 =

A 13

B 14

C 15

D 16

24. 119 ÷ 9 =

A 13 R1

B 13 R2

C 14 R1

D 14 R2

25. 96 ÷ 10 =

   A 9 R6

   B 9 R9

   C 10 R1

   D 10 R6

26. 13,000 ÷ 100 =

   A 13

   B 130

   C 1,300

   D 13,000

27. Devin has $2.00. How many $0.05 erasers can he buy?

   A 10

   B 20

   C 30

   D 40

28. What figure is shown?

   A rectangle

   B square

   C triangle

   D pentagon

29. Which triangle is shown?

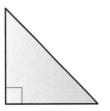

   A acute

   B right

   C obtuse

   D equilateral

30. What figure is shown?

A square

B rectangle

C pentagon

D hexagon

31. What figure is shown?

A sphere

B cube

C cone

D cylinder

32. Which fraction is equivalent to $\frac{2}{3}$?

A $\frac{4}{5}$

B $\frac{4}{6}$

C $\frac{4}{7}$

D $\frac{4}{9}$

33. What is the chance of the spinner landing on 2?

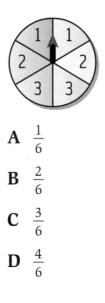

A $\frac{1}{6}$

B $\frac{2}{6}$

C $\frac{3}{6}$

D $\frac{4}{6}$

34. Julie is meeting her friend in 20 minutes. It is now 11:15. At what time will Julie meet her friend?

A 11:20

B 11:25

C 11:30

D 11:35

> **Read each passage and the questions that follow. Answer the questions in complete sentences. Show your work.**

35. Order the numbers from least to greatest.

127, 59, 118

_____

36. Write 4,893 in expanded form.

_____

37. Create a math problem to add the coins. Write the amount.

_____

38. Show 1:53 on the clock.

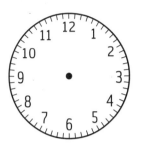

39. Anna's piano lesson starts at 3:20 P.M. Her lesson lasts for 45 minutes. Use the clock below to show what time Anna's lesson will end.

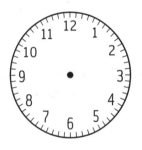

40. Measure the line segment to the nearest centimeter.

•————————————•

_____

41. Write a subtraction sentence using the same family of facts as shown below.

> 8 + 5 = 13

42. Mrs. Patel's class made vegetable soup. They used more carrots than potatoes in their soup. Write "carrots" and "potatoes" to complete the chart to show the correct amounts used in the soup.

Vegetable	Amount Used
	$\frac{1}{3}$ cup
	$\frac{1}{2}$ cup
Celery	$\frac{1}{4}$ cup

43. Write a math sentence to show another way to write 4 + 4 + 4 + 4 + 4.

44. Peter's family ordered 3 boxes of apples. There are 12 apples in each box. Write a math problem to find the total number of apples. Solve the math problem.

45. Mr. Ingram has 27 fish and 3 aquariums. He has the same number of fish in each aquarium. Write a math problem to find the number of fish Mr. Ingram has in each aquarium. Solve the math problem.

46. Draw a line. Label it *LM*.

47. Draw a ray. Label it *GH*.

48. Find the perimeter. Show your work.

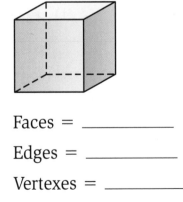

4 in.

3 in. 3 in.

4 in.

_____

49. Use the cube to fill in the missing numbers.

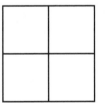

Faces = _____

Edges = _____

Vertexes = _____

50. Name each figure shown.

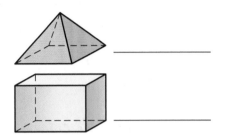

_____

_____

51. Order from least to greatest.

$\frac{1}{2}$ $\frac{2}{3}$ $\frac{1}{4}$ $\frac{3}{4}$

_____

52. Use your pencil to color $\frac{1}{4}$ of the square.

53. Use your pencil to color $\frac{2}{3}$ of the circle.

54. Marsha asked 30 people what their favorite color was. The bar graph shows the results. Use the bar graph to answer the questions.

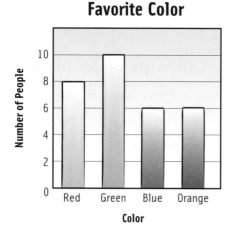

Favorite Color

Which was most people's favorite color?

_____

Which colors were chosen as favorites by the same number of people?

_____

_____

55. Ryan recorded the number of sunny days each month from May through September.

May = 13, June = 18, July = 26, August = 28, and September = 19

Draw a pictograph showing the number of sunny days in each month.

56. Graph each ordered pair.

(3, 4) (6, 2) (5, 1) (2, 6)

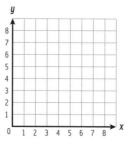

1. Which of the birds' feet belongs to a bird that has adapted to water?

   A

   B

   C

   D

2. This symbol shows that an item—

   A has renewable resources.

   B can be made without trees.

   C can be recycled.

   D is biodegradable.

3. What safety equipment should be worn when riding a bike?

   A seat belt

   B goggles

   C helmet

   D wrist bands

4. Which type of matter is described in the notes?

   | 1. Made up of atoms |
   | 2. Red color |
   | 3. Shape and size do not easily change |

   A solid

   B liquid

   C compound

   D gas

5. What does the drawing show?

   A a lunar eclipse

   B phases of the moon

   C constellations of the sun

   D a solar eclipse

6. Which part of soil is made from decayed plants and animals?

A rocks

B nutrients

C minerals

D humus

7. What kind of simple machine is Jose using to put the box on the moving truck?

A inclined plane

B lever

C pulley

D wheel and axle

8. Which of these is a nonliving part of a desert ecosystem?

A rattlesnake

B cactus plant

C sand

D lizard

9. Which organism in the food chain is a producer?

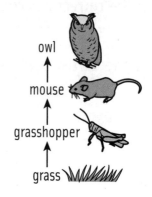

A mouse

B grasshopper

C owl

D grass

10. Sensory receptors in your skin are most important for—

A sight.

B hearing.

C smell.

D touch.

11. Which animal can be added to the list of invertebrates?

> 1. Turkey
> 2. Fish
> 3. _____

   A lobster

   B horse

   C tiger

   D whale

12. In which habitat are deer usually found?

   A deserts

   B forests

   C oceans

   D seashores

13. Which foods have the most calcium?

   A fruits

   B vegetables

   C bread and rice

   D milk and cheese

14. Which of these activities uses an involuntary muscle?

   A bending over and picking up a ball

   B turning the page of a book

   C breathing in and out

   D walking across the room

15. Which is the best way to get vitamins and nutrients?

   A eat only foods from one food group

   B eat many different kinds of foods each day

   C eat only fruits and vegetables

   D eat only foods you see advertised on TV

16. Which sentence is true about tropical rain forests?

    A Tropical rain forests are increasing in size.

    B Tropical rain forests are spreading across countries.

    C Tropical rain forests are less popular with owners of plants and animals.

    D Tropical rain forests are losing many plants and animals to growing business.

17. Through which material would sound waves move the slowest?

    A water

    B air

    C wood

    D metal

18. Which word best describes the liquid in the glass?

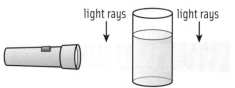

    A transparent

    B reflective

    C translucent

    D opaque

19. Which of these will cause slow changes in Earth's landforms?

    A rock slide

    B volcano

    C glacier

    D earthquake

Answer the questions in complete sentences.

---

20. List two kinds of bones.

    _____

    _____

21. Label the missing parts of the food pyramid.

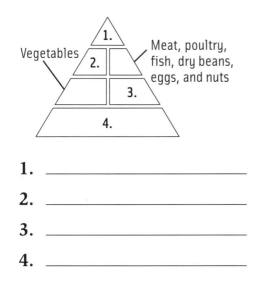

1. _____

2. _____

3. _____

4. _____

22. What information is missing in the section on nosebleeds?

_____

_____

_____

23. What should be written in the emergency phone numbers section?

_____

Use for 22–23.

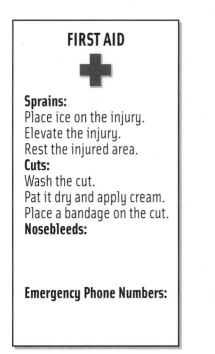

FIRST AID

Sprains:
Place ice on the injury.
Elevate the injury.
Rest the injured area.
Cuts:
Wash the cut.
Pat it dry and apply cream.
Place a bandage on the cut.
Nosebleeds:

Emergency Phone Numbers:

Use for 24–25.

9:00 AM   Noon

24. Why did the puddle change appearance?

_____

_____

_____

25. Is the change in the puddle physical or chemical? What tells you this?

_____

_____

_____

_____

_____

Use for 26–27.

26. What three things are needed to make a shadow like the one in the picture?

_____

_____

_____

27. Where does the light energy in this picture come from?

_____

_____

_____

_____

_____

Use for 28.

28. Label the layers of Earth.

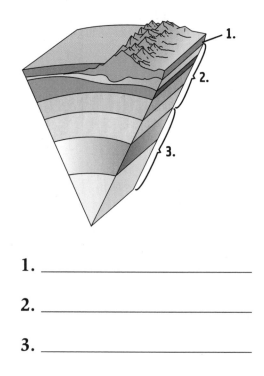

1. _____

2. _____

3. _____

Read each question and the answer choices that follow. Circle the letter of the correct answer.

1. A community is usually made up of several—

   A states.

   B neighborhoods.

   C nations.

   D people.

2. What type of community includes farms and open spaces, with long distances between places?

   A rural

   B urban

   C international

   D national

3. Climate is—

   A the type of weather of a place over time.

   B the number of people in a specific place.

   C the type of landforms that surround a place.

   D the number of cities in a specific state.

4. Something found in nature that people use is called a—

   A fruit.

   B vegetable.

   C natural resource.

   D natural material.

5. Iron, salt, and diamonds are examples of—

   A plants.

   B organisms.

   C landforms.

   D minerals.

6. Which type of transportation existed before 1800?

   A wagons

   B automobiles

   C airplanes

   D trains

7. Which communication device was invented by Samuel Morse?

   A telegraph

   B satellite

   C Internet

   D telephone

8. Why do most people work?

   A because they are bored

   B to invent new things

   C to make money to buy goods and services

   D because they like handling goods and services

9. A group of workers and machines all working together to make a final product is called a—

   A farm.

   B mine.

   C neighborhood.

   D monarchy.

10. Which group of Native Americans lived in Mesa Verde, Colorado, and built pueblos for protection?

    A Anasazi

    B Blackfoot

    C Dakota

    D Crow

11. Who was the leader of the English colony at Jamestown?

    A Pocahontas

    B Christopher Columbus

    C John Smith

    D George Washington

12. In what U.S. city did the Spanish set up missions to teach their religion to others?

A New York

B San Antonio

C Los Angeles

D Portland

13. Which early American wrote *Poor Richard's Almanac*?

A Benjamin Franklin

B John Smith

C John Adams

D Thomas Jefferson

14. Who was the first president of the United States?

A Abraham Lincoln

B Benjamin Franklin

C Thomas Jefferson

D George Washington

15. Why did pioneers use the Oregon Trail?

A to move east

B to move west

C to escape from British troops

D to leave the United States

16. Someone who comes from one country to live in another is called—

A a traveler.

B an immigrant.

C a citizen.

D an explorer.

17. Which city had an immigration center on Ellis Island?

A San Antonio

B Portland

C Los Angeles

D New York

18. Which of these is the capital of the United States?

   A Seattle

   B Alexandria

   C Washington, D.C.

   D New York

19. What is one way to be a good citizen?

   A vote

   B litter

   C break laws

   D damage property

20. Which of these listed the reasons why the colonies should be free?

   A U.S. Constitution

   B Magna Carta

   C Bill of Rights

   D Declaration of Independence

> **Read each selection and the questions that follow. Answer the questions in complete sentences.**

Use for 21–24.

The delegates who wrote the Constitution were doing something that no one had ever done before. They were making rules to create a new nation. The fifty-five delegates at this meeting were smart and well educated. Many of the most important people in the United States at that time were delegates, including George Washington, James Madison, Alexander Hamilton, and Benjamin Franklin. We now call these people the *Framers,* for framing the rules for our government.

21. What new thing did the delegates who wrote the U.S. Constitution do?

_____

_____

_____

22. How many delegates met to write the Constitution?

_____

_____

_____

23. Name four people who helped write the Constitution.

_____

_____

_____

24. Why do we call the people who wrote the Constitution the *Framers*?

_____

_____

Use for 25–28.

The right to vote is so important that it has been the subject of several other amendments. Originally, the states allowed only men to vote. The 19th Amendment, in 1920, gave women the right to vote. Some states would charge taxes to prevent poor people, particularly people of color, from voting. The 24th Amendment, in 1964, protected the right of citizens to vote even if they cannot pay the tax. In 1971, the 26th Amendment settled the question of how old people must be to vote. It says that citizens who are 18 years old and older have the right to vote.

25. Who were the only people originally allowed to vote?

_____

_____

_____

_____

_____

26. What did the 19th Amendment do?

_____

_____

_____

27. What did the 24th Amendment do?

_____

_____

_____

28. What did the 26th Amendment do?

_____

_____

_____

_____

_____

_____

_____

Read the documents in Part A and answer the questions. Then read the directions in Part B and write your essay.

Part A: Short Answer

Use for 29–32.

The Constitution is a remarkable document. When it was written, it created a new nation and a new form of government. Nothing like it had ever been written before. Now, the government it created has lasted more than 200 years. Many other countries model their constitutions on ours.

The Constitution creates a system of government that gives you many freedoms and protections that people in other countries do not have. Some countries have a single, all-powerful leader who makes all the laws. In our country, the Constitution makes the president share much of the decision-making power with Congress. In addition, the courts make sure laws agree with the Constitution.

29. What did the Constitution do when it was written?

_____

_____

_____

30. How has the U.S. Constitution affected other countries?

_____

_____

_____

31. How is the leader of the United States different from the leaders of some other countries?

_____

_____

_____

32. What do the U.S. courts do?

_____

_____

_____

Use for 33.

In some countries, the government tells you which religion to practice and punishes people who do not practice that religion. In our country, the Constitution says that you can practice any religion—or no religion.

In some countries, the government punishes people who complain about the government. In our country, the Constitution says you may speak and write freely, even if the government does not like it.

In some countries, the government arrests people, puts them into jail, and punishes them for no reason. In our country, the Constitution says the government must follow many rules to protect the rights of people who are charged with crimes.

33. What are three rights that the U.S. Constitution gives people?

_____

_____

_____

Use for 34–35.

The Constitution protects your rights. Protecting these rights also means you have important responsibilities. One responsibility is to vote so you can choose leaders and lawmakers who will act wisely and protect your rights. Another responsibility is to serve on juries, to protect the right to jury trials. Another responsibility is to pay taxes so that the government gets the money it needs to do its many jobs.

34. What does the Constitution do besides protect your rights?

_____

_____

_____

_____

_____

_____

35. What are three responsibilities of U.S. citizens?

_____

_____

_____

_____

_____

_____

_____

_____

_____

_____

_____

_____

_____

_____

Part B: Essay

> Use the information from the documents. You may also use your knowledge of social studies. Write an essay. Include an introduction, two supporting paragraphs, and a conclusion.

36. **Task:** Use information from the documents to write an essay on the U.S. Constitution. Your essay should—

   1. describe how the Constitution was written.

   2. tell how it created a new nation and government.

   3. list the rights and responsibilities the Constitution gives U.S. citizens.

   4. describe how the Constitution makes the U.S. government different from the governments in some other countries.

_____

_____

_____

_____

_____

_____

_____

_____

_____

Assessment Answers

1.	B	13.	A
2.	C	14.	D
3.	B	15.	A
4.	A	16.	B
5.	D	17.	B
6.	D	18.	D
7.	C	19.	B
8.	C	20.	A
9.	C	21.	A
10.	D	22.	B
11.	D	23.	B
12.	C	24.	C

25. How old are you?

26. Sally had a bowl of cereal, an apple, and a glass of orange juice for breakfast.

27. My best friend lives in St. Louis, Missouri.

28. My favorite day of the week is Saturday.

29. My family went on a trip to Washington, D.C. It took us eight hours to get there. We visited the White House, the Capitol, and the Washington Monument. We visited many other sites, too. We stayed in Washington, D.C., for five days.

30. The main heading is Blue Whale.

31. The details are: mammal; largest animal ever, up to 100 feet long; found in all oceans; almost extinct; only 5,000 left in the world.

Scoring Rubric for Questions 32–33:

2 POINTS
Both contractions are correct.

1 POINT
One contraction is correct.

0 POINTS
Both contractions are incorrect.

Scoring Rubric for Question 34:

4 POINTS
The paragraph demonstrates correct usage of quotation marks to show dialogue. All grammar, spelling, punctuation, and capitalization errors are corrected.

3 POINTS
The paragraph demonstrates correct usage of quotation marks to show dialogue. Most grammar, spelling, punctuation, and capitalization errors are corrected.

2 POINTS
The paragraph contains errors in the usage of quotation marks to show dialogue. Some grammar, spelling, punctuation, and capitalization errors are corrected.

1 POINT
The paragraph demonstrates incorrect usage of quotation marks to show dialogue. Few grammar, spelling, punctuation, and capitalization errors are corrected.

0 POINTS
The paragraph does not demonstrate correct usage of quotation marks to show dialogue. No grammar, spelling, punctuation, and capitalization errors are corrected.

35. The purpose is to tell someone how to build a snowman.

36. Answers vary. Possible answer: The balls of snow will get really big and heavy, so it's easier if you have more people.

Scoring Rubric for Question 37:

4 POINTS
The three main steps are listed in order.

3 POINTS
The three main steps are listed, but there is an error in the order.

2 POINTS
One step is incorrect and the order is incorrect.

1 POINT
More than one step is incorrect and the order is incorrect.

0 POINTS
All of the steps are incorrect.

Scoring Rubric for Question 38:

4 POINTS
The paragraph vividly describes a person, place, event, or object. It includes a topic sentence, supporting details, and descriptive words. It is well organized and there are no errors in grammar, spelling, punctuation, or capitalization.

3 POINTS
The paragraph describes a person, place, event, or object. It includes a topic sentence, supporting details, and descriptive words. There is good organization and there are a few minor errors in grammar, spelling, punctuation, and capitalization.

2 POINTS
The paragraph does not include a full description of a person, place, event, or object. The topic sentence and supporting details are not clear. There are not many descriptive words. The

Assessment Answers

organization is not clear and there are significant errors in grammar, spelling, punctuation, and capitalization.

1 POINT
The paragraph is only marginally descriptive. There is no topic sentence or organizational structure. There are numerous errors in grammar, spelling, punctuation, and capitalization.

0 POINTS
The paragraph is not descriptive. It does not have a topic sentence or supporting details, and there are few, if any, descriptive words. The organization is poor and there are many errors in grammar, spelling, punctuation, and capitalization.

Scoring Rubric for Question 39:

4 POINTS
The thank-you note uses the proper opening and closing. It mentions each item that was received. It is well organized and there are no errors in grammar, spelling, punctuation, or capitalization.

3 POINTS
The thank-you note uses the proper opening and closing. It mentions each item that was received. There is good organization and there are a few minor errors in grammar, spelling, punctuation, and capitalization.

2 POINTS
The thank-you note does not use the proper opening and closing. It mentions each item that was received. The organization is not clear and there are significant errors in grammar, spelling, punctuation, and capitalization.

1 POINT
The thank-you note does not use the proper opening and closing. It does not mention each item that was received. There are numerous errors in grammar, spelling, punctuation, and capitalization.

0 POINTS
The thank-you note does not use the proper opening and closing. It does not mention each item that was received. The organization is poor and there are so many errors in grammar, spelling, punctuation, and capitalization that it is unreadable.

Scoring Rubric for Question 40:

4 POINTS
The paragraph gives steps that have a clear order. It is well organized and there are no errors in grammar, spelling, punctuation, or capitalization.

3 POINTS
The paragraph gives steps that have a clear order. There is good organization and there are a few minor errors in grammar, spelling, punctuation, and capitalization.

2 POINTS
The paragraph gives steps, but the order is not completely clear. It is not well organized and there are significant errors in grammar, spelling, punctuation, and capitalization.

1 POINT
The paragraph has steps that are difficult to follow and the order is not clear. The organization is poor, and there are numerous errors in grammar, spelling, punctuation, and capitalization.

0 POINTS
The paragraph gives no steps to follow. The organization is poor and there are many errors in grammar, spelling, punctuation, and capitalization.

MATH

1. B		18. C	
2. D		19. B	
3. A		20. B	
4. C		21. C	
5. B		22. C	
6. C		23. A	
7. B		24. B	
8. D		25. A	
9. A		26. B	
10. A		27. D	
11. D		28. A	
12. C		29. B	
13. A		30. D	
14. D		31. C	
15. B		32. B	
16. C		33. B	
17. D		34. D	

35. 59, 118, 127

36. 4,000 + 800 + 90 + 3

37. .25 + .25 + .10 + .10 + .10 + .05 + .01 + .01 + .01 + .01 = $0.89

38. The clock's hour hand is pointing to 11 and the minute hand is pointing to 3 second marks past the 10.

Assessment Answers

39. The clock's hour hand is pointing to 4 and the minute hand is pointing to 1.

40. The line measures 11 centimeters.

41. $13 - 5 = 8$ or $13 + 8 = 5$

42. potatoes $= \frac{1}{3}$ and carrots $= \frac{1}{2}$

43. 5×4

44. $3 \times 12 = 36$

45. $27 \div 3 = 9$

46. Check that student draws a line and labels it *LM*.

47. Check that student draws a ray and labels it *GH*.

48. $3 + 4 + 3 + 4 = 12$

49. faces $= 6$, edges $= 12$, vertexes $= 8$

50. in order shown: pyramid and rectangular prism

51. $\frac{1}{4}, \frac{1}{2}, \frac{2}{3}, \frac{3}{4}$

52. Check that student shades in 1 box of the square.

53. Check that student shades in 2 parts of the circle.

54. most favorite color: green; colors that were favorites of same number of people: blue and orange

55. Check art representing number of sunny days for May (13), June (18), July (26), August (28), and September (19).

56.

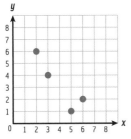

20. Student should name two of the following types of bones: long, short, flat, irregular.

21. 1 = fats, oils, sweets; 2 = milk, yogurt; 3 = fruit; 4 = bread, cereal, rice, pasta

Scoring Rubric for Question 22:

4 POINTS
Answer includes: to treat a nosebleed, sit down, lean forward, pinch your nostrils shut, wash your hands after the bleeding stops, seek medical attention if the bleeding does not stop after 30 minutes.

3 POINTS
Answer includes four of the five elements listed above.

2 POINTS
Answer includes two or three of the five steps listed above.

1 POINT
Answer includes one of the steps listed above.

23. 911

24. The puddle changed its appearance because some of the water evaporated.

25. Evaporation is a physical change. The change is due to the sun's light shining on the puddle and drying it out, making it physically smaller.

26. To make a shadow like the one in the picture, you must have a source of light, something opaque to block the light, and a surface for the shadow to be seen on.

27. The light energy comes from the sun.

28. 1 = crust, 2 = mantle, 3 = core

SCIENCE

1. A		11. A	
2. C		12. B	
3. C		13. D	
4. A		14. C	
5. B		15. B	
6. D		16. D	
7. A		17. D	
8. C		18. A	
9. D		19. C	
10. D			

SOCIAL STUDIES

1. B		11. C	
2. A		12. B	
3. A		13. A	
4. D		14. D	
5. D		15. B	
6. A		16. B	
7. A		17. D	
8. D		18. C	
9. B		19. A	
10. A		20. D	

21. They made rules to create a new nation.

22. Fifty-five delegates met to write the Constitution.

Assessment Answers

23. George Washington, James Madison, Alexander Hamilton, and Benjamin Franklin helped write the Constitution.

24. They are called the *Framers* because they framed the rules of our government.

25. Men were the only people originally allowed to vote.

26. The 19th Amendment gave women the right to vote.

27. The 24th Amendment gave people the right to vote even if they cannot pay the voting tax.

28. The 26th Amendment said that citizens who are 18 years or older have the right to vote.

29. It created a new nation and a new form of government.

30. Many other countries model their constitutions on ours.

31. Some countries have a single, all-powerful leader who makes all the laws. In our country, the Constitution makes the president share much of the decision-making power with Congress.

32. The courts make sure laws agree with the Constitution.

33. The Constitution gives people the right to choose a religion, the right to complain about the government, and the right to be treated fairly when accused of a crime.

34. The Constitution gives you important responsibilities.

35. U.S. citizens have a responsibility to vote, serve on juries, and pay taxes.

Scoring Rubric for Question 36:

4 POINTS

The essay is well written, well organized, and demonstrates a clear understanding of the U.S. Constitution. It describes how the Constitution was written and how it created a new nation and government, lists the rights and responsibilities the Constitution gives to citizens, and describes how the Constitution makes the U.S. government different from the governments in some other countries. Each paragraph is well organized and contains a topic sentence.

3 POINTS

The essay has a few minor flaws in grammar and organization but demonstrates a good understanding of the U.S. Constitution.

2 POINTS

The essay has some significant flaws in grammar and organization. It demonstrates some understanding of the U.S. Constitution.

1 POINT

The essay has major flaws in grammar and organization. There is very little understanding of the U.S. Constitution.

0 POINTS

The essay is poorly written and organized. There is no understanding of the U.S. Constitution.

Answers

PROMOTING LITERACY

Lesson 1.1   *Student Learning Page 1.A*

Answers will vary. Picture and rest of story should reflect a possible continuation of the story.

Lesson 1.2   *Student Learning Page 2.A*

1. ?
2. !
3. .
4. .
5. The children watch the game.
6. I love to eat apples!
7. Save your money to buy a bike.
8. How big is the balloon?
9–12. Each type of sentence should be written correctly.

Lesson 1.3   *Student Learning Page 3.A*

Answers will vary. Possible answers: Plants and animals drink water. Water makes things grow. Some animals and plants live in water.

Lesson 1.4   *Student Learning Page 4.A*

"Hi," the boy said. "My name is Max. What's your name?"

"Well, it's nice to meet you. Are there a lot of kids that live in this neighborhood?" Max asked.

"I think I'm really going to like it here," Max said. "It seems like a really nice place to live. What do you do for fun around here?"

Max said, "I'm glad that we moved in next to you. I hope that we can be friends!"

"Oh, there's my brother. I think he needs help bringing boxes in the house," Max said quickly. "It was really nice meeting you."

Lesson 1.5   *Student Learning Page 5.A*

2. is
3. will
4. have
5. are
7. she will
8. does not

9. here is
10. Answers will vary. At least one contraction should be used.

Lesson 1.6

Student Learning Page 6.A

1. February 22, 1988
2. June 26, 1951
3. March 14, 2003
4. Tuesday, December 19, 2004
5. Labor Day is the first Monday in September.
6. The mall first opened on April 5, 2000.
7. My aunt visited us last Tuesday, July 4, 1996.
8. My birthday is Friday, August 12, 1999.

Student Learning Page 6.B

1. added, will/shall add
2. invited, will/shall invite
3. painted, will/shall paint
4. cleaned, will/shall clean
5. planted
6. looks
7. will bloom
8. will watch

Lesson 1.7   *Student Learning Page 7.A*

Answers will vary.

Lesson 1.8   *Student Learning Page 8.B*

1. wonderful and powerful
2. Wasis
3. no one
4. everyone
5. Answers will vary. Possible answer: because she knows things that the chief doesn't; she knew that the chief couldn't outsmart a baby

Lesson 1.10   *Student Learning Page 10.A*

1. Effect: She never went on to medical school.
2. Cause: Stephanie Kwolek invented a new fiber called Kevlar.
3. Effect: She became one of the most important chemists in the nation.

Answers

4. Cause: You must repeat and repeat until you notice the unusual.

Lesson 1.11 *Student Learning Page 11.B*

2. David's arms were amputated below the elbows because of an accident he had when he was two years old.

3. David can bat without hands by holding the bat between his left upper arm and chest and using his right arm to push the bat.

4. Josh made the glove for David by making a model of the glove out of paper, then sewing a glove from leather.

5. When his prosthetic glove worked, David started playing right field for the Spring Branch Mustangs.

Lesson 1.12 *Student Learning Page 12.A*

Answers will vary. Chart should be filled in accurately depending on section of research chosen.

Lesson 1.13

Student Learning Page 13.A

1. cucumbers, tomatoes, lettuce
2. Put the two slices of bread side by side.
3. Spread mayonnaise on the bread.
4. first, next, then, finally

Student Learning Page 13.B

Smith, Elm, Elm, Grand, Grand

Student Learning Page 13.C

1. D
2. B
3. A
4. F
5. C
6. E

Lesson 1.14 *Student Learning Page 14.A*

Answers may vary. Possible answer:

March 13, 2002

Dear Aunt *K*atherine,

Thank you so much for the new pair of skates. I have been hoping to get new skates all year! I am glad that you chose purple because it is my favorite color. I *can't* wait for spring to come so I can go skating!

Maybe the next time that you come over, we can go skating together. Now that *I'm* nine, I think that I can keep up. Thanks again for the great gift.

Love,

*K*aelyn

Lesson 2.1 *Student Learning Page 1.A*

1. D
2. B
3. C
4. A
5. 85,392; eighty-five thousand, three hundred ninety-two
6. 30,439; thirty thousand, four hundred thirty-nine
7. 59,300; fifty-nine thousand, three hundred
8. 22,096; twenty-two thousand, ninety-six

Lesson 2.2 *Student Learning Page 2.A*

1. 12
2. 14
3. 92
4. 68
5. 966
6. 247
7. 382
8. 506
9. 801
10. 787

Lesson 2.3 *Student Learning Page 3.A*

1. 0
2. 448
3. 1,883
4. $89

Lesson 2.4 *Student Learning Page 4.A*

1. Answers will vary.
2. Answers will vary.
3. Answers will vary.
4. Answers will vary.

Answers

5. $1.62

6. $1.95

7. $2.85

8. 2 dimes, 5 nickels, 5 pennies

Lesson 2.5 *Student Learning Page 5.A*

1. 9:15

2. 1:50

3. 6:30

4. 7:10

5. 4:00 or 4 o'clock

6. on the 6

7. on the 5

8. 5:45

Lesson 2.6

Student Learning Page 6.A

1. a

2. a

3. b

4. b

5. a

6. b

7. a

8. 8

9. Jordan

10. $16.50

Student Learning Page 6.B

Answers will vary. The two columns should be relatively close in weight.

Student Learning Page 6.C

1. 44°C

2. 53°C

3. 95°F

4. 30°C

5. 20°C

6. Answers will vary. Calculations should be accurate.

Lesson 2.7 *Student Learning Page 7.A*

1. $3 \times 7 = 21$

2. $5 \times 4 = 20$

3. $5 \times 10 = 50$

4. 12

5. 21

6. 5

7. 0

8. 24

9. 16

Lesson 2.8 *Student Learning Page 8.A*

1. 138

2. 567

3. 495

4. 2,728

5. 1,086

6. 6,354

7. $20 \times 6 = 120$

8. $200 \times 4 = 800$

9. $700 \times 8 = 5,600$

10. $400 \times 4 = 1,600$

Lesson 2.9

Student Learning Page 9.A

1. 4

2. 6

3. 4

4. 5

5. 8

6. 7

7. 6 R2

8. 0

9. mental math; 4

10. mental math or calculator; 16

11. mental math; 9

12. calculator; 20 players

Student Learning Page 9.B

1. 9 balloons for each friend

2. 3 pencils for each student

3. 10 sandwiches on each tray

4. 6 flowers in each row

Lesson 2.10 *Student Learning Page 10.A*

1. 50

2. 80

3. 13

4. 22

5. 19 R2

Answers

6. 12 R6
7. 4
8. 9
9. 7 R3
10. 32 R5
11. 11
12. 4
13. 34

Lesson 2.11   Student Learning Page 11.A

1. Answers will vary.
2. Answers will vary.
3. Answers will vary.
4. red: $\frac{4}{12}$, black: $\frac{8}{12}$
5. $\frac{1}{3}$ of 12 = 4; $\frac{2}{3}$ of 12 = 8; $\frac{2}{3}$ is larger than $\frac{1}{3}$
6. Giving 15 checkers would not be a reasonable answer. Student can use the 20 checkers and divide them into roughly 3 groups to help find this answer.

Lesson 2.12   Student Learning Page 12.A

1. Bar graph should be completed accurately.
2. Pictograph should be completed on separate sheet: Maria should have 6 trees, Kim 3, and Randy 5.
3. $\frac{1}{2}$
4. $\frac{1}{3}$
5. Tree diagram should be completed on separate sheet; $\frac{1}{6}$.

Lesson 2.13

Student Learning Page 13.A

1. Answers will vary. Check student's drawing.
2. Answers will vary. Check student's drawing.
3. letters with one line of symmetry: A, B, C, D, E, M, T, U, V, W, Y; letters with two lines of symmetry: H, I, O, X
4. one fold equals one line of symmetry; two folds equals four lines of symmetry
5. Answers will vary. Check student's drawing.
6. a. obtuse triangle; b. hexagon; c. quadrilateral or rectangle; d. right triangle

Student Learning Page 13.B

1. 5 miles
2. 1.5 square miles
3. perimeter
4. 2.5 miles

SCIENCE

Lesson 3.1   Student Learning Page 1.A

The chart should be completed accurately.

Invertebrates: earthworm, turtle, crab, lobster, spider, slug, octopus

Vertebrates: zebra, bat, goat, wolf, hawk, whale, alligator, lizard, tiger, shark, toad, snake, gorilla

Traits will vary.

Lesson 3.2   Student Learning Page 2.A

1. seeds
2. cones
3. spores
4. neither
5. spores
6. neither
7. seeds
8. flowers

Lesson 3.3   Student Learning Page 3.A

The animals should be accurately identified as producers, consumers (plant-eaters or meat-eaters), or decomposers.

Lesson 3.4   Student Learning Page 4.A

The drawing should accurately reflect the habitat and its organisms. The paragraph should accurately explain the drawing.

Lesson 3.5   Student Learning Page 5.A

Answers will vary. Possible answers: The owl is using the tree for shelter. The squirrel is gathering acorns from the tree for food. The deer is drinking water from the pond. The duck lives by the pond. She used things near the pond to build her nest. She also swims in the pond, eats fish from the pond, and drinks water from the pond.

Answers

Lesson 3.6

Student Learning Page 6.A
The chart should be completed accurately.

Student Learning Page 6.B
The page should be completed accurately.

Student Learning Page 6.C
1. Litter: Garbage in the water can harm fish and other living things and block water flow.
2. Oil: Harms plants, animals, and people who drink the water.

Lesson 3.7   Student Learning Page 7.A
1. smooth, involuntary
2. cardiac, involuntary
3. skeletal, voluntary
4. skeletal, voluntary
5. skeletal, voluntary
6. skeletal, voluntary
7. skeletal, voluntary

Lesson 3.8   Student Learning Page 8.A
1. bread, cereal, rice, and pasta group: 6–11 servings
2. vegetable group: 3–5 servings
3. fruit group: 2–4 servings
4. milk, yogurt, and cheese group: 2–3 servings
5. meat, poultry, fish, dry beans, eggs, and nuts group: 2–3 servings
6. fats, oils, and sweets: use sparingly

Lesson 3.9   Student Learning Page 9.A
man: shoes and goggles
girl: helmet and knee, elbow, and wrist pads

Lesson 3.10

Student Learning Page 10.A
The drawings and labels should match the page. The tongue should show where the student tasted bitter, salt, sweet, and sour. The eye should match the color of one of the student's eyes.

Student Learning Page 10.B
1. nose

2. mouth
3. eyes
4. ears
5. skin

Lesson 3.11

Student Learning Page 11.A
Drawings should be completed and properties should be listed accurately.

Student Learning Page 11.B
Experiment should be completed and sample colors should be drawn in notebook.

Lesson 3.12   Student Learning Page 12.A
1. translucent
2. opaque
3. transparent
4. translucent
5. opaque
6. opaque

Lesson 3.13   Student Learning Page 13.A
1. pulley
2. wheel and axle
3. lever
4. inclined plane
5–7. Answers will vary.

Lesson 3.14   Student Learning Page 14.A
Student should find that the bar magnet is much stronger than the nail and that the magnetized nail loses magnetic power over time and when dropped.

Lesson 3.15   Student Learning Page 15.A
The answers and drawing should be completed accurately depending on planet chosen.

Lesson 3.16

Student Learning Page 16.A
The volcano should "erupt" with "lava" flowing down the sides.

Student Learning Page 16.B
Student should describe accurately what he or she found with the soil he or she collected.

Answers

Lesson 4.1 *Student Learning Page 1.A*

1. police station, main road
2. B3
3. post office
4. C1
5. A1

Lesson 4.2

Student Learning Page 2.A

The correct locations on the map should be colored in when directed.

Student Learning Page 2.B

1. south
2. southeast
3. northeast
4. east
5. south
6. west
7. compass rose
8. legend

Lesson 4.3 *Student Learning Page 3.A*

The story about Sandra should accurately describe life in an urban community. The story about Justin should accurately describe life in a rural community.

Lesson 4.4 *Student Learning Page 4.A*

Map should be colored correctly.

Lesson 4.5 *Student Learning Page 5.A*

Map symbols should be colored accurately.

Lesson 4.6 *Student Learning Page 6.A*

1. Interstate Highway 77
2. New Mexico, Texas, Oklahoma
3. Answers may vary. Possible answers: Interstate Highways 90, 82, 84, 80
4. Answers may vary. Possible answers: Maine, New Hampshire, Massachusetts, Connecticut, Rhode Island, New York, Vermont

5. Interstate Highway 70

Lesson 4.7 *Student Learning Page 7.A*

Paragraph and drawing should be completed accurately using knowledge the student learned.

Lesson 4.8 *Student Learning Page 8.A*

Student's drawing of Jamestown settlement should accurately show walls, buildings, people, and areas.

Lesson 4.9 *Student Learning Page 9.A*

1. Answers may vary. Possible answers: fruit, seeds, nuts, beans, roots, rabbits, deer
2. Answers may vary. Possible answers: spinning, weaving, fishing, hunting, collecting foods, cooking
3. Answers will vary.
4. Answers will vary.
5. Answers will vary.
6. Make sure the clues are accurate for the item of clothing.

Lesson 4.10

Student Learning Page 10.A

Answers will vary. Check student's drawing and description.

Student Learning Page 10.B

1. b
2. d
3. a
4. c

Lesson 4.11 *Student Learning Page 11.A*

Journal entry and drawing should depict accurately pioneer travel and pioneer life.

Lesson 4.12 *Student Learning Page 12.A*

The speech should include reasons why these rights are important.

Lesson 4.13 *Student Learning Page 13.A*

Answers will vary. Student's symbols and facts should be accurate for your state.

GLOSSARY

Like any other specialty area, teaching and homeschooling have their own unique vocabulary. We've included some terms we thought might be helpful.

accelerated learning

when a student completes a certain set of lessons faster than most students; this can happen due to a student's natural motivation or in a more structured manner, such as continuing lessons throughout the year versus taking the summer off

assessment

a review of a student's learning progress and comprehension; traditionally done through tests or grades; assessments in progressive learning environments such as homeschooling take on many different forms, including summary discussions, demonstrative projects, and oral questions and answers; formalized assessment is included in this book, beginning on page 303

auditory learner

an individual who absorbs new information most effectively by listening; an auditory learner will remember information that is spoken or related through sound such as musical lyrics, reading aloud, or audiocassettes

child-centered learning

a type of learning in which the teaching style places the child at the center of his or her learning, meaning that a child begins and proceeds with new subjects, such as reading, as he or she is ready; this style of teaching requires intimate awareness of the student by the teacher

correlated to state standards

a phrase that means that something meets or exceeds a particular state's mandatory educational requirements for the intended grade level

critical thinking skill

the ability to assess information, make independent judgments, and draw conclusions; this skill is independent of and goes beyond the memorized information that a student has learned

curriculum

an ordered list of specific topics of study that is used as a teaching map

distance learning

a type of instruction in which classes are completed at a different physical location than at the school that offers them; formerly known as correspondence classes, this term now includes video and Internet classes

graphic organizer

a way to visually organize information for the purpose of learning enhancement; usually referring to charts and graphs, these can be useful for visual learners; several graphic organizers are included in this book: Venn Diagram, Comparison Chart, Web, and Sequence Chain

inclusive

a homeschool group that is inclusive and welcomes anyone who homeschools regardless of religious or educational beliefs or practices; as homeschooling becomes more popular, more inclusive groups have been formed; in the traditional classroom setting, an inclusive school is focused on reaching out to the increasingly diverse student populations to provide a supportive and quality education to all students regardless of economic status, gender, race, or disability

kinesthetic learner

an individual who absorbs new information most effectively through experience; a kinesthetic learner will understand information by completing hands-on exercises, doing, and moving

learning style

the singular manner and rate that each child naturally pursues his or her education; educators have identified three primary ways of describing learning styles: auditory, kinesthetic, and visual

lesson plan

a detailed description of the part of the curriculum one is planning to teach on a certain day

multicultural

adapted to relate to diverse cultures; many teachers incorporate multicultural learning materials into their lessons to encourage exposure to different traditions

real books

books you get at the library or the bookstore that aren't textbooks; some homeschoolers work almost exclusively from real books and don't use textbooks at all; this book provides a curriculum that's based on reading and research with real books

scoring rubric

a measurement tool used to assess student work that includes a system of scoring levels of performance; scoring rubrics are used with some lessons in this book and with the formalized assessment section in the back of this book

self-directed learner

an individual who is free to pursue education by his or her own means and guidance versus through traditional classes or schools; a term often used in homeschool literature

self-teaching

when an individual naturally learns about a topic of particular interest on his or her own,

without formal instruction and usually as a result of natural attraction to or talent in the subject matter

standardized test

a test is considered standardized when it is given in the same manner, with the same directions to children of the same grade level across a school district, state, or country; the test shows how your student is doing compared to other students; the assessment section beginning on page 303 offers examples of standardized test questions

teaching strategy

a creative way to motivate and inspire students, such as using a visual aid, entertaining or humorous delivery, interactive activity, or theme-based lessons; if your student is bored, he or she might benefit from a change in teaching strategies

unschooling

a teaching philosophy first identified by educator John Holt that's based on the idea that the child directs his or her own learning based on his or her own interests; works under the assertion that textbook-type teaching can dull a child's natural zest for learning and the belief that a student will learn more when he or she is engaged, uninterrupted, and enjoying

visual learner

an individual who absorbs new information most effectively through the sense of sight; a visual learner will comprehend information by reading, watching a video, using a visual computer program, and looking at pictures in books

Waldorf

a method of education that was developed by Rudolph Steiner and attempts to teach the whole child: physical, emotional, and academic; Waldorf schools are located throughout the country, and there is also a network of Waldorf homeschoolers

Venn Diagram

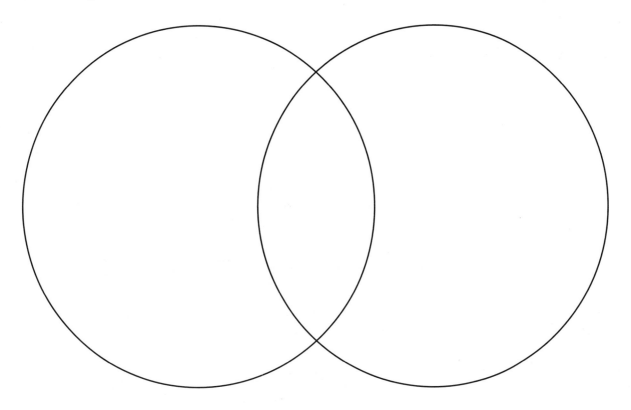

Comparison Chart

Issue:_____	A: _____	B: _____
I.	1.	2.
II.	3.	4.
III.	5.	6.

Web

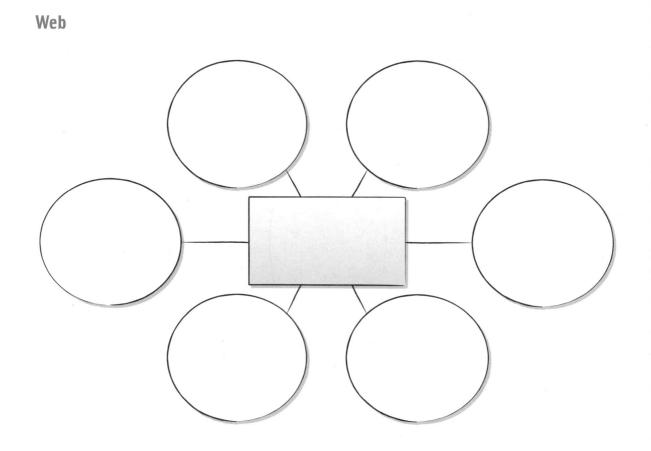

Sequence Chain

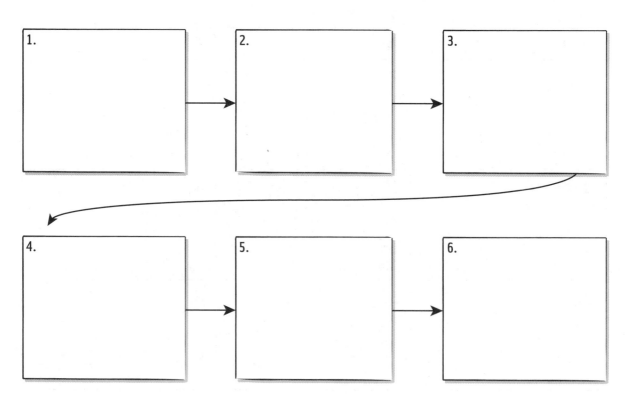

Making the Grade: Everything Your 3rd Grader Needs to Know

Index

Note: Page numbers in bold indicate the definition of a term.

Note: Page numbers in bold indicate the definition of a term.

Index

Note: Page numbers in bold indicate the definition of a term.

Note: Page numbers in bold indicate the definition of a term.

Index

Note: Page numbers in bold indicate the definition of a term.

W

Wagon train exercise, 287
Warm-blooded animals, **157,** 158
Washington, D.C., 289–291, 295
Water
    bodies of, 254
    pollution, 181–182, 185
Web graphic organizer, 298, 354
Wedge, **215,** 216, 217
Weight units of measure, 105, 108
Wheel and axle, **215,** 216, 217
White House, 289–290, 294
Wind erosion, **179**
Word form for writing numbers, 85
Word wall activity, 10
Work, **215**
    jobs and services, 240, 263–264
    of simple machines, 215–216
World wars, Navajo code and, 39
Writing activities
    Anasazi-related, 269, 270
    animal postcard, 160
    autobiographical book, 18
    biography, 54
    comic strip, 22
    conversational dialogue, 22
    dialogue, 21–22
    diary entries, 192
    game directions, 72
    habitat exercise, 173
    letter, 256, 274
    poetry, 196
    science fiction chapter exercise, 37
    travelogue, 278
Writing process
    dates, 27, 29
    dialogue, 19–21
    main ideas and details exercise, 65
    notetaking, 61–63
    optional activities, 66
    proofreading exercise, 75
    research reports, 61–66
    stages, 63–64
    thank-you notes, 73–76
    verb tenses, 27–28, 30

Z

Zoologists, 158

Credits

Art & Photo Credits

Promoting Literacy
Background/Icon: © Dynamic Graphics
Opener (page 1): © PhotoDisc
Page 6, 7, 8: © PhotoDisc; **9:** PP/FA, Inc.; **14:** Precision Graphics; **17, 18:** Carol Stutz Illustration; **21:** Precision Graphics; **22, 25:** Carol Stutz Illustration; **26, 27:** Precision Graphics; **30:** Digital Stock; **33:** Lisa Zador/Artville, LLC; **35, 36, 37, 38, 40, 43:** Carol Stutz Illustration; **47:** Digital Stock; **48:** Carol Stutz Illustration; **51:** © PhotoDisc; **52:** Carol Stutz Illustration; **53:** PP/FA, Inc.; **57, 58, 60:** Carol Stutz Illustration; **62:** Library of Congress, Prints & Photographs Division, HABS, Reproduction number HABS, DC,WASH,461A–; **65:** PP/FA, Inc.; **66, 69:** Carol Stutz Illustration; **70, 71, 72, 73, 75, 76:** Precision Graphics

Math
Background/Icon: © PhotoDisc
Opener (page 79): © PhotoDisc
Page 85: Precision Graphics; **86:** Carol Stutz Illustration; **87:** Precision Graphics; **88:** © Image 100/Royalty-Free/CORBIS; **90, 92, 93, 97:** Precision Graphics; **98:** Carol Stutz Illustration; **101:** Precision Graphics; **103:** © PhotoDisc; **104, 106:** Precision Graphics; **108:** Carol Stutz Illustration; **109, 112, 115 (top):** Precision Graphics; **115 (middle, bottom), 116:** Carol Stutz Illustration; **118:** © PhotoDisc; **121:** Carol Stutz Illustration; **122:** Precision Graphics; **123:** © EyeWire, Inc.; **127:** Carol Stutz Illustration; **130, 131, 132, 137, 138, 139 (top):** Precision Graphics; **139 (bottom):** © CORBIS; **140:** Precision Graphics; **141:** © PhotoDisc; **144, 146, 147, 148, 149, 151:** Precision Graphics

Science
Background/Icon: © PhotoDisc
Opener (page 155): © PhotoDisc
Page 157: Precision Graphics; **158:** © PhotoDisc; **159:** PP/FA, Inc.; **160:** © Ryan McVay/Getty Images; **163 (top left):** © Photodisc Collection/Getty Images; **163 (top right):** © CORBIS; **163 (bottom left):** © Royalty-Free/CORBIS; **163 (bottom right):** © Photodisc Collection/Getty Images; **167 (top left):** Digital Stock; **167 (top right):** Creatas LLC; **167 (bottom right):** Digital Stock; **169:** PP/FA, Inc.; **172:** National Park Service; **174, 177:** Carol Stutz Illustration; **183, 184:** PP/FA, Inc.; **185:** Carol Stutz Illustration; **186:** PP/FA, Inc.; **188:** © Digital Vision; **189:** Precision Graphics; **191, 192, 195:** PP/FA, Inc.; **196, 199, 200:** Carol Stutz Illustration; **203, 204:** Precision Graphics; **206:** © PhotoDisc; **207:** Carol Stutz Illustration; **209:** PP/FA, Inc.; **210:** Precision Graphics; **212:** © PhotoDisc; **213:** Precision Graphics; **217 (top left):** Copyright © 2003 PP/FA, Inc. and its licensors. All rights reserved.; **217 (top right):** © Photodisc Collection/Getty Images; **217 (bottom left):** © CORBIS; **217 (bottom right):** © Royalty-Free/CORBIS; **218:** © Oscar White/CORBIS; **221, 222:** Carol Stutz Illustration; **224:** © CORBIS; **225 (top):** Mike Hill/Alamy; **225 (bottom), 228:** © CORBIS; **230:** Precision Graphics; **231, 233:** National Park Service; **234:** © L. Clarke/CORBIS

Social Studies
Background/Icon: © Wes Thompson/CORBIS
Opener (page 237): © PhotoDisc
Page 240: Carol Stutz Illustration; **241, 245:** Precision Graphics; **248 (left):** © Scenics of America/PhotoLink/Getty Images; **248 (middle):** © CORBIS; **248 (right):** © Photodisc Collection/Getty Images; **251:** Carol Stutz Illustration; **254:** National Park Service; **255:** Mapping Specialists, Ltd.; **258:** © Photodisc Collection/Getty Images; **259:** Mapping Specialists, Ltd.; **263, 265:** Precision Graphics; **267:** National Park Service; **269:** © Macduff Everton/CORBIS;

272: © Bettmann/CORBIS; **274:** © Dave G. Houser/CORBIS; **276:** © Randy Faris/CORBIS; **278:** © PhotoDisc; **281 (top):** National Oceanic and Atmospheric Administration/Department of Commerce; **281 (bottom):** PP/FA, Inc.; **285:** © PhotoDisc; **287:** Mapping Specialists, Ltd.; **288:** Precision Graphics; **290:** National Park Service; **291 (left):** © Royalty-Free/CORBIS; **291 (right):** © Jim Zuckerman/CORBIS; **294:** National Park Service; **296:** © Paul Wootton Associates; **298:** Precision Graphics; **299:** PP/FA, Inc.; **300:** © PhotoDisc

Page 306: Carol Stutz Illustration; **307:** PP/FA, Inc.; **308:** Carol Stutz Illustration; **310, 315:** Precision Graphics; **317:** © PhotoDisc; **318:** Precision Graphics; **319, 320, 321 (bottom right):** PP/FA, Inc.; **321 (left, top right, middle right), 322, 323 (top left):** Precision Graphics; **323 (bottom left, right), 324 (right):** PP/FA, Inc.; **324 (left), 325 (top left, right):** Precision Graphics; **325 (bottom left), 326 (left):** Carol Stutz Illustration; **326 (right), 328, 329 (bottom left, right):** Precision Graphics; **329 (top left):** PP/FA, Inc.; **330 (left):** Carol Stutz Illustration; **330 (right):** Precision Graphics; **334:** © Royalty-Free/CORBIS; **343, 353, 354:** PP/FA, Inc.

Literature Credits

5–8, From *Tick Tock Tales* by Margaret Mahy. Text copyright © 1993 by Margaret Mahy. Published by Orion Children's Books. Reprinted by arrangement with Orion Children's Books.

35–36, From THE WONDERFUL FLIGHT TO THE MUSHROOM PLANET by Eleanor Cameron. Copyright © 1954 by Eleanor Cameron; Copyright © renewed by Eleanor Cameron. By permission of Little, Brown and Company, (Inc.)

41–42, From *World Folktales: An Anthology of Multicultural Folk Literature* by Anita Stern. Copyright © 1994 by NTC/Contemporary Publishing Company. Published by National Textbook Company, a division of NTC/Contemporary Publishing Company. Reprinted by arrangement with the McGraw-Hill Companies.

47, R. Gerry Fabian. Reprinted by permission of the author.

47, "Butterfly", from SILVER SEEDS by Paul Paolilli and Dan Brewer, illustrated by Steve Johnson and Lou Fancher, copyright © 2001 by Paul Paolilli and Dan Brewer, text. Used by permission of Viking Penguin, an imprint of Penguin Putnam Books for Young Readers, a division of Penguin Putnam Inc. All rights reserved.

51–52, From *Women Inventors 4* by Jean Blashfield © *1996 by Bridgestone Books,* an imprint of Capstone Press. Used with permission.

57–58, From *The Kids' Invention Book* by Arlene Erlbach. Copyright 1997 by Arlene Erlbach. Used by permission of the publisher, Lerner Publications Company, a division of Lerner Publishing Group. All rights reserved.

334–338, From *The U.S. Constitution and You* by Syl Sobel. Copyright © 2001 by Barron's Educational Series, Inc. Reprinted by arrangement with Barron's Educational Series, Inc.